TORRES

✓ SKIM – FAST
Read.

2/21/17

6/16/17 –

EXCELLENCE GAPS
IN EDUCATION

EXCELLENCE GAPS IN EDUCATION

**Expanding Opportunities
for Talented Students**

Jonathan A. Plucker

Scott J. Peters

HARVARD EDUCATION PRESS
CAMBRIDGE, MASSACHUSETTS

Paperback ISBN 978-1-61250-992-1
Library Edition ISBN 978-1-61250-993-8

Library of Congress Cataloging-in-Publication Data
Names: Plucker, Jonathan A., 1969– author. | Peters, Scott J., 1983– author.
Title: Excellence gaps in education : expanding opportunities for talented
    students / Jonathan A. Plucker, Scott J. Peters.
Description: Cambridge, Massachusetts : Harvard Education Press, [2016]
Identifiers: LCCN 2016021408| ISBN 9781612509921 (pbk.) | ISBN
    9781612509938 (library edition)
Subjects: LCSH: Gifted children—Education—United States. | Children of
    minorities—Education—United States. | Poor children—Education—
    United States. | Gifted children—United States—Identification. |
    Education and state—United States. | Educational evaluation.
Classification: LCC LC3993.9 .P58 2016 | DDC 371.95—dc23
    LC record available at https://lccn.loc.gov/2016021408

Published by Harvard Education Press,
an imprint of the Harvard Education Publishing Group

Harvard Education Press
8 Story Street
Cambridge, MA 02138

Cover Design: Wilcox Design
Cover Photo: Blend Images - Hill Street Studios/Getty Images

The typefaces used in this book are Berkeley Oldstyle and Gotham.

To Julia Link Roberts, who has supported this work from the beginning and uses it to help improve the lives of so many students.
—JAP

To every child who just wants to be challenged.
—SJP

CONTENTS

PART FOUR

Taking a Big Swing at It

PREFACE

EXCELLENCE GAPS are differences between subgroups of students performing at the highest levels of achievement. These gaps are among America's most pressing educational problems: they are economically damaging over the long haul; they hurt families and communities—particularly those from disadvantaged backgrounds; and they cast a dark shadow of lost potential over American culture and educational systems. Yet few educators and policymakers, let alone members of the general public, are aware of their existence or their importance. Indeed, probably the only groups that have noticed are affected students and the parents who have to watch their children's abilities and passions go un-nurtured and underdeveloped.

We were motivated to write this book for a number of reasons. Jonathan became concerned in the early years of the No Child Left Behind era that nearly all of the discourse surrounding education policy was focused on achievement gaps at the basic proficiency level. Many of the thought leaders in American education policy discussed advanced achievement and excellence gaps only rarely, and if they did, often expressed hostility toward these topics. But a quick look at the available education data showed that achievement gaps were large and, by some measures, growing at the advanced levels of achievement. This realization began a decade's worth of research that is reflected in this book. Scott approached this topic frustrated by the double-talk of the American educational system, which speaks elegantly about growth for all while simultaneously focusing almost exclusively on remediation. If we as a society truly believe that everyone can achieve and that everyone should have the opportunity to learn in school, then our practices need to reflect that belief across the full range of student achievement.

We both were attracted to the topic of excellence gaps—and, indeed, to the prospect of writing this book—because this work addresses an important question that both general education and gifted education have often avoided: How well does what we advocate for work, and for whom? Too rarely, educational policy is approached from a general perspective of outcomes, with no consideration of differential outcomes across racial groups, income groups, or groups starting at different levels of readiness. This blind spot in educational policy cannot continue.

WHY THIS BOOK?

In our view, excellence gaps have not received the attention they deserve, from educators, policy makers, or the public at large. We find this especially troubling given how often educational policy makers speak of equality and equal opportunity. To help rectify this oversight, this book has dual purposes: to provide an overview of the problem and to suggest potential interventions. In part 1, we review American education policy and how it has—and has not—addressed the needs of advanced students and educational excellence over the past several decades. We discuss the state of educational excellence and excellence gaps in the United States, both in terms of how students have performed academically and how their needs are traditionally met (or not). In part 2, we review the ways in which American educational institutions and educators have attempted to promote educational excellence, including a discussion of terminology, specifically involving the use of various labels to refer to advanced achievement and advanced learners.

Part 3 provides a close examination of various interventions that policy makers and educators have identified as potential ways to shrink excellence gaps. We examine and evaluate a diverse range of interventions from outside the K–12 spectrum as well as outside the American educational context. There are many examples of institutions setting out to decrease excellence gaps—though often not calling them by this name—but only recently has this topic garnered broader, significant attention in K–12 education.

Finally, in part 4, we bring the lessons learned together and propose a path forward for addressing excellence gaps. Our goal throughout the book, and especially in this last section, is to provide a clear, frank, and provocative perspective on the relevant issues. In our view, any obfuscation would only serve to divert attention away from the students, families, and communities suffering from excellence gaps, and that has been allowed to occur for far too long.

PART ONE

Why Excellence Gaps?

1

Setting the Table for Excellence

TO BEGIN our analysis of excellence gaps, we would like to sketch out some examples of how a range of factors combine to create very large gaps between what otherwise similar children can achieve and actually are achieving. These examples should be viewed as hypothetical illustrations, although many of the details are drawn from talented students with whom we've worked.

To begin, consider Chloe's situation. She was a fourth grader in a large, suburban elementary school in an upper-middle-class part of her state. Although English was not her first language (she had been adopted from South Korea the previous year), her intellectual and musical talents were easy to see. On one occasion, the principal stuck his head in the classroom and said, "I love this music you're playing! What is it?" The teacher directed his attention to the piano in the corner of the room, where Chloe was impressing everyone in the room with her skills. Chloe also excelled in both math and reading, in class and on standardized tests. She had the good fortune to be placed with an experienced teacher who was skilled at differentiating instruction and the curriculum based on Chloe's particular needs. This opportunity also helped her develop a strong interest in science. The school had a small but well-designed gifted program, and Chloe's parents were a frequent—but not overbearing—presence in the school to make sure her needs were being met. All of this combined to make for a learning environment that provided numerous opportunities for Chloe to develop her talents—opportunities of which she readily took advantage.

Chloe had a first-rate preschool and early elementary experience before moving to the United States, and her ability to consume new information and excel when faced with challenging work sharply increased as her vocabulary improved. On the rare occasions when the school could not provide specific services that her parents felt necessary, they found and paid for resources outside of the school, including extra tutoring in English, a private piano teacher, and weekend enrichment courses in science and math.

Contrast Chloe's experiences with those of Kevin, a lower-middle-class black sixth grader in a suburban district. He and his brother lived with their mother, his father having little or no role in his life. But Kevin's biggest hurdle was his dyslexia—writing a sentence was a painful experience for him, and he spent a lot of time in the school's resource room with the special education teachers.

At the same time, Kevin had amazing spatial skills. He could build just about anything, think in three dimensions with ease, and understand any spatial problem—and usually offer a good solution. Kevin's primary sixth-grade teacher quickly noticed Kevin's abilities and called them to the attention of the school's enrichment coordinator. Together, they pushed hard to provide Kevin with opportunities that would stretch and further develop his intellectual strengths. The sixth-grade teacher was one of the school's instructional leaders, and it's worth noting that Kevin had a very pleasant demeanor and was generally well liked.

However, despite the teachers' best efforts, Kevin made little progress. This was partly a labeling problem. In one instance, the enrichment coordinator couldn't find Kevin and eventually tracked him down in the resource room. When the coordinator walked into the room, the other teachers froze. The special education director walked the coordinator into the hall and gently asked what he was doing in the resource room, cautioning him that classroom teachers would not be happy if they saw him "crossing the lines" between special education, the regular classroom, and gifted education. Kevin had severe learning disabilities, therefore he could not be intellectually talented. It was suggested that Kevin needed to focus on overcoming his dyslexia before he could "go have fun" in the enrichment program and even begin to think about developing his spatial talents.

Kevin's family did not have the socioeconomic means of most other families in the community, denying him many of the out-of-school opportunities available to other students. The impact of these cultural, status, and resource issues became glaringly clear during the sixth-grade science fair. Like millions of American science fair participants, many students chose the classic topic of "Why Popcorn Pops," and Kevin was among them. But in the days leading up to the fair, it became clear that Kevin fully grasped the physics of the topic, while most of his classmates did not. The night of the science fair, the judges commented that they wished just one student could correctly describe the science behind a popping kernel. Kevin's teachers looked at each other quizzically: Did Kevin make a mistake? Did he get nervous and describe things incorrectly? They went to talk to him . . . and found an empty spot where his project should have been. The next morning, they found out that Kevin's mother had been working, so he had no way to get back to the school for the science fair. He was embarrassed about imposing on others and therefore had never asked anyone—a teacher, a neighbor, a classmate, a friend—for help. Perhaps more to the point, no one in Kevin's life thought to ask.

The difference between Chloe and Kevin's experiences is stark but complex. Both attended well-resourced public schools in suburban areas, and they both had loving families and supportive educators—hardly worst-case scenarios. But as these examples show, those advantages only get a talented student so far. Years of distinctly different opportunities, levels of support, and levels of resources—all against the backdrop of racial, socioeconomic, and perhaps gender bias (some unintentional, some not)—create very different educational experiences for talented students. Those experiences are additive over time and can result in students of similar initial ability achieving at very different levels. When students attend poorly resourced schools, lack family support, or don't have access to high-quality educators, the differences between these levels of achievement can become enormous. The disparities get wider over time as some students continue to benefit from in- and out-of-school resources while others do not. In this book, we refer to these differences as *excellence gaps*.

The story of Chloe and Kevin is the story of educational excellence gaps and how they come into existence before and continue to grow after a child enters formal K–12 education. When educational opportunities at any level are not offered as part of the public education system, then some families will seek them out at their own cost and some will not. This is one of the reasons that educational achievement and family income are so highly correlated—money is often directly linked to access to educational opportunity. Families who are aware of supplementary options, can afford them, have the time to seek them out and enroll their children, and are willing to do so even when such content is not part of the local school's curriculum will take advantage of such opportunities in order to further their child's learning. All parents would want to provide enrichment for their talented children but only some have that option due to financial, cultural, logistical, or political barriers.

Although the strong association between socioeconomic status and opportunity is evident in the United States, it is not written in stone. In fact, as Finn and Wright discuss in their recent book on the topic, this association is not present in many other developed nations.[1] We will explore this phenomenon in more depth in chapter 2, but for now it will suffice to note that growing up poor stacks the talent development deck against students, but that doesn't mean they stand no chance to develop their talents.

Of course, substantial minimum proficiency and excellence gaps exist even before students arrive in kindergarten or first grade. Students from low-income or otherwise underprivileged families often have less access to high-quality preschool than their higher-income peers; this, combined with access to fewer resources during the school years and, on average, enrollment in lower-quality schools, further exacerbate excellence gaps.

A brief note on terminology before we dive into excellence gaps. It has become fashionable of late, in some circles, to talk about "white/Asian privilege," "upper-class privilege," or more globally, "majority privilege." These phenomena certainly exist and have been documented. But we strongly believe that such language is divisive and off-putting to many people who would otherwise be eager to tackle the issues of excellence gaps. For this reason, we will talk about accumulated *advantages* that many students have, and that many students do not.

THE AMERICAN INFATUATION WITH ACHIEVEMENT GAPS

The American educational system, with its federalist organization and spirit, is often hard for people from other countries to understand. Jonathan often works in China, and he dreads an all-too-common question: "Can you explain how American schools are organized?" The direct answer is "No," but he tries to be a good sport and provide an answer, usually with a description of the tradition of local control set within the context of states' rights, casually noting that the US Constitution doesn't mention education. This explanation usually results in a conversation-killing silence as his colleagues try to figure out how it can all possibly work.

But the organization of the American public education system explains a great deal of why most state and national education policy focuses on struggling students. Lengthy tomes have been written on this topic and a detailed description here would be a distraction.[2] But it is worth a quick review to set the stage for a discussion of excellence gaps. Broadly, the federal government's role in education has largely been one of remediation—filling in the gaps in our education system, primarily in an effort to improve the quality of education for low-income and minority students. This level-the-playing-field approach, which cuts across federal agencies, has clearly had an impact on American children. Policies from the National School Lunch Program to Head Start to Title I have helped reduce child hunger, provided critical preschool experiences, and pushed critical funding to schools with high percentages of low-income students—all in an attempt to close various gaps in access, readiness, and opportunity between advantaged and disadvantaged groups.[3] We can debate the extent to which these efforts have been successful, or whether they are funded nearly at the level required to fully address the problems of low-income students, but there is little debate that students are much better off with these programs than in their absence.

Although the idea of "achievement gaps" has likely been around as long as there have been public school systems, it emerged as a catalyst for US educational policy in the 1964 Civil Rights Act.[4] Most in education might be surprised to think of civil rights legislation as sparking a wide-spread interest in testing and achievement disparities, but a little-known section of the Civil Rights Act mandated a survey be conducted by the Commissioner of the Office of Education (then part of the Department of Health, Education, and Welfare) "concerning the lack of availability of equal educational opportunities for individuals by reason of race, color, religion, or national origin in public educational institutions at all levels in the United States."[5] We can't imagine that anyone realized at the time just how influential this section would be for the next fifty years of American educational policy.

The results of this survey were presented to the president and Congress in the form of a report entitled "Equality of Educational Opportunity," more commonly known as the Coleman Report after its lead author, sociologist James S. Coleman.[6] In undertaking their charge, the committee, led by Coleman, tackled a key question: What is equality and what does it mean for schools to offer "equal educational opportunities"? The report noted that equality was measured by such factors as the level of teacher training and availability of resources. What the authors of the report either assumed or simply decided on their own was that these resources and opportunities were always examined with regard to helping students reach minimum, grade-level proficiency—reaching advanced levels of achievement or even just continued growth were never considered. For example, the survey was interested in the age of the main school building, how many students were in each classroom, and whether the schools had sufficient textbooks. Although the report did include measures of access to AP courses and college-credit-bearing courses, this topic was assessed in two questions of the 120-item survey. Far more common were questions on how many times the student had changed schools or talked to a guidance counselor. The survey was focused on minimum competency and the disproportionality with which various subgroups reached this educational threshold.

The focus of the Civil Rights Act and the Coleman Report was on (1) differential access for students to grade-level materials leading to basic proficiency and (2) differential rates of achievement of basic proficiency. Although this may seem unsurprising, we can't help but wonder why equality at advanced levels of performance was barely considered or why Congress didn't consider academic growth as a metric of equality.

Why is it when American audiences turn to achievement or achievement "gaps" as a measure of equality, they look primarily to basic proficiency gaps? The Coleman Report was entitled "*Equality* of Educational Opportunity" [emphasis added], yet this was operationalized as equality of achievement at basic or grade-level proficiency. This operationalization of "equality" has been the rudder of federal educational policy for at least the last fifty years, with implications that American schools are still dealing with today. As we discuss below, this emphasis has continued and expanded under the No Child Left Behind Act (NCLB), the more recent NCLB waivers, Race to the Top, the Every Student Succeeds Act (ESSA), and other federal and state education initiatives.

The Elementary and Secondary Education Act

It was not by coincidence that the Civil Rights Act and the Coleman Report both came out within a year of another piece of legislation that would have profound effects on American schools: the first passage of the Elementary and Secondary Education Act (ESEA), which included the goal "The purpose of this title is to ensure that all children have a fair, equal, and significant opportunity to obtain a high-quality education and reach, at a minimum, proficiency on challenging State academic achievement standards and state academic assessments."[7]

A later section of ESEA, also entitled the State and Local Flexibility Demonstration Act, included the intent "to narrow achievement gaps between the lowest and highest achieving groups of students so that no child is left behind."[8] Implied in this initiative is that "leaving no child behind" means that no child fails to reach minimum proficiency. The fact that some students would quite literally be "left behind" as states and teachers focused their efforts on below-proficiency students never appeared to enter into the equation for equity. Even today, as many states move toward value-added models of teacher evaluation, many of them only focus on growth or value added if it means growth toward minimum proficiency. Some states allocate points for growth above proficiency, but many are still stuck in the basic proficiency mind-set established by ESEA over fifty years ago.

Despite the criticisms that ESEA has received regarding its negative educational effects on advanced students, its *stated* purpose contains little that directly discourages advanced educational programs. For example, the Act refers to "challenging standards" and a "high-quality education," and even includes a specific statement that state-level standards, however challenging, should be seen as a floor and not a ceiling (that is, "at a minimum"). Those familiar with the Common Core State Standards will recognize this emphasis—that standards are levels of basic proficiency and that they should not be seen as the highest aspiration of learning.[9] The US Department of Education set a level of basic proficiency as a criterion and then recommended that all schools seek to go beyond this. The ESEA legislation even included funding for AP courses. As with Common Core, there is little that can be taken as explicitly hostile toward advanced levels of performance, yet the law was interpreted as setting basic proficiency as the goal, not the first milestone on a journey to advanced achievement. In later versions of ESEA, the focus on minimum proficiency strengthened, until the sole focus became closing these minimum competency achievement gaps and increasing the number of students who reached grade-level proficiency. Similarly, the Common Core has been presented at times as not allowing students to move beyond the grade-level expectation—that the standards are so rigorous that no student will ever be beyond them. Of course, this isn't true.

The Soft Bigotry of Minimum Competency

Two major aspects of the ESEA have had the greatest influence on American K–12 school practice: (1) the emphasis on grade-level proficiency as the standard for judging educational quality and (2) the goal of closing achievement gaps. We have already described the textual basis for the first provision; the second was taken from the stated goal of "closing the achievement gap between high- and low-performing children, especially the achievement gaps between minority and nonminority students, and between disadvantaged children and their more advantaged peers."[10] As of 1965, the federal government had crafted a new set of educational principles via the ESEA: (1) increase all student achievement up to state-set minimum-proficiency standards and (2) narrow the differential rates in achievement of those standards that exist between income and racial/ethnic groups.

As schools proceeded to augment their existing offerings with courses and resources focused on remediation and expanded their focus on math and reading (as the primary tested subjects), this had the unintended consequence of also cutting back on programs or services for advanced learners. Given that the expanded funding through NCLB was directed at remediation toward grade-level proficiency, it is not surprising that this is where schools focused their efforts. Little if any incentive was provided to develop students' abilities, even within the tested content areas, beyond minimum proficiency. As attention was drawn away from moving beyond those standards, advanced learners had fewer places to develop their talents unless their families could afford out-of-school resources. The larger purpose of a K–12 education became reaching grade-level proficiency.

Doubling Down (Literally) on Minimum Competency

This primary, if not sole, focus on minimum proficiency gaps was only expanded with NCLB, the 2001 reauthorization of ESEA. Signed into law on January 8, 2002, the Act upped the ESEA ante, so to speak, adding highly prescriptive provisions—nearly all of which focused on minimum competency achievement gaps—in much more explicit fashion than did the original 1965 ESEA.[11]

The strongly bipartisan NCLB, passed easily by both houses of Congress, was the most extensive overhaul of ESEA since its inception. The primary goal of NCLB remained to address widespread disparities in educational opportunity within the United States, especially those that led to significantly poorer academic outcomes by minority and economically vulnerable students. In particular, the concept of achievement gaps, reflecting differences between demographically defined groups of students, was popularized, with the broader intent of NCLB being the elimination of those gaps by 2014, at which point every public school student was expected to reach grade-level proficiency. Little mention was made in NCLB of any focus on advanced learners or even on what to do with minority or disadvantaged students who were already at grade level, how they would continue to be challenged, or even how they would be prevented from regressing as they continued to be taught content they had already mastered.

NCLB's goals were to be accomplished via an emphasis on increased accountability, more consistent achievement testing across states, improved education data systems, enhanced public school choice, and improvements in teacher quality. To support implementation of NCLB, federal K–12 education funding increased sharply during its early years, almost 100 percent of which was focused on interventions for helping schools reach the grade-level proficiency goal.

Republican legislatures in several states were hesitant about this new federal role in education, which had previously been largely a state concern. That said, despite a rattling of sabers in several legislatures, NCLB was eventually implemented in all fifty states, and the basic mechanisms largely remained in place for roughly a decade. In 2011, the Obama administration allowed states to apply for waivers from some NCLB requirements, an option of which more than forty states took advantage. However, very few states proposed waiver provisions that moved their state away from a focus on minimum competency or addressed educational excellence in any meaningful way. To the contrary, many states made changes to their K–12 accountability and educator evaluation systems that only strengthened the role of minimum competency as the overarching goal of K–12 public education.

A number of NCLB benefits and weaknesses have become apparent over the past dozen years. On the positive side, access to education data significantly increased, certain achievement gaps narrowed, and performance on widely respected assessments, such as the National Assessment of Educational Progress (NAEP) steadily improved (though modestly in most cases and more so in math than reading).[12] Weaknesses included concerns about the expanding federal role in K–12 education, narrowing of the curriculum due to the testing focus on mathematics and reading, highly complicated mechanisms for determining adequate performance in schools and districts, and the heavy emphasis on student testing.[13] Further, NCLB failed to address the services students should receive once they reach grade level proficiency or if they are already achieving grade level proficiency.

From our perspective, the major strength and weakness of NCLB was the focus on minimum competency–based achievement gaps and the lack of *any* attention to gaps at higher levels of achievement. On the one hand, the focus on basic proficiency achievement gaps and not leaving any children behind was a welcome acknowledgment that improving the achievement of disadvantaged students should be a national education priority. On the other hand, the basic accountability mechanism of NCLB—letting states create their own standards, assessments, and passing cut scores, with remedies and penalties for poor performance created by the federal government—proved to be largely unworkable and ineffective, with some states creating weak standards and low cut scores, allowing most states to avoid the actual changes the Act was meant to spur. These emphases and requirements codified the primary importance of closing minimum competency achievement gaps above all others. Complicating matters further, influential think tanks such as The Education Trust assertively pushed the basic competency perspective, discouraging attempts to broaden the focus of NCLB to high-ability students.

The Every Student Succeeds Act (ESSA), passed in late 2015, was the long-overdue reauthorization of the ESEA.[14] ESSA differs from its ESEA and NCLB predecessors by including several provisions for advanced learners. First, the law authorized the Javits Gifted and Talented Students Education Program with a priority focus on at-risk and low-income students. For over twenty years, the Javits Program has funded demonstration projects seeking to meet the needs of gifted and talented students, particularly students traditionally underrepresented in gifted programs. Although Congress still needs to appropriate funds for the program, the inclusion of the Javits Program in ESSA will prevent the program from constantly needing to be reauthorized (which led in the past to periods of sharply reduced or no funding). This program will help states, schools, and researchers develop and research interventions targeted at advanced learners from disadvantaged populations. In the most recent funding cycle, multiple Javits-funded projects related to excellence gaps.

What's even more important about ESSA is its state and district requirements. For the first time, the law makes it clear that individual districts are allowed to use Title I funds to identify and serve advanced learners. Districts that receive any Title II funding for professional development must also show how these funds were used to address the learning needs of advanced learners ("all students" specifically includes gifted and talented students). Both states and individual districts must disaggregate achievement data by level, allowing outside stakeholders to evaluate the growth of high-performing students and thus making these data widely visible for the first time. At the time of this writing, many of the final regulations are still being negotiated, so it is far too early to tell what effect these new federal policies will have, both on the number of advanced learners or the size of American excellence gaps. But these changes are certainly improvements over previous national policies.

We Can Focus on More Than Competency

Our aim is not to imply that NCLB and related efforts focusing on minimum competency are misplaced or misguided. Rather, we want to emphasize that (1) they are an outgrowth of the traditional view of state and especially national education policy, and (2) there has been little or no attention to structuring these policies in a way that encourages educational excellence or the shrinking of excellence gaps.

Minimum proficiency standards are useful and important. However, in being necessary, they should not be seen as sufficient. These standards help schools and states plan scopes and sequences for learning, purchase curriculum, and (in theory) avoid unnecessary repetition of curriculum. How important is minimum proficiency achievement? The Organisation for Economic Co-operation and Development (OECD) estimated that bringing all American students up to minimum proficiency would lead to massive economic benefits, perhaps into the trillions of dollars.[15] Based on these economic benefits and the ethical responsibility to educate all of our children, the importance of getting all students to *at least* minimum proficiency is clear.

One issue with NCLB's focus on gaps are the criteria used to determine success. Standards—even minimum competency ones—did not beget achievement gaps, nor do they cause students to be low-achieving. As a result of NCLB, many states lowered their grade-level standards so that a larger number of students would test at or above grade-level minimum proficiency expectations.[16] Yet despite this dumbing down of proficiency, achievement gaps between student subgroups remained. The reason is simple: if two people are standing ten feet apart, then changing how a "foot" is measured will have no effect on how far apart they actually are. Over the past decade, some educators and advocacy organizations have argued for raising academic standards across the board, with the implication being such action would increase the quality of education all students receive. This is the movement that yielded the Common Core State Standards and college- and career-ready standards in place of minimum proficiency standards. But this would have (and has had) no effect on achievement gaps. All that redefining the standard does is change how far a given student is from it. Put simply, the placement of the goal post might make one group seem closer to it than another (or could even make both groups seem past the goal), but it has no effect in how far apart the two groups are from each other. It takes more than a name change to close performance gaps between students.

Gaps between student subgroups exist long before students ever begin formal K–12 education, which is part of the reason they are so hard to close. In a widely reported study, Hart and Risley found that children of professional parents were read to approximately three times as much as children of parents on welfare.[17] By age three, the former group had a vocabulary was twice as large than the latter. More recently, Kornrich and Furstenberg looked at parental spending as a source of preschool differential educational opportunity.[18] Families in the lowest tenth of income spent approximately $750 per year on their child, whereas families in the two highest tenths spent $3,701 and $6,673 per year, respectively. To be sure, parental spending and reading are not the sole sources of achievement gaps, but they are major factors in creating gaps that are very difficult to eliminate once students are in school.

Wherever we set the standards, there will always be students far below and far above them for whom instruction based on those standards is not educationally beneficial. A 2013 study noted that despite 95 percent mastery of concepts such as basic counting and shape recognition by American kindergarteners, teachers reported spending about thirteen days per month re-teaching these topics.[19] Think about that for a minute. There are roughly twenty instructional days in a month, and nationwide, on average, teachers reported spending at least part of thirteen out of these available days teaching content nearly everyone had already mastered. Why? Because that's what was in the grade-level standards! What ESEA accomplished (intentionally or not), and NCLB took to a whole different level, was the idea that "goodness" or effectiveness in K–12 teaching and learning was a result of progress toward these grade-level standards. Students who were already at grade-level proficiency received far less attention (their "points" toward "goodness" were already in the bank), as did those students who were too far below grade level to ever make it across the finish line in a single year. This is where minimum proficiency standards have gone wrong. Taking the focus of minimum proficiency and adding "closing of gaps" to the equation for goodness, policymakers gave their implicit blessing to decades of neglect of those students who were already at grade-level proficiency.

WHY FOCUS ON EXCELLENCE GAPS?

We see several reasons why the traditional, exclusive focus on minimum or basic competency achievement gaps poses problems for our students, schools, and society at large. First, achievement gaps exist at many levels. Minimum competency gaps are prioritized because of the traditional national and state policy focus described above, but there is no reason why differences in achievement couldn't also be a focus of education and policy at higher levels of performance. The emphasis placed on minimum competency is manifested in state accountability systems, how test results are interpreted and used at the school and classroom level, and how teachers are evaluated. When advanced achievement and closing excellence gaps are not considered educational priorities, it should not be surprising that high-ability students and their education receive relatively little attention.[20]

Second, overall rates of advanced performance within the United States are low relative to other industrialized countries, and excellence gaps are big and, by some estimations, growing—or at best shrinking very slowly. This is important to note because, contrary to the belief that "a rising tide raises all ships," progress in shrinking minimum competency gaps does not necessarily translate into shrinking excellence gaps.

Third, closing the other, more traditional achievement gaps probably won't lead to the social and economic progress claimed by advocates. Although minimum proficiency may have been sufficient to get a job and support a family at some point in the previous century, in the increasingly globalized economy of today, such basic skills are just that— basic.[21] Getting all students working up to basic grade-level achievement is an ethical requirement and certainly has economic benefits. But a society of students working at grade level, with little advanced achievement, will not be an economic growth and innovation machine.

Finally, and perhaps most importantly, failing to address excellence gaps will almost certainly cause them to grow over the long term as some families continue to develop the skills of their children outside of the public educational system. As the anecdotes at the beginning of this chapter illustrate, and the data in chapters 2 and 3 will show, students with knowledgeable, well-resourced families will often find the extra support needed to develop their talents and achieve success; their less well-supported peers often do not get that extra support, which over time widens gaps. Of course, advantaged families should not be faulted for providing advanced resources to their children, but their doing so combined with the relatively small attention advanced learners receive in public schools exacerbates excellence gaps.

2

How Excellent Are We?

EDUCATIONAL EXCELLENCE can be operationalized and assessed in several ways—we could probably write a book just on potential definitions and approaches to measurement. But you don't want to read that book any more than we want to write it, so we are going to keep things rather simple, focusing on excellence as high levels of traditional academic achievement. This success would include but not be limited to successful AP experiences, graduation from challenging colleges, or good grades in middle and high school honors classes.

Over the years, when we've talked about gaps in advanced achievement, we have had people ask us versions of the "But what about . . . " question (for example, "But what about creativity?" "But what about critical thinking?" "But what about twenty-first-century skills?"). We generally have two responses. First, we would use alternative measures if we had them, but we really don't. For example, if we had large-scale creativity measures, this book would primarily be focused on creativity and innovation gaps and how to shrink them. But we just do not have solid, large-scale data in that area. Second, even if we had great, scalable measures of those other constructs, traditional student achievement would still be important and would likely continue to dominate most educational policy discussions because (1) it is easily understood by most policymakers, educators, and parents, (2) content knowledge has long been seen as a goal of K–12 education, and (3) traditional student achievement is important.

Therefore, for the purposes of this book, and similar to how others have conceptualized it, educational or academic excellence is defined as the percent of students who score at advanced levels on international and national achievement tests.[1] Plucker and Burroughs have noted the various ways that excellence can be measured using assessment results, with the two most meaningful measures being ninetieth percentile scores or the percentage of students scoring above a specific threshold.[2] In general, the ninetieth percentile method has statistical advantages, while the percentage scoring advanced approach is more effective in policy settings. We will discuss the implications of these different approaches when we share data on excellence gaps in chapter 3, but for now we will assume that the percent of American students who score at advanced levels of standardized achievement tests matters, and matters a lot. As you will read in this chapter, the news is not good when it comes to American excellence. Students in the United States hardly lead the world in advanced performance (although grade 4 students perform at higher levels than grade 8 students).

Percentages Matter

Salzman and Lowell, offering a dissenting perspective, argue that the percentage of advanced performers matters less than the total number of high performers.[3] They suggested that the United States, though it has a low percentage of high scorers, produces large numbers of those students, which is the more important statistic. They have a point here, as the United States, with the third-largest population in the world, has a lot of students. Therefore, in their logic, the relatively poor US performance on that international assessment was actually an indicator of relative success. They further argue that focusing on top performers is ill-advised, and that the focus of national-level policy should be reducing the number of low-performing students.

This criticism does have face validity. If all 475,000 of Singapore's students performed at advanced levels in science, they would still be dwarfed in size by the roughly 8 million US students (roughly 12.5 percent) performing at advanced levels.[4] But Salzman and Lowell's analysis is based on two questionable assumptions. First, they ignore the size of each country's economy. The US economy is nearly forty times larger than that of Singapore, and it could be argued that the United States needs forty times as much talent to maintain and grow its economy.[5] It is also reasonable to assume that countries with relatively large economies have a large need for talent compared with smaller economies, making the production of talent across the board a critical contributor to quality of life. Put more bluntly, if rates of advanced performance don't matter and, therefore, the United States has enough talented students, why is there so much pressure by the business community to import more talent each year?[6]

Second, Salzman and Lowell assume that countries cannot create education systems that address the needs of all students, arguing instead that we must prioritize one group of students (for example, struggling students) over another (high-performing students). This default to the classic equity-or-excellence argument, as we discussed in chapter 1, feels weak: Why prioritize achievement gaps at one level but not another? Equity is equity, regardless of the students' potential.

Measuring Excellence

The following section uses a range of international and American assessment data to provide evidence of the excellence level of American students. International data are drawn from the most recent, 2011 administration of the Trends in Mathematics and Science Study (TIMSS) organized by the International Association for the Evaluation of Educational Achievement (IEA), using scale scores of 625 or higher to represent advanced achievement and educational excellence.[7] TIMSS is one of the two major international assessments, with the OECD's Programme for International Student Assessment (PISA) being the other. Much ink has been spent analyzing the differences between the two assessment programs, but for our purposes that would be getting into the weeds.[8] Suffice it to say that both programs have considerable strengths and, of course, flaws, but we use TIMSS because it is grade-based rather than age-based and because it uses the same assessment framework as the US national test (NAEP).

At this point, some of you are probably thinking, "Tests, tests, tests—I hate tests so much. Why are they using test data?" As we've said, they are our best options for data right now. But also, as one of our colleagues recently noted (and he's hardly a lover of standardized tests) these tests don't produce a lot of false positives.[9] In other words, if you do well on an achievement test, the odds are pretty good that you have learned quite a bit. And when we're comparing countries or states, false negatives (that is, bright students who don't test well) probably balance each other out in most of those comparisons. Having large percentages of students who know lots of stuff is not a bad thing.

HOW EXCELLENT ARE WE?

International Comparisons

Given increasing global competition for talent, Plucker noted that it is worthwhile to examine how countries compare in producing high-achieving students.[10] The results generally show that US students perform relatively well in math and science in grade 4, but the differences in advanced achievement between the United States and other countries widens considerably as students move into later grades. In the following sections, both cross-sectional and quasi-longitudinal data are presented for selected countries on the TIMSS grade 4 and grade 8 science and mathematics assessments of 2003, 2007, and 2011. Figures 2.1–2.5 depict trends in the percentage of students scoring at the TIMSS advanced level between 2003 and 2011. Taking descriptive data with a grain of salt is always a good idea, which is why assumptions about testing conditions across countries in large-scale international assessments are occasionally questioned.[11] The most notable caveat for the data in these figures is that not every country has consistently participated in the three TIMSS assessments since 2003. That said, several observations can be drawn from these descriptive data. First, the range in performance among countries is considerable, extending from the low single digits for a handful of countries to the high teens and twenties for others. The range is much larger in mathematics (with nearly 50 percent of students reaching the advanced level in some countries) than in science (with only 20 to 25 percent) of students nearing this level in the top-performing countries).

Second, the relative rankings for countries vary based on subject and grade level, but the differences are not large. For example, in addition to the usual countries at the top of the table (Taiwan, Japan, South Korea, Singapore), Russia, England, and the United States perform relatively

FIGURE 2.1   Grade 4 science advanced achievement
(percent scoring 625+) on TIMSS

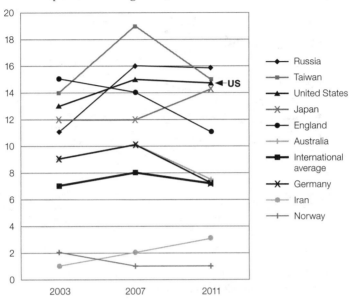

Source: Adapted from Jonathan A. Plucker, *Advanced Academic Performance: Exploring Country-Level Differences in the Pursuit of Educational Excellence* (Policy Brief 7) (Amsterdam: International Association for the Evaluation of Educational Achievement, 2015), http://www.iea.nl/fileadmin/user_upload/Policy_Briefs/IEA_policy_brief_Aug2015.pdf.

well in grade 4 and grade 8 science and grade 4 mathematics. Russian students also perform at high levels in grade 8 mathematics, but American and English students less so.

Third, although regression to the mean (the statistical fact that very low or high performers tend to move toward the group average over time) is often a complicating factor in studies of education excellence, it does not appear to be a major factor in these analyses, given that roughly the same number of countries exhibit declining and increasing percentages of advanced students.[12]

Cohort Trends in Excellence by Country

The unique sampling framework for TIMSS (that is, testing every four years in grades 4 and 8) allows us to answer the question, How did the percent of advanced scorers change from grade 4 in 2007 to grade 8 in

FIGURE 2.2 Grade 8 science advanced achievement
(percent scoring 625+) on TIMSS

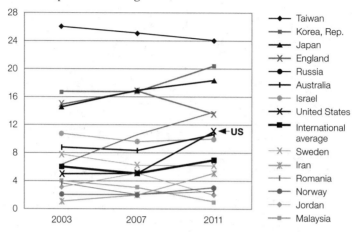

Source: Adapted from Jonathan A. Plucker, *Advanced Academic Performance: Exploring Country-Level Differences in the Pursuit of Educational Excellence* (Policy Brief 7) (Amsterdam: International Association for the Evaluation of Educational Achievement, 2015), http://www.iea.nl/fileadmin/user_upload/Policy_Briefs/IEA_policy_brief_Aug2015.pdf.

FIGURE 2.3 Grade 4 and mathematics advanced achievement
(percent scoring 625+) on TIMSS

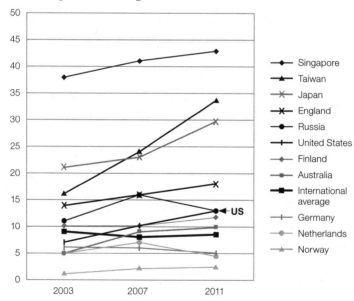

Source: Adapted from Jonathan A. Plucker, *Advanced Academic Performance: Exploring Country-Level Differences in the Pursuit of Educational Excellence* (Policy Brief 7) (Amsterdam: International Association for the Evaluation of Educational Achievement, 2015), http://www.iea.nl/fileadmin/user_upload/Policy_Briefs/IEA_policy_brief_Aug2015.pdf.

FIGURE 2.4   Grade 8 mathematics advanced achievement (percent scoring 625+) on TIMSS—Countries with over 20 percent advanced

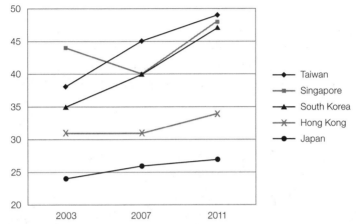

Source: Adapted from Jonathan A. Plucker, *Advanced Academic Performance: Exploring Country-Level Differences in the Pursuit of Educational Excellence* (Policy Brief 7) (Amsterdam: International Association for the Evaluation of Educational Achievement, 2015), http://www.iea.nl/fileadmin/user_upload/Policy_Briefs/IEA_policy_brief_Aug2015.pdf.

FIGURE 2.5   Grade 8 mathematics advanced achievement (percent scoring 625+) on TIMSS—Countries with less than 15 percent advanced

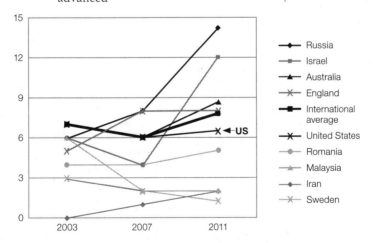

Source: Adapted from Jonathan A. Plucker, *Advanced Academic Performance: Exploring Country-Level Differences in the Pursuit of Educational Excellence* (Policy Brief 7) (Amsterdam: International Association for the Evaluation of Educational Achievement, 2015), http://www.iea.nl/fileadmin/user_upload/Policy_Briefs/IEA_policy_brief_Aug2015.pdf.

2011? Or, more to the point, Is there an "excellence value-added" from fourth to eighth grade in certain countries? Table 2.1 includes cohort comparison data for mathematics, table 2.2 for science.

For math, three of the four highest-scoring countries significantly increased the percentage of students scoring at the advanced level from grade 4 to grade 8, while the percentage in some low-scoring countries declined further by grade 8. In science, the number of advanced students

TABLE 2.1   Advanced scorers (625+) on TIMSS mathematics: 2007 grade 4 versus 2011 grade 8

	2007 grade 4		2011 grade 8		Cohort differences		
Jurisdiction	Percent advanced	SE	Percent advanced	SE	Percent advanced	95% CI	
Taiwan	24	(1.2)	49	(1.5)	+25	21.64	28.98
Singapore	41	(2.1)	48	(2.0)	+7	1.28	12.64
Japan	23	(1.2)	27	(1.3)	+4	0.71	7.49
Iran	0	(0.1)	2	(0.5)	+2	0.74	2.88
Slovenia	3	(0.4)	4	(0.4)	+1	−0.48	1.90
Georgia	1	(0.4)	3	(0.3)	+1	0.33	2.27
International average	11	(0.2)	11	(0.2)	0	−0.85	0.40
Australia	9	(0.8)	9	(1.7)	0	−3.81	3.48
New Zealand	5	(0.5)	5	(0.8)	0	−2.08	1.65
Hungary	9	(0.8)	8	(0.7)	−1	−3.28	0.75
Norway	2	(0.3)	1	(0.2)	−1	−1.72	−0.41
Russia	16	(1.8)	14	(1.2)	−2	−5.93	2.60
Italy	6	(0.7)	3	(0.5)	−2	−3.75	−0.44
United States	10	(0.8)	7	(0.8)	−3	−5.64	−1.27
Lithuania	10	(0.7)	5	(0.6)	−5	−6.45	−2.85
Hong Kong	40	(2.2)	34	(2.0)	−6	−11.80	−0.25
England	16	(1.2)	8	(1.4)	−8	−11.75	−4.58

Source: Adapted from Jonathan A. Plucker, *Advanced Academic Performance: Exploring Country-Level Differences in the Pursuit of Educational Excellence* (Policy Brief 7) (Amsterdam: International Association for the Evaluation of Educational Achievement, 2015), http://www.iea.nl/fileadmin/user_upload/Policy_Briefs/IEA_policy_brief_Aug2015.pdf.

Notes: Countries with estimates of 0% in both years are omitted. The cohort differences may appear incorrect due to rounding. SE = Standard error, CI = Confidence interval.

TABLE 2.2   Advanced scorers (625+) on TIMSS science:
2007 grade 4 versus 2011 grade 8

	2007 grade 4		2011 grade 8		Cohort differences		
Jurisdiction	Percent advanced	SE	Percent advanced	SE	Percent advanced	95% CI	
Slovenia	6	(0.6)	13	(0.8)	+7	4.98	9.01
Japan	12	(1.0)	18	(1.1)	+6	3.06	8.78
Taiwan	19	(1.0)	24	(1.4)	+5	2.02	8.60
Singapore	36	(1.9)	40	(1.7)	+4	−0.91	9.17
Lithuania	3	(0.4)	6	(0.7)	+3	1.24	4.45
Iran	2	(0.3)	5	(0.7)	+3	1.42	4.54
New Zealand	8	(0.5)	9	(1.0)	+1	−0.84	3.37
Norway	1	(0.4)	3	(0.4)	+1	0.33	2.53
Australia	10	(0.7)	11	(1.6)	0	−3.08	3.88
International average	9	(0.2)	9	(0.2)	0	−0.81	0.33
Georgia	1	(0.2)	0	(0.1)	0	−0.50	0.36
England	14	(1.2)	14	(1.5)	−1	−4.49	3.06
Russia	16	(1.9)	14	(1.1)	−2	−6.38	2.31
United States	15	(0.9)	10	(0.7)	−5	−7.26	−2.70
Hong Kong	14	(1.4)	9	(1.1)	−5	−8.55	−1.48
Hungary	13	(1.0)	9	(0.8)	−5	−7.15	−2.10
Italy	13	(1.0)	4	(0.5)	−9	−11.07	−6.80

Source: Adapted from Jonathan A. Plucker, Advanced Academic Performance: Exploring Country-Level Differences in the Pursuit of Educational Excellence (Policy Brief 7) (Amsterdam: International Association for the Evaluation of Educational Achievement, 2015), http://www.iea.nl/fileadmin/user_upload/Policy_Briefs/IEA_policy_brief_Aug2015.pdf.

Notes: Countries with estimates of 0% in both years are omitted. The cohort differences may appear incorrect due to rounding. SE = Standard error, CI = Confidence interval.

in three high-scoring countries increased from grade 4 to grade 8, but no country with below-average results in grade 4 experienced a significant decline over the ensuing four years. These results suggest that a handful of countries were able to add to already high levels of excellence. Specifically, Taiwan, Singapore, and Japan should be the subject of further investigation, as the percentages of students reaching advanced level in these countries increased in both math and science.

These international data on excellence lead to several conclusions. First, the percentage of students scoring at the advanced level at grades 4 and 8 and in mathematics and science ranges widely (some would say wildly) from several countries that have essentially no students performing at advanced levels to a handful of countries in which a quarter to a half of students routinely score advanced.

At a broader policy level, research should focus on the extent to which high-scoring countries have comprehensive national excellence policies for education and, eventually, workforce development. Do high-scoring countries emphasize educational excellence more than low-scoring countries; for example, by including data on advanced performance in national reports? There have always been robust research programs on educational excellence around the world, but research on country-level education policies for excellence is much rarer.[13] Of course, the lack of national-level excellence strategies is a limitation on such research.[14]

Second, several countries routinely see increases in their percentage of high-scoring students, which flies in the face of regression to the mean. At the same time, a smaller number of lower-performing countries have experienced consistent decreases in the percentage of high-scoring students; both groups should be the subject of additional research to determine the potential causes for the unexpected increases and decreases in advanced performance.

National Wealth, Inequality, and Educational Excellence

One possible interpretation of these data is that national wealth and prosperity are the main drivers behind a country's percentage of students scoring at advanced levels: more mature, richer nations may have more resources to devote to moving their students to excellent performance. At the same time, it can be reasonably argued that less wealthy, developing countries may see educational excellence as a strategy for talent development, innovation, and economic growth, prioritizing excellence over other forms of educational success.

We can begin to investigate this by looking at indicators of national wealth and income inequality. Figures 2.6–2.9 plot countries' 2010 per capita GDP versus their percent of advanced scorers in grade 4 math (figures 2.6 and 2.7) and grade 8 science (figures 2.8 and 2.9). Preliminary analyses found evidence that the data perform differently for the

FIGURE 2.6 Grade 4 math advanced scorers versus per capita GDP:
G20 countries, 2011

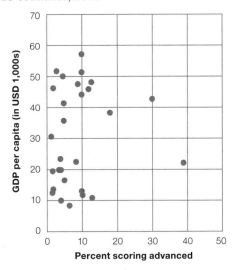

Source: TIMSS data from the International Association for the Evaluation of Educational Achievement, http://www.iea.nl/480.html; World Bank Gini Index Estimates, http://data.worldbank.org/indicator/SI.POV.GINI.

FIGURE 2.7 Grade 4 math advanced scorers versus per capita GDP:
Non-G20 countries, 2011

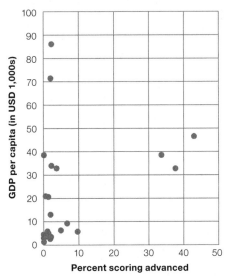

Source: TIMSS data from the International Association for the Evaluation of Educational Achievement, http://www.iea.nl/480.html; World Bank Gini Index Estimates, http://data.worldbank.org/indicator/SI.POV.GINI.

FIGURE 2.8   Grade 8 science advanced scorers versus per capita GDP:
G20 countries, 2011

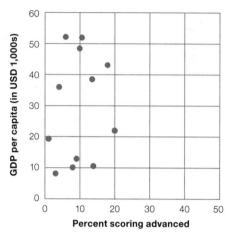

Source: TIMSS data from the International Association for the Evaluation of Educational Achievement, http://www.iea.nl/480.html; World Bank Gini Index Estimates, http://data.worldbank .org/indicator/SI.POV.GINI.

FIGURE 2.9   Grade 8 science advanced scorers versus per capita GDP:
Non-G20 countries, 2011

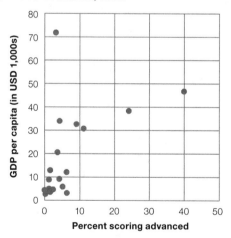

Source: TIMSS data from the International Association for the Evaluation of Educational Achievement, http://www.iea.nl/480.html; World Bank Gini Index Estimates, http://data.worldbank .org/indicator/SI.POV.GINI.

world's largest economies, leading to separate figures for G20 and non-G20 countries. (For the purposes of this chapter, the G20 figures include all countries in the G20 plus any EU member states given the EU membership in the G20).

For G20 countries (figures 2.6 and 2.8), there appears to be little relationship between per capita GDP and educational excellence. The situation for non-G20 (figures 2.7 and 2.9) nations is more complex. If high-GDP, low-performance outliers are removed (Qatar, Norway), there appears to be a small but positive relationship between economic strength and educational excellence. If the moderate-GDP, high-performance countries are treated as outliers and removed, there would be little evidence of a correlation.

Even assuming the high-GDP, low-performance countries are the outliers, issues of causality need to be addressed: Does national wealth lead to academic excellence? Is academic excellence the driver of national wealth? Or are there other variables that better explain the possible correlation between per capita GDP and percent of advanced scorers in non-G20 nations? Answering these questions is beyond the scope of this volume but deserves further investigation.

Yet another possible influence on academic excellence is economic inequality.[15] This argument has been used to explain performance on international assessments.[16] For the purposes of this analysis, each country's percentage of advanced scorers was plotted against its Gini coefficient (an approximation of income inequality largely calculated using the percentage of national wealth concentrated in the wealthiest individuals in a society; a Gini index of 0 indicates perfect equality whereas a Gini index of 100 equals perfect inequality.[17] The Gini coefficient is controversial as it was designed as a rough measure of economic dispersion. Because any definition of what counts as value or access to capital can be argued as being imperfect, the coefficient is imperfect or at least arguable as a measure of inequality. However, it is widely considered a rough estimate of economic equality in a country, with larger values representing more inequality.[18] There are large gaps in the data for 2010 Gini coefficients, but we judged the available information to be sufficient for these exploratory analyses. Figure 2.10 shows the Gini coefficient versus advanced scorers for grade 4 mathematics, and figure 2.11 for grade 8

FIGURE 2.10   Grade 4 mathematics advanced scorers versus
Gini coefficient, 2011

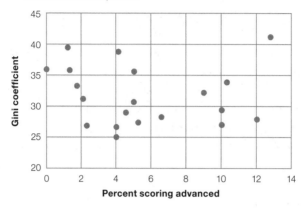

Source: TIMSS data from the International Association for the Evaluation of Educational Achievement, http://www.iea.nl/480.html; World Bank Gini Index Estimates, http://data.worldbank
.org/indicator/SI.POV.GINI.

FIGURE 2.11   Grade 8 science advanced scorers versus Gini coefficient, 2011

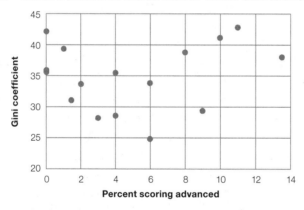

Source: TIMSS data from the International Association for the Evaluation of Educational Achievement, http://www.iea.nl/480.html; World Bank Gini Index Estimates, http://data.worldbank
.org/indicator/SI.POV.GINI.

science (grade 8 mathematics and grade 4 science data are not included
due to space limitations, but they are similar to the grade 4 mathematics
data in figure 2.10).

The data do not point to any definitive conclusions but suggest the
need for future research. If the one outlier is removed from figure 2.10

(the United States, with a Gini coefficient of 41.1 and 13 percent scoring advanced), there may be a slight negative relationship. Figure 2.10 suggests a possible parabolic relationship between the two variables, which could mean that higher levels of inequality may be associated with both lower- and higher-performing students at the advanced level.

Economic wealth may have a complex relationship to educational excellence. Does one lead to the other? Is there a reciprocal relationship? Or is any observed correlation spurious? The data presented here provide limited evidence of a relationship (especially among non-G20 nations), but the nature of that relationship needs considerable additional study. Furthermore, a more complex research program is required to determine if there is a minimum amount of educational excellence needed to develop an economy, expand a mature economy, or develop certain industries, such as biotechnology. For example, do low levels of advanced performance in some Nordic countries matter less in their mature economies than in smaller, developing economies? Or are these countries importing talent via immigration or outsourcing, or relying on natural resources rather than human capital to maintain their quality of life?

That said, we often run into critics who suggest that the United States' high levels of income inequality make shrinking excellence gaps very difficult, if not impossible. The data presented in this section, although hardly conclusive about the exact relationship between inequality and educational excellence, strongly suggest that inequality does not preclude a country from having relatively small excellence gaps.

US Excellence

Up to this point, the international data suggest that a respectable if not overwhelming amount of American students perform at the advanced level in mathematics and science in grade 4, but at a less impressive rate in grade 8. Furthermore, the various cross-sectional and longitudinal data presented in the figures so far in this chapter provide evidence that the percent of advanced scorers slips in both subjects between grade 4 and grade 8. The data on the relationship between national economic wealth and inequality, although preliminary, suggest that those variables do not have appreciable relationships with a country's ability to produce students who perform at advanced levels.

But what about national and state-level data within the United States? We have the advantage of world-class, long-term achievement testing programs and, therefore, relatively deep storehouses of student data. What do these data sets tell us about educational excellence within the United States?

The US and state data we examined are drawn from recent administrations of the National Assessment of Educational Progress, which, as mentioned above, is based on a similar framework to TIMSS. NAEP tests students periodically in a range of content areas and annually in math and reading/language arts in grades 4, 8, and 12 (less often in twelfth grade). As with TIMSS (and any other international or national assessment), not every student takes the NAEP exam, but the National Center for Education Statistics (which oversees NAEP) estimates of student performance at the state and national level are considered to be of high quality. In this book, national-level NAEP data include both public and private school students; state-level data include only public school students (but given that public schools serve over 90 percent of American preK–12 students, that doesn't affect our conclusions).

NAEP scores are reported in different ways, but the format that gets the most attention in policy circles, and which we will use here, is to present the percentage of students who score in each of four performance bands: Below Basic, Basic, Proficient, and Advanced. Table 2.3 presents an example of the expectations for student performance within each performance category.

TABLE 2.3   Descriptions of NAEP achievement levels in general and for specific assessments

	Basic	Proficient	Advanced
General	Partial mastery of prerequisite knowledge and skills that are fundamental for proficient work at each grade assessed. NAEP also reports the proportion of students whose scores place them below the *Basic* achievement level.	Solid academic performance for each grade assessed. Students reaching this level have demonstrated competency over challenging subject matter, including subject-matter knowledge, application of such knowledge to real-world situations, and analytical skills appropriate to the subject matter.	Superior performance at each grade assessed.

(continued)

TABLE 2.3 Descriptions of NAEP achievement levels in general and for specific assessments (*continued*)

	Basic	Proficient	Advanced
Reading grade 4	Students should be able to locate relevant information, make simple inferences, and use their understanding of the text to identify details that support a given interpretation or conclusion. Students should be able to interpret the meaning of a word as it is used in the text.	Students should be able to integrate and interpret texts and apply their understanding of the text to draw conclusions and make evaluations.	Students should be able to make complex inferences and construct and support their inferential understanding of the text. Students should be able to apply their understanding of a text to make and support a judgment.
Mathematics grade 8	Students should exhibit evidence of conceptual and procedural understanding in the five NAEP content areas. This level of performance signifies an understanding of arithmetic operations—including estimation—on whole numbers, decimals, fractions, and percents.	Students should apply mathematical concepts and procedures consistently to complex problems in the five NAEP content areas.	Students should be able to reach beyond the recognition, identification, and application of mathematical rules in order to generalize and synthesize concepts and principles in the five NAEP content areas.
Science grade 12	Students should be able to describe, measure, classify, explain, and predict phenomena at multiple scales, from atomic/molecular to interstellar. They should be able to design and critique observational and experimental studies, and they should be able to propose and critique solutions to problems at local or regional scales.	Students should be able to demonstrate relationships and compare alternative models, predictions, and explanations. They should be able to design and critique observational and experimental studies, controlling multiple variables, using scientific models to explain results, and choosing among alternative conclusions based on arguments from evidence. They should be able to compare scientific costs or risks and benefits of alternative solutions to problems at local or regional scales.	Students should be able to use alternative models to generate predictions and explanations. They should be able to design and critique investigations that relate data to alternative models of phenomena. They should be able to compare costs or risks and benefits of alternative solutions to problems at local, regional, and global scales.

Source: All information in this table drawn from various sources at www.nationsreportcard.gov.

A fair question at this point would be: But what should the data look like? Based on the international averages, getting at least 10 percent of American students scoring in the Advanced range feels like a reasonable starting point. However, as the data below indicate, even this low-hanging fruit is well beyond our current reach in most content areas.

In general, few US students in public or private schools score advanced on the various NAEP assessments (table 2.4). By far the best performance is found in mathematics and reading, which is not surprising, given the focus of American schools in the NCLB era with its narrowing of the curriculum. But even in these areas, the percentage of students scoring advanced is not impressive. And the percentage in other subject areas—from civics and economics to US history and science—ranges from negligible to tiny.

We are sensitive to the fact that one can question the content of these tests, whether "knowing stuff" is really that important, and (again) whether tests in general are a good indicator of an education system's

TABLE 2.4   Percent scoring advanced on most recent NAEP test by subject area

	Grade 4	Grade 8	Grade 12
Civics	2% (2010)	2% (2014)	4% (2010)
Economics			3% (2012)
Geography	2% (2010)	3% (2014)	1% (2010)
Mathematics	7% (2015)	8% (2015)	3% (2013)
Reading	9% (2015)	4% (2015)	5% (2013)
Science		2% (2011)	
US history	2% (2010)	1% (2014)	1% (2010)
Writing		3% (2011)	3% (2011)

Source: Format adapted from www.nationsreportcard.gov. All data from NAEP data explorer: http://nces.ed.gov/nationsreportcard/naepdata/.

performance. Indeed, we have raised these questions in roughly similar contexts ourselves. But our view is that having few students graduating high school with advanced understanding of economics and geography, for example, is hard to view as a good thing. Knowledge and understanding matter, and as the international data suggest, it is possible to get large percentages of students to advanced levels of content-specific understanding. We've just historically not accomplished this in the United States.

That said, the recent weak performance has substantially improved over the past generation, at least in the more frequently tested areas of math and reading (see table 2.5 and figures 2.12–2.14). The percentage of advanced scorers in math has increased significantly in grades 4 and 8 since 1996. But math progress is much more muted in grade 12 math and in all grades for reading. We will not consider progress in other tested content areas, such as US history and writing, since so few students perform at advanced levels.

TABLE 2.5　Percent scoring advanced on NAEP math and reading assessments, 1996–2015

	Math			Reading		
	Grade 4	Grade 8	Grade 12	Grade 4	Grade 8	Grade 12
1996	2	4	2			
1998				7	3	6
2000	3	5	2	7		
2002				7	3	5
2003	4	5		8	3	
2005	5	6	2	8	3	5
2007	6	7		8	3	
2009	6	8	3	8	3	5
2011	7	8		8	3	
2013	8	9	3	8	4	5
2015	7	8		9	4	
Change 1996–2015	+5%	+4%	+1%	+2%	+1%	–1%

Source: Format adapted from www.nationsreportcard.gov. All data from NAEP data explorer: http://nces.ed.gov/nationsreportcard/naepdata/.

FIGURE 2.12   Percent scoring advanced on NAEP mathematics assessments, selected years

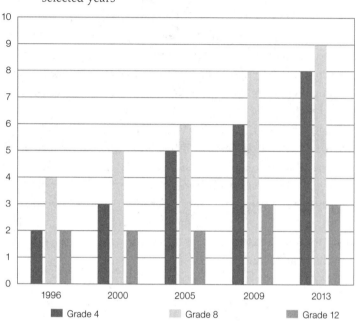

Source: All data from NAEP data explorer: http://nces.ed.gov/nationsreportcard/naepdata/.

Advanced Performance at the State Level

The national data are rather depressing, but the role of education in our federalist system often produces wide variations in state education systems, making an examination of state data worthwhile. Figures 2.15 and 2.16, which depict advanced scoring rates by state, provide evidence that performance at the advanced level is highly variable. We provide only two maps, as the basic trends are similar: mostly mediocre, with more variance on some tests and grade levels than at others. For example, in grade 4 reading, a handful of states are doing well, three are doing poorly, and the rest are mediocre; in grade 4 mathematics, there is more of a spread from top to bottom, but fewer than 10 percent of students are performing at the advanced level in the majority of states have. On NAEP assessments with low excellence rates (including grade 8 reading, every level of science, US history, writing) one finds little state-level variation, because advanced performance rates are uniformly poor.

FIGURE 2.13   Percent scoring advanced on NAEP reading assessments, selected years

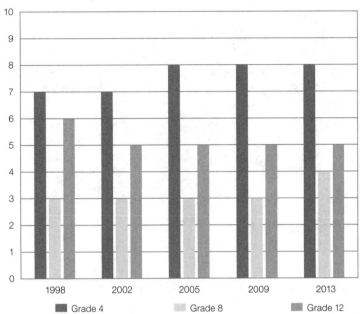

Source: All data from NAEP data explorer: http://nces.ed.gov/nationsreportcard/naepdata/.

FIGURE 2.14   Percent scoring advanced on other recent NAEP assessments

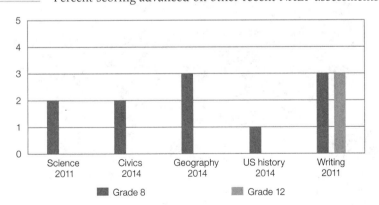

Source: All data from NAEP data explorer: http://nces.ed.gov/nationsreportcard/naepdata/.

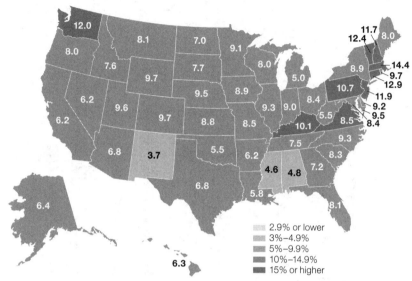

FIGURE 2.15   NAEP 2015 grade 4 reading, percent scoring advanced by state

Source: All data from NAEP data explorer: http://nces.ed.gov/nationsreportcard/naepdata/.

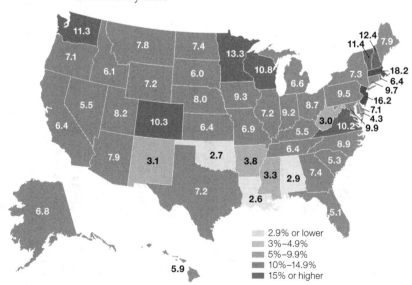

FIGURE 2.16   NAEP 2015 grade 8 mathematics, percent scoring advanced by state

Source: All data from NAEP data explorer: http://nces.ed.gov/nationsreportcard/naepdata/.

Socioeconomic Status Matters

As with the international data, it is possible to examine the relationship between socioeconomic status and academic excellence. As one moves from the country level to the student level, socioeconomic status becomes harder to measure and researchers generally use proxy variables associated with overall family income and social status. One such variable, which we use in figure 2.17 below, is parent education level (defined by NAEP as the highest level of education achieved by either parent). Not surprisingly, parent education is clearly correlated with advanced performance.

CONCLUSIONS ABOUT AMERICAN EDUCATIONAL EXCELLENCE

The data in this chapter can be sliced and diced in infinite ways, but they tell pretty much the same story any way you look at them: the United States—in both public and private K–12 schools—produces too few students performing at educationally excellent levels. This is true both in absolute (the overall percentages of advanced scorers) and relative terms

FIGURE 2.17   NAEP grade 8 mathematics percent advanced by parent education

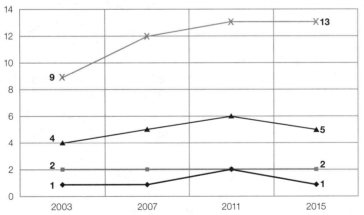

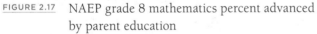

Source: All data from NAEP data explorer: http://nces.ed.gov/nationsreportcard/naepdata/.

(the percentages compared with other countries). Within the United States, state-by-state variation is considerable, but in the vast majority of states, fewer than 10 percent of students are performing at advanced levels in reading and math at any grade level and fewer than 5 percent score advanced in other content areas at any grade level.

We have had critics ask an important and reasonable question: If our country has produced so few advanced performers for such a long period of time, how can you argue that educational excellence is so important? After all, the United Stated is still the world's largest economy.

Simply put, we imported our talent.[19]

Largely lost in current debates about immigration is the fact that the United States has long satisfied its tremendous thirst for talent by importing the world's best and brightest. These individuals often came to the United States for higher education, then stayed for (and thrived in) our combination of soft power, economic opportunity, and social mobility. Whether those factors are still attractive is a debate beyond the scope of this book, but geopolitics and worldwide economic growth have changed the context for the global competition for talent. When one of us first began teaching at a university some twenty-odd years ago, his international students strongly preferred to remain in the United States after graduation. But as time has marched on, many countries have greatly expanded economic opportunities, and the perception is that obtaining visas and green cards to remain in the United States has become more difficult. Although the United States still imports much of its talent, its ability to do so over the next several decades—when international competition for such talent will likely become even more intense—is highly uncertain.

This situation has led us to refer to the United States as a great place to be talented but not a great place to develop one's talents. With changing immigration patterns, we can no longer accept this situation. We must do a better job of pushing our students to perform at advanced levels.

3

Excellence Gaps

ONE WAY to get more advanced students is fairly obvious: we need to start shrinking excellence gaps. Before we get into potential strategies for doing so, we need to explore what excellence gaps look like and how have they changed over time. In this chapter, we provide several examples, but we avoid getting too far into the weeds—more detailed and extensive examples are provided in a recent report on excellence gaps, a recent research paper on excellence gaps across countries, and the original excellence gap research report, in addition to Finn and Wright's analyses.[1] Our analyses and these reports all point in the same direction: the United States has large excellence gaps.

READING THE TEA LEAVES OF EXCELLENCE GAPS

To get started, let's take a look at table 3.1, showing the percentages of lower-income students who score advanced on NAEP assessments.

We have heard responses to these data like "Yikes!" "That can't be right!" and our favorite, stunned silence. And these are reasonable. The most troubling response has been, "But I have had plenty of poor students who performed at very high levels." Well, that's probably not accurate, according to all of the available data. Of course, NAEP results are estimates (that is, not every student in the country takes each test), and a zero represents an estimate that "rounds to zero." In a country with over 60 million K–12 students, even 0.4 percent of students in a given grade level can represent a significant number of students.

TABLE 3.1   Percent of students eligible for free or reduced-price lunch scoring advanced on most recent NAEP test by subject area

	Grade 4	Grade 8	Grade 12
Civics	0% (2010)	0% (2014)	1% (2010)
Economics			0% (2012)
Geography	0% (2010)	1% (2014)	0% (2010)
Mathematics	2% (2015)	2% (2015)	0% (2013)
Reading	3% (2015)	1% (2015)	2% (2013)
Science		0% (2011)	
US history	0% (2010)	0% (2014)	0% (2010)
Writing		1% (2011)	1% (2011)

Source: All information in this table drawn from various sources at www.nationsreportcard.gov.

All of that said, very few low-income students, as identified by eligibility for free or reduced-price lunch, score at the advanced level on any national tests. Now compare the data in table 3.1 with that for non-eligible (that is, higher-family-income) students in table 3.2.

The differences in math and reading are stark; in other content areas, the differences are significant but not nearly as large. This probably is a result of NCLB's narrowing of the curriculum and/or narrow focus on improving math and reading test scores.[2] However, it is safe to conclude that students' odds of performing at high levels greatly increases if their families are of higher rather than lower means.

Large excellence gaps also exist based on race and ethnicity. For example, figure 3.1 includes data for specific racial/ethnic groups of students on the NAEP grade 4 math assessment. Although the percentage of students scoring advanced on these tests has increased for most groups, Asian American and white students have seen sharply increased their rates of advanced achievement, while Hispanic, black, and Native American students have seen very small increases in the number of advanced

TABLE 3.2   Percent of students not eligible for free or reduced-price lunch scoring advanced on most recent NAEP test by subject area

	Grade 4	Grade 8	Grade 12
Civics	3% 2010	3% 2014	5% 2010
Economics			4% 2012
Geography	3% 2010	5% 2014	1% 2010
Mathematics	13% 2015	13% 2015	4% 2013
Reading	15% 2015	6% 2015	7% 2013
Science		3% 2011	
US History	4% 2010	2% 2014	1% 2010
Writing		5% 2011	4% 2011

Source: All information in this table drawn from various sources at www.nationsreportcard.gov.

scorers. Figure 3.2, showing grade 4 reading assessment results by lunch status, paints a similarly depressing picture.

State-Level Excellence Gaps

State data are again illustrative, especially because some states with relatively high rates of advanced students also have very large excellence gaps. Figures 3.3 and 3.4 present an estimate of excellence gaps for each state on various assessments, calculated as the percentage of free or reduced-price lunch–eligible students scoring advanced divided by the percentage of non-eligible advanced scorers (for example, if a state has 2.5 percent of eligible students scoring advanced versus 10 percent non-eligible, the excellence gap index would be .25; in other words, low-income students are performing at advanced levels at a quarter the rate of higher-income students).

A good example of this is Massachusetts, a state that has rightfully received praise for sharp increases in test scores, including increases in the percentage of students scoring advanced on many state and NAEP

FIGURE 3.1   NAEP grade 4 math percent advanced, by race/ethnicity

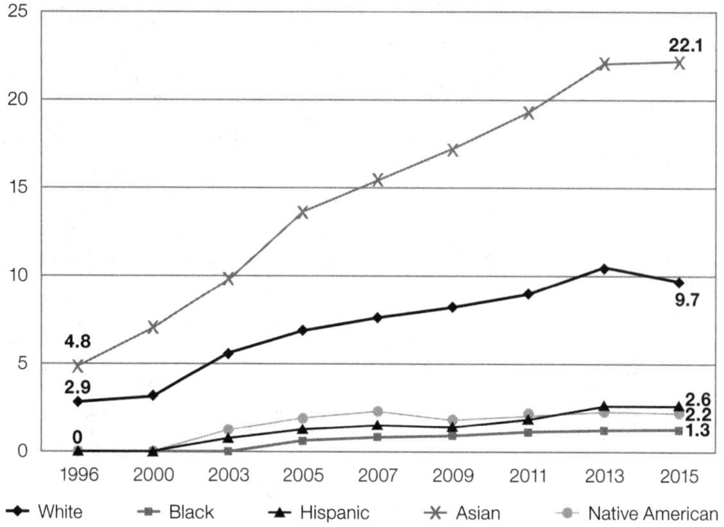

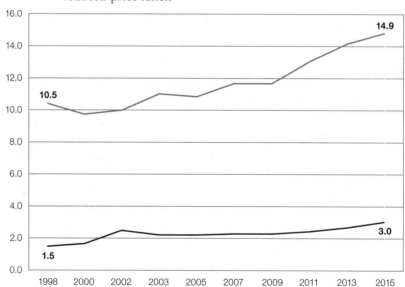

Source: All data from NAEP data explorer: http://nces.ed.gov/nationsreportcard/naepdata/.

FIGURE 3.2   NAEP grade 4 reading percent advanced, by eligibility free or reduced-price lunch

Source: All data from NAEP data explorer: http://nces.ed.gov/nationsreportcard/naepdata/.

FIGURE 3.3 NAEP 2015 grade 4 mathematics excellence gaps by lunch status, eligible students scoring advanced as a proportion of non-eligible students scoring advanced

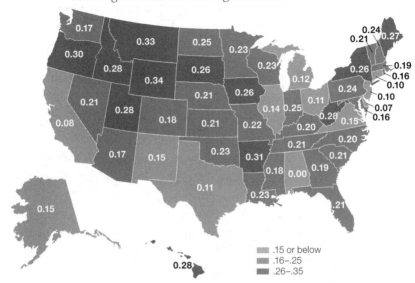

Source: All data from NAEP data explorer: http://nces.ed.gov/nationsreportcard/naepdata/.

FIGURE 3.4 NAEP 2015 grade 4 reading excellence gaps by lunch status, eligible students scoring advanced as a proportion of non-eligible students scoring advanced

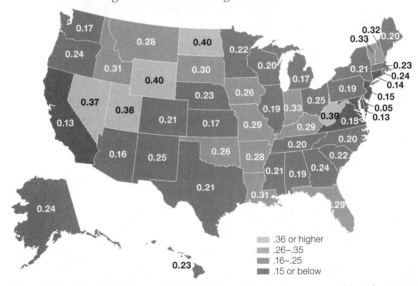

Source: All data from NAEP data explorer: http://nces.ed.gov/nationsreportcard/naepdata/.

assessments. At the same time, Massachusetts also suffers from some of the largest excellence gaps in the country. A rising tide may lift all ships, but it clearly doesn't lift them all to the same level.

International Excellence Gaps

We have little recent research on international excellence gaps, with most the recent conducted in the United States and United Kingdom. Rutkowski, Rutkowski, and Plucker used TIMSS data from eighty-two education systems and found evidence of shrinking gender excellence gaps and persistent but small immigration excellence gaps (academic performance of immigrant versus nonimmigrant students).[3] To date, little research appears to have been conducted on excellence gaps across countries based on student socioeconomic status, in part because of how difficult it is to obtain a comparable metric of income of wealth across nations. This is certainly an area worth of further research.

Finn and Wright took a different approach to uncover comparative excellence gaps. Using PISA data, they compared the percentage of high-scoring students from the top and bottom quartiles of socioeconomic status (SES), as measured by PISA's Index of Economic, Social, and Cultural Status (ESCS). Figure 3.5 shows a clear relationship between the percentage of poorer versus wealthier students who score at high levels, and cleverly took these data further by calculating a ratio of high-SES advanced performers to low-SES advanced performers. For the selected countries, ratios ranged from 2.9:1 to 18.0:1, with low ratios representing smaller socioeconomic excellence gaps. The United States had a higher ratio than all but Hungary in math and reading, and only Hungary and Taiwan had higher ratios in science. So not only do excellence gaps exist in every country, they are much larger in the United States than in the other countries included in figure 3.5.[4] This is discouraging news.

It's Not All About Poverty

In reviewing these data, it is tempting to lay the blame for excellence gaps at the feet of poverty. Although economic vulnerability is almost certainly a major contributor to excellence gaps (and a promising focus for interventions), the data paint a more complex picture: race/ethnicity has a notable influence on these gaps. We plotted excellence rates for

FIGURE 3.5   Percentage of international students at levels 5 or 6, PISA math, by socioeconomic status

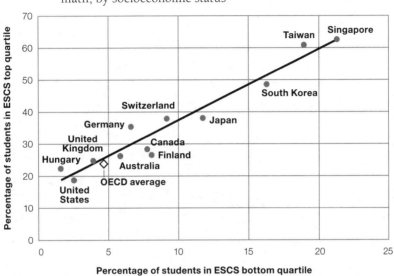

Source: From Chester E. Finn and Brandon L. Wright, *Failing Our Brightest Kids: The Global Challenge of Educating High-Ability Students* (Cambridge, MA: Harvard Education Press, 2015), figure 2.6, p. 34. Used with permission.

NAEP grade 8 math from 1996 through 2015 by free or reduced-price lunch status, but with an important twist: we compared results of Asian American and white students who qualified for free or reduced price-lunch against results for black, Hispanic, and Native American students who did not qualify in order to try and single out the effect of race separate from that of income (see figure 3.6).

This approach is admittedly crude and imprecise, but is enlightening nonetheless. More sophisticated approaches to this topic tend to find similar results. These data suggest that even when controlling for socioeconomic status, excellence gaps by race/ethnicity may still exist. This suggests that, at least in the United States with regard to excellence gaps, race still matters. It further suggests that any interventions to address excellence gaps that focus on poverty reduction may not fully address persistent excellence gaps.

Figure 3.7, depicting lunch status advanced scoring rates by parent education, illustrates the complexity of socioeconomic gaps further.

FIGURE 3.6   Big racial excellence gaps even when controlling for socioeconomic status

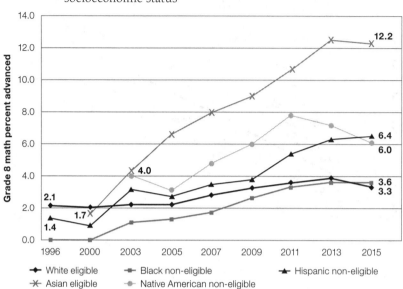

Source: All data from NAEP data explorer: http://nces.ed.gov/nationsreportcard/naepdata/.

Children who have a parent who has completed college have significantly higher excellence rates compared with those whose parents have less education; but the socioeconomic excellence gap is actually *larger* for the most educated families. Data such as these provide evidence that excellence gaps are complex phenomena, and therefore call into question the efficacy of narrow interventions, such as those focused on only one potential cause, to close or eradicate them.

CONCLUSIONS ABOUT AMERICAN EXCELLENCE GAPS

These and related data led Plucker and colleagues to refer to the existence of a persistent talent underclass in the United States made up of black, Native American, Hispanic, and low-income students.[5] *Underclass* is admittedly a strong term, but how else to refer to entire demographic groups of students whose academic talents have not been developed for at least a generation, and almost certainly several generations? And

FIGURE 3.7   Socioeconomic status excellence gaps have an interesting
relationship with parent education

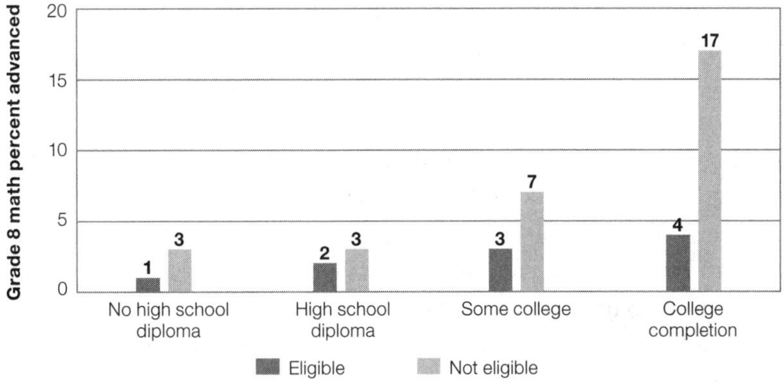

Source: All data from NAEP data explorer: http://nces.ed.gov/nationsreportcard/naepdata/.

excellence gaps are not closing on their own. On the contrary, many
are growing, with the implication that our talent underclass may also
be growing.

As of the 2015–2016 school year, 51 percent of US public K–12 students qualified for free or reduced-price lunch, and white and Asian
American students constitute only 56 percent of K–12 public school students (a percentage projected to decline through at least 2024).[6] These
data points provide clear evidence that the K–12 student population is
changing, and that in the near future the majority of American students
will be non-white, non-Asian American, and economically vulnerable.
Although all countries suffer from excellence gaps, we now have data
suggesting that the United States has considerably larger gaps than most
other industrialized countries. We question whether the American economy, and therefore the American way of life, can continue to thrive with
the majority of our most academically accomplished students coming
from a shrinking portion of our children. There is a clear and pressing
need for programs and interventions that better develop the skills and
talents of students from black, Native American, Hispanic, and low-income families.

There is nevertheless reason for optimism. The United States is a very
large country, with the third-largest population in the world. Even small
improvements in the percentage of students scoring advanced will add

thousands to the rank of high performers. For example, in fall 2015, the United States had approximately 50 million K–12 public school students, of whom slightly more than 50 percent were eligible for free or reduced-price lunch.[7] Of that 25 million, very few performed at advanced levels, as noted above. Getting just 3 percent of those students to move to advanced level (which would shrink some but hardly all of most excellence gaps) would result in 750,000 more high-achieving students. That's roughly the same number of international students enrolled in US postsecondary institutions.[8] Such an influx of talent would not only be a powerful form of economic stimulus, but would also be a means for community development and personal improvement. After all, helping poor, urban students perform at very high levels clearly will benefit these students, but it is also likely to benefit their families, their community, and our national economy. Everyone gains when talented students are able to learn and achieve at their full potential.

PART TWO

How Is Educational Excellence Fostered?

4

The Identification of Excellence

BEFORE EXAMINING potential strategies for shrinking excellence gaps, we need to review some important aspects of traditional practice with students in this area. Part 2 is devoted to this review. We begin in this chapter by examining the labels applied to high-potential students, along with an analysis of how those labels are usually operationalized and applied. In chapter 5, we dive into traditional approaches for teaching for academic excellence.

Labels are not inherently good or bad, but they take on value judgments over time. Nowhere is this more true than with the label of "gifted" in K–12 education. It is human nature to classify things that share certain characteristics into groups or schema in order to make for more efficient mental processing. In this sense, labels are meant to be a positive thing for both educational systems and the students they serve. The general idea seems to be that by diagnosing and labeling all students who share a common need or characteristic, the educational system can more quickly and more appropriately respond to their needs. Little about this seems objectionable, although we will return to the construct validity of some of these labels and how they are determined later.

The essential question is whether or not the positives that come from being labeled outweigh any potential negative side effects. For example, does labeling a student as "learning disabled," which brings a wealth of positive interventions, outweigh the negative stigma, lower expectations, and social implications that come along with it? This is an unanswerable question (at least empirically), but we will discuss these issues with a specific focus on gifted education in this chapter.

CRITERIA FOR THE "GIFTED" LABEL

Regarding students who are learning above grade level or have the potential to do so, labels most commonly attributed include gifted, talented, high-ability, high-potential, or advanced. For simplicity's sake, we refer to this group of labels under the term gifted. Our reason for focusing on these terms is that they often carry the widest range of definitions and criteria, especially when compared with terms like college ready, which are often based on very clear predictive criterion (for example, a certain probability of earning a certain grade in a first-year college course). In table 4.1, we present how long some of the most common terms have been in use. In most cases, they have been around for a long, long time, and this may explain why they are often used interchangeably, with little attention to the implications of their specific definitions. Rather than focus on those definitions, we will emphasize how they are actually operationalized and measured with a focus on the implications for excellence gaps.

National Practices

Unlike special education labeling, which is federally mandated for all schools and in the same fashion regardless of student population, state, or district, the criteria for labeling students as gifted are left to states. Two good sources for how giftedness is measured and on what basis the label is applied are the National Association for Gifted Children's biannual *State of the States* report and a national survey of gifted programs conducted by the University of Virginia (UVA).[1]

In the *State of the States* report, thirty-two of the thirty-nine responding states reported that identification of gifted and talented student was required by state law or administrative rule. In twenty-one of those states, the criteria for assigning the label were determined solely at the individual district level. This points to one of the strengths and challenges of labeling students as gifted with regard to K–12 education and to narrowing excellence gaps. Although local operationalization means

TABLE 4.1   Somewhat arbitrary analysis of common terms to refer to excellent students

Term	Google Scholar citations 1990–2016	Earliest academic use	Citation
Gifted	~25,200	1889, but probably used decades earlier	Francis Galton, "On head growth in students at the University of Cambridge," *Journal of Anthropological Institute of Great Britain and Ireland* 18 (1889): 155–156.
Talented	~18,500	1832	J. J. Park, "Legal Education," *American Jurist and Law Magazine* 8 (1832): 247.
High-ability	~10,800	1889	T. H. Stafford, "Astronomy in the United States," *Sidereal Messenger* 8 (1889): 70–77.
College ready	~741	1978, but general concept used at least two decades earlier	D. M. Knoell, "Growth Through Positive Planning," *New Directions for Community Colleges* 22 (1978): 75–84.
More able	~5,510	1914, clouded by changing use of the term in recent decades	S. A. Courtis, "Standard Tests in English," *The Elementary School Teacher* 14, no.8 (1914): 374–392.
Advanced	~28,000	1827	C. A. Goodrich and C.F. Hachenberg, *Elements of Greek Grammar: Used in Yale College* (Hartford, CT: Cooke and Co., 1827).

Note. Citation counts are based on searching for "<term> student." The earliest academic use was determined by searching Google Search results backward in time by decade until no other uses of a term were found, or until we grew tired of searching.

that schools can decide which students are the most in need of additional challenge, it also means there are more chances for identification systems to be implemented poorly or even not at all. How states identify students as gifted in K–12 schools varies widely. Some states, such as New Mexico, require an intelligence test score at a certain level before any funds are allocated to the district for use in gifted education. In this case, the level of need is irrelevant—all that matters is whether or not a student scores two standard deviations or higher on an IQ test. Contrast this with a state like Georgia, where a student might be identified as gifted on the basis of a high teacher rating, an ninetieth percentile or higher score on a creativity measure, and a ninetieth percentile or higher score on an academic achievement measure. In both these examples, the general criteria are required for use by all districts in the states. States like Minnesota require identification (though strangely, no services, although this phenomenon is not limited to that state) but leave the identification process completely up to the local districts. The wide range of criteria by which students are labeled as gifted only serves to obfuscate issues related to talent development and the mitigation of excellence gaps.

The 2013 UVA survey based its data on different methodology than the *State of the States* report. Rather than rely on surveys of each state education agency, the UVA report relied on a more complex sampling of school districts to arrive at a nationally representative sample of school district practices. One of the first practices noted (which was also noted in the *State of the States* report) was that teacher nomination or referral was the most common starting point for identification. In other words, no identification processes or procedures were put into action until a student was recommended by his or her teacher. Following this screening or nomination stage, 60 percent of districts assessed students using a standardized assessment or set of assessments. A set cut score was then used to determine who qualified for services. This two-stage model is very common in gifted identification.

The UVA report also noted wide variations in what data districts collected in addition to the assessments. Some included additional ability or achievement tests while others included informal/homemade teacher checklists or portfolios. Often a student was required to meet multiple hurdles in order to be labeled as gifted—a practice that is especially exclusive and results in greater numbers of students who are qualified going unidentified.[2] The survey also noted a range of participation by committees. In some cases, committees took all available data into account to make the final decision about labels or programming.

IMPLICATIONS OF LABELS FOR EXCELLENCE GAPS

One of the most common practices in gifted and talented identification is also one of the most problematic from the standpoint of excellence gaps. As of 2012, 51 percent of American K–12 students were white, 16 percent were black, 24 percent were Hispanic, 5 percent were Asian or Pacific Islander, and the rest were Native American or multiracial.[3] Despite these racial/ethnic breakdowns, the teachers who were involved in the nominations in 2012 were 82 percent Caucasian, 7 percent black, 8 percent Hispanic, 2 percent Asian, and 1 percent Native American or multiracial.[4] Peterson noted that cultures perceive and manifest talents differently based on their own cultural values.[5] This calls into question whether teachers who are from different cultural backgrounds than the students they're evaluating can be effective in nominating those students as gifted; in fact, a 2016 study found that black students were significantly less likely to be referred by their teacher for gifted services when their teacher was not black.[6] If it is indeed true that teachers who do not share the same cultural background of their students have difficulty seeing gifts and talents in those students, then states with diverse teaching forces should see higher rates of diverse students being nominated.

But that's not how it turns out. Georgia has one of the most diverse teaching forces in the nation, with 76 percent of teachers being white and 17 percent black. Nevertheless, McBee still found that black and Hispanic students were much less likely to be nominated by their teachers than white or Asian students.[7] And when a large Florida district replaced teacher nominations with universal screening as the first assessment stage, the diversity of students labeled as gifted greatly increased.[8] If typical gifted education programs do help students achieve at high levels (something we are skeptical of but will address in chapter 5), and if classroom teachers are the initial gatekeepers to such programs, then the fact that teachers are likely to choose overwhelmingly white and Asian American students as gifted is likely to contribute to excellence gaps. This does not mean that teachers cannot be useful in the process of identifying gifted students, rather it points to the need to be very careful in how their input is used and what weight it is given in labeling decisions.

Intelligence, group ability, and academic achievement tests are ubiquitous in gifted student identification. For example, the UVA survey lists the Cognitive Abilities Test and Otis Lennon School Ability Test as the two most common instruments, whereas the *State of the States* report lists achievement and intelligence tests as the most common. What is not addressed directly by either report is whether the majority of the identification decisions made using these tests are based on national norm comparisons. For example, one UVA survey respondent stated that students must receive scores at or above the ninety-sixth percentile on two approved measures to be identified as gifted. Our personal experience tells us this means on national norms and believe this is the most common approach, though we have found no definitive data on this fact.

But the use of national norms for gifted identification is a problem for excellence gaps, since it will result in some schools having very large percentages of their populations labeled as gifted while others (likely low-SES schools) having very small to none of their student population identified. Because students from black, Hispanic, Native American, and low-income families receive lower observed scores on nearly all tests of academic ability and achievement, any cut score based on a general, national norm will result in the underrepresentation of students from those populations.[9] If the interventions provided under the label of *gifted* result in increased rates of advanced achievement, then this process will exacerbate excellence gaps. In a sense, the use of national norms for advanced educational programs serves to continue to advance those students who are already advanced. This becomes a vicious cycle where the only students who receive a program are those who were advanced to begin with. Clearly this will not close excellence gaps.

The point about students from certain student subgroups receiving lower average scores is important for a second reason. These scores are, for the most part, not indicative of bias in assessment.[10] Rather, they are an indication that educational opportunity and opportunity to learn are not equally distributed across all racial, ethnic, and income groups. This is perhaps the greatest challenge to mitigating excellence gaps. When many of the students from these subgroups have access to fewer educational opportunities, then they have fewer chances to develop their talents. When schools identify students based on their current level of achievement (or ability as influenced by achievement), these students are often not labeled as gifted.

Unfortunately, there are few options for how to directly address this problem as long as educational opportunity is strongly correlated with family income. Not only will this fail to develop the talents of those students who were not already high achieving at the time of identification, but it will also further develop the skills of the already-advanced peers further exacerbating excellence gaps. This does not mean that existing talents should not be developed, but it does mean something needs to change if excellence gaps are to be closed—assuming that whatever is provided to the students successfully labeled as gifted increases student rates of high achievement or student growth.

POTENTIAL SIDE EFFECTS OF LABELING

When students enter a classroom, a number of factors influence the teacher's perception of each student. Although what teachers might know about their students ahead of time can vary widely, one thing most of them are likely to know is any special education identification and required curricular modifications or accommodations. Because of the legal requirements for individualized education plans that accompany special education labels, these labels carry actual weight. They also carry baggage. Teacher expectations have long been studied with regard to how they influence student performance. For example, in 2015 Friedrich and colleagues found that the "Pygmalion effect"—higher teacher expectations lead to higher student performance (and vice versa)—was a significant predictor of student grades and achievement test scores.[11] This supports the idea that expectations, however derived, do influence academic performance.

Labeling effect or labeling bias is the concept that an educational label (such as special or gifted education) creates expectations regarding a student so labeled.[12] To evaluate the degree to which special education labels influence expectations, Allday and colleagues presented 122 undergraduate education majors with a series of videos of grade school and high school students in classrooms. These subjects were then asked to total on- and off-task behaviors they observed.[13] They were then randomly assigned into four groups, and each group was given different additional information about the students in the videos: (1) that they had no exceptionality, (2) that they had been diagnosed with ADHD, (3) they had been diagnosed with oppositional defiant disorder, or (4) that they had been labeled as gifted and talented. The observers were more likely to score students as off task if they were also labeled as oppositional defiant disorder and less likely to score students as off task if they were labeled as gifted and talented (partial-eta square of .11). Although in this case, the negative side effect of the label was rather small, it does highlight how changing nothing but the label has an effect on how educators perceive students' behavior, including when students are labeled as gifted or otherwise advanced.

To focus more on the actual child and his or her learning needs while simultaneously focusing less on the label, the fields of special and gifted education have shifted the terminology to "students with special needs" or "children with gifts and talents," thereby putting the student first in the discussion. Gates presented the idea that students who are labeled as "gifted" begin believe that they should perform well at all things or be advanced in all areas—including in emotional or psychosocial development.[14] As a result, educators can forget to consider how to support advanced learners as they take on new content because they are expected to never need help.

One of the greatest concerns in this area is that once labeled as such, gifted students begin to see their abilities as fixed (as opposed to malleable) and to exhibit a performance goal orientation as opposed to one based on mastery. One study of 1,743 high-ability students found that being identified as gifted at any point in a student's K–12 career was associated with identifying more with entity views of intelligence and ability (perception of ability or intelligence as fixed and stable) as opposed to incremental views (perception of ability as malleable and fluid).[15] This points to a potential concern that labels involving advanced performance or "giftedness" could have the unintended side effect of making students feel more as though they have no control over their ability or achievement in a given area—that effort or hard work is ineffective or irrelevant.

The larger research base on whether or not being identified gifted increases a person's entity view of ability is mixed. However, most of this work has focused on how students labeled as gifted perceive their talents as opposed to what effect being identified had on this perception. For example, one study sought to answer the question "Do gifted students tend to view their giftedness as a fixed entity?" rather than looking at how the label changed the students' views.[16]

Although labels related to special and gifted education are applied only to certain segments of the population—those students with exceptionalities—what has become a far more ubiquitous practice is labeling students according to their overall achievement level based on standardized tests or other academic criteria. Labels such as *proficient*, *college ready*, or *grade level* are commonplace in K–12 education, yet relatively little work has been done in evaluating how these labels influence students' attitudes, learning, and motivation. As with other labels, achievement performance labels could be seen as a good thing as they allow students to better understand how they might fare in a university or other postsecondary training program. In this fashion, students whose abilities might be higher than they think could be encouraged to pursue higher education. Likewise, students who thought they would perform well in higher education might instead pursue a post-secondary educational program focused more on the world of work. However, performance data are imperfect and students may make decisions that don't take such imperfection into account.

One study looked at Massachusetts, where students are labeled as either *failing, needs improvement, proficient,* or *advanced* based on three different cut points on the state achievement test. The authors wanted to see whether the classification influenced students' postsecondary decisions even when the test score otherwise carried no significance to the students. Using a natural experiment facilitated by state policy changes, the authors found that these labels do influence decisions. For example, a child who just met the advanced threshold on the state math test was five percentage points more likely to attend college than a peer who just missed this threshold and was labeled as proficient. The result was even stronger for those students who, before being labeled, reported that they did not plan to attend college. Being labeled as advanced increased their likelihood of attending college by ten percentage points.[17] Importantly, this entire study was conducted using only data from low-income students attending urban schools. This carries profound implications for excellence gaps as it suggests that the data being collected in order to evaluate excellence gaps also potentially contributes to them when students not categorized as advanced are discouraged from seeking out advanced educational opportunities. This doesn't mean that such data should not be collected, rather that it should be used carefully and with caution lest low-income, high-potential students see less than advanced performance as an indication that gifted or advanced programs are not for them.

Carol Dweck, famous for her work on mindset and goal orientation theory, has long cautioned that the term *gifted* has the feel of a fixed mind-set. In this sense, individuals who are labeled as gifted can begin to see their skills or abilities as something they were born with and of which they must constantly demonstrate and prove to others. For example, if Bobby has been labeled gifted in science and is frequently praised for being a good science student, then he will begin to see that ability as innate. He will also begin to assume that always doing well in science is expected, and that any struggle or failure is a reflection on him as a person. This is a negative side effect of the label. Keep in mind that many of students singled out as gifted don't ever have to work hard while in K–12. They've been under challenged for a long time, they've received reinforcement that tells them they should never have to challenge because they are so smart, and eventually they will head to college or the world of work where challenge and failure are realities.

With regard to the label of *gifted*, the essential question, as it is with special education labels, is whether or not the potential benefits outweigh potential negative side effects. There are several clear positives to using the label. For example, in the roughly 70 percent of states that have some financial support for gifted education, at least some (for example, Alabama, New Mexico) provide these funds based on the number of identified students. There are also at least thirty-two states that have some form of state requirement to identify and serve gifted students. Both of these seem like clear examples of "giftedness" helping advanced learners within K–12 schools.

What isn't clear is whether or not these benefits can be realized without any of potential negatives that come with the label. Negative side effects are rarely evaluated or reported on in the scholarly literature. Below we consider some of the potential or empirically supported negative side-effects or barriers that come with the use of the term gifted (these are summarized in table 4.2).

Its Arbitrary Nature. Although many states have a definition or conception of giftedness that they use as the basis for identification, it is rarely made clear why these students, such as those scoring above the ninety-eighth percentile on a test, require specialized services and not those at the ninety-seventh or the ninetieth percentile. It seems relatively accepted that such services are important for high-potential students to grow and learn, but it's less clear why *only* those students at or above

TABLE 4.2   Summary of issues and key questions for the label "gifted" ✔

Issue	Key questions
The label can be arbitrary.	Does use of the label represent all students who would benefit from services tied to the identification process?
Use of the label varies widely.	Does the label accurately reflect the services being offered by the program?
The label may be perceived negatively by those who don't have it.	Does programming deliver the desired outcomes, justifying the use of the label?
The label may reinforce stereotypes.	Do identification strategies result in labeled students having demographics similar to the total school population?
The label may exacerbate excellence gaps.	How can programming be designed to foster talents of advanced learners from underrepresented/ underperforming subgroups?

certain criteria require those services. Is there something special about the ninety-eighth percentile? Are these students inherently different in some key way from those at the ninety-seventh? The fact is that there are far more underchallenged students than just those above the ninety-eighth percentile. This lack of a coherent argument renders the term gifted as rather arbitrary and is a significant hurdle for gifted education and its advocates. How can one ask for more funding, support, or attention if one cannot answer "Why these students but not those students?"

Its Widely Varied Nature, Often by Design. The diverse areas in which states or schools allow students to be identified as gifted is both a strength and a weakness. Many schools include domains such as academics, leadership, performing arts, creativity, and motivation, as those in which a student can be identified as gifted. It is a good thing to allow for a wide range of talents to be recognized and nurtured. However, when skills in any one of these areas all lead to a generic label of gifted, the label becomes instructionally useless. If a teacher looks at her class list and sees three students for next fall are identified as gifted, what does that mean? Do they require math that is above grade level? Would they learn best via independent projects as opposed to group work? Are they world-class musicians? In contrast to labels such as oppositional defiant disorder, the label of gifted is almost instructionally useless for the classroom teacher.

There is also the problem of teacher ratings and nominations. Even if identification is limited to a single content area, such as those students who are advanced in math, if teachers are involved in the identification process through recommendations or ratings, then they will all look for slightly different things. Each teacher's operational definition of what a "gifted math student" looks or acts like will be slightly different because each teacher is different. Although there are positives to this natural diversity of perspective, it does decrease the reliability of teacher ratings and makes for a more varied population in terms of math needs. This means that even if the widely varied nature of "giftedness" is addressed via a focus on a specific domain, there is still the challenge in what raters are actually looking for when they use the term gifted. Some will only nominate the once-in-a-lifetime students, while others will nominate anyone who turns his or her work in on time and is respectful in class. This variance in what is perceived as gifted translates to an identified population that has a wider range of educational needs for the program or service into which they are placed.

Its Perception by the "Non-Gifted." Several authors in the field have noted the potential for the gifted label to upset or generally turn off people, especially those people whose children have not had the label bestowed on them.[18] As researchers and advocates in the field of advanced education, we have spent our careers trying to explain away the initially negative connotations that come with the term. Many equity-minded educators see the term as elitist at worst or a barrier to full inclusion of "non-gifted" children at best. As we noted in the previous section, the field of gifted education has never made it clear why "these kids," whoever they are, require a special service that would not be beneficial to everyone else. If gifted education programs are highly effective and yield tangible benefits to identified students, then maybe they are worth any potential hurt feelings or stigma that they confer to others. That said, the assumption of lots of positive benefit is questionable at best.

Its Magnification of Racial/Ethnic and Income Inequality. Most of the underrepresentation of minorities and lower-income students in identified gifted populations is not due to malicious racism, classism, or any other explicitly negative intent. Instead, the inequality in gifted education is a symptom of much larger societal inequality and often overlaps with race, ethnicity, and economic status combined with some ill-advised assessment practices. Despite the wide acceptance by American society that educational opportunity is not equally distributed across all economic and cultural groups, there is still widespread outrage at the rates of representation among Native American, Hispanic, black, and low-income students in identified gifted populations. Because of this, a major downside to the label of gifted is the spotlight it places on this inequality and the potential stereotypes it reinforces. The label has placed gifted education on the front lines of the inequality wars in which equity-minded individuals want to see greater proportionality despite the large underlying inequality that preceded it, whereas gifted education backers want to see all students challenged. Gifted education did not cause this inequality but its presence in K–12 schools often magnifies its extent.

Its Potential to Exacerbate Excellence Gaps. If the populations that benefit from traditional gifted education tend to be more often white, and Asian, and come from more affluent backgrounds than the larger K–12 student population, and if gifted education programs increase rates of high achievement, then it is possible that such programs could make excellence gaps worse. But this is not a reason not to have them. The fact that some students are learning at a faster rate and a higher level, which in turn places a spotlight on systematic inequality, does not mean that those high-performing students should be slowed down in order to make inequality look less bad. Yet we have heard this exact logic time and time again. School district administrators are often concerned that having any kind of advanced programming or gifted education could make their achievement gaps worse. This makes them hesitant to include such programs. But the real solution isn't to get rid of any advanced programs. Rather, the goal should be finding a way to better foster the talents of advanced learners from traditionally underrepresented populations.

It may seem that by presenting these negative side effects that we believe attention to advanced learners is not appropriate or, up to this point, ineffective. But nothing could be further from the truth. We present this information as a context for considering the following question: Are the positives that come with "giftedness" and "gifted" education worth the price we pay in negative side effects? No label is free of baggage, and the issue for educators, policymakers, and scholars is to determine if it is worth carrying the baggage because the destination is worthwhile.

Our big takeaways from the labeling research and the study of identification policies and practices are that (1) labels matter, (2) they can exert both positive *and* negative pressure on student outcomes, and (3) there may be ways to use labels' positive aspects to help shrink excellence gaps, thereby reducing some of the negative aspects. Several of the example programs we will discuss in the next chapter do just that, as do some of the potential interventions discussed in part 3.

5

Approaches to Talent Development

ALTHOUGH IN THIS BOOK we approach talent development and excellence gaps very broadly (including higher education and early childhood gaps), the primary focus is on mitigating excellence gaps within the context of K–12 schools. To that end, no discussion of excellence gaps would be complete without an overview of the field best known as *gifted and talented* or *high-ability* education. We present this content because it highlights where some gifted education programs might exacerbate or help mitigate excellence gaps and also provides a structure through which to consider the interventions we will present in parts 3 and 4.

PARADIGMS OF TALENT DEVELOPMENT

Dai and Chen classified the models used to address gifted or high-ability learners in K–12 schools as falling into one of three paradigms: the *gifted child* paradigm, the *talent development* paradigm, and the *differentiation* paradigm.[1] We provide a brief overview of each in the following pages with additional commentary on how each might relate to K–12 excellence gaps.

The Gifted Child Paradigm
The gifted child paradigm is by far the oldest of the three, and anecdotal evidence suggests it to be the most commonly practiced by K–12

schools. In this paradigm, "giftedness" is a human trait that exists in certain individuals and can be best measured with a high degree of accuracy by intelligence (IQ) or other general ability tests. The idea behind giftedness is that individuals who possess it are likely to have the greatest potential for significant achievement and contributions to society and therefore supporting them is a good investment of resources. Further reinforcing this view of giftedness as a trait is the assumption that gifted individuals are qualitatively and inherently different from "non-gifted" individuals in ways that necessitate special services in K–12 education.

Because of its use of intelligence tests or other typical academic ability tests, this particular model has the clearest implications for underrepresented learners and excellence gaps. Programs within the gifted child paradigm, in general, expect the smallest number of students identified as gifted and requiring specialized services. In practice, these identified children are much less likely to be from black, Native American, Hispanic, or low-income families.[2] Because the gifted child paradigm is so closely tied to IQ, and because of similarities to special education (a field dealing with human exceptionalities) cut scores of 130 or two standard deviations above the norm are typical for identification. This is turn results in the very small numbers of identified students (~2 percent) overall, although, since talent is viewed as a characteristic of certain people who are not likely to be represented evenly across schools, districts, or even states, some schools have very large numbers of identified students while others have none. When the intercorrelations between race/ethnicity, socioeconomic status, and academic achievement are taken together, the influence of models under this paradigm on excellence gaps become obvious. High-income individuals from dominant cultural groups are seen as having talents whereas low-income members of other student subgroups are seen as not having gifts or talents. This resulting state of affairs has been a barrier for gifted education advocacy for decades.

Although the gifted child paradigm is commonly practiced in K–12 schools, it has fallen out of favor in the scholarly literature. Scholars such as Borland, Subotnik, Olszewski-Kubilius, and Worrell and one of the authors of this book have called for its rejection in favor of alternative models that are more inclusive and equitable but are also more defensible in line with what is known about psychological science.[3] Perhaps the greatest limitation of this paradigm is that it leaves the talents of so many students from low-income, black, Native American, and Hispanic families underdeveloped in schools, as these students are far less likely to be identified for and placed in K–12 gifted programs. As we noted in chapter 3, research has shown K–12 excellence gaps increasing over time with a dramatic increase coming after the passage of NCLB.[4] Plucker and colleagues have suggested that part of this is due to fewer and fewer advanced educational opportunities being made available to students from traditionally underrepresented populations.[5] There have also been questions as to whether or not programs designed under this paradigm are actually effective when it comes to raising student achievement even when they are provided to those underrepresented students who need them (a question we will return to later in this chapter).[6]

Services and programs designed around the gifted child paradigm tend to be very exclusive in the sense that they are often completely separate from the rest of the "regular" educational system. Such services tend to include pull-out enrichment and self-contained gifted programs that are assumed to provide content that is targeted specifically at the trait of giftedness. Thus instruction often includes critical and creative thinking as well as more in-depth problem solving. When these advanced topics are much more commonly provided to students from dominant-culture and high-income families, an expansion of excellence gaps is a result.

The Talent Development Paradigm

The talent development paradigm, developed in the 1970s and 1980s in direct response to the challenges and limitations of the gifted child paradigm, made several important changes. First, it broadened the conception of talent to include far more than general or specific academic ability to include nearly any area of human potential. This necessitated broader identification efforts to match with the expanded focus. Second, the assumption of giftedness as a primarily genetic or inherent trait was jettisoned in favor of much more nuanced "gifted behaviors" with specific domains.[7] The talent development paradigm instead views talent as capable of being developed—that gifted behaviors can and are meant to be nurtured over time.

Identification within the talent development paradigm is much more domain-specific than in the gifted child paradigm: students are identified for some specific intervention or talent development program rather than as "gifted" per se. This flexibility allows students to move in and out of services or programs as needed and the expanded domains also allow for a wider range and number of students to participate. All of this is done to facilitate the paradigm's chief goal: "to cultivate a broader, more diverse range of strengths and interests and to help students achieve excellence in their chosen areas."[8]

Arguably the most widely known and broadly implemented program that falls under the talent development paradigm is Renzulli and Reis's Schoolwide Enrichment Model (SEM).[9] SEM embodies many of the major tenets of the talent development model by (1) including a far larger number of students than typical gifted education, (2) providing a range of services based on each student's level of readiness, and (3) facilitating students' talents in their own areas of interest and passion. The model begins with Type I enrichment, meant to expose students to new ideas and topics in order to spark their interest in particular areas. This component involves the largest number of students so that latent talents, interests, and abilities can come to the forefront in order to be developed at higher levels: Type II enrichment, where students engage in group training related to their area of interest; and Type III enrichment, where students engage in individualized independent projects. A wide body of research has been conducted on SEM, which we will present after discussing the third and final paradigm.

The Differentiation Paradigm

The differentiation paradigm is in many ways the newest of the three. The idea and practice of differentiation is nothing new but where the paradigm is unique is in its use of differentiation as a large-scale instructional and programmatic model for all students—including advanced learners. In differentiation models advanced learners are provided exactly what should be provided to all learners—an appropriately challenging educational experience that is tailored based on their present need. In this sense they are similar to educational models such as response to intervention, where evidence of student need is used to determine an appropriate intervention related to academics, behavior, or social-emotional support.[10] A benefit to the differentiation paradigm over the gifted child paradigm is its focus on full-time, appropriately challenging education for advanced learners. Whereas the gifted child paradigm often involved part-time pull-out classes or ability groups for certain students, the differentiation paradigm gives rise to a larger model in which all students should be appropriately matched with their level of readiness as often as is possible. This makes it appealing to both advocates and skeptics as it argues for a single best practice for all students. In doing so, it deemphasizes the importance of identifying the gifted as a separate class. With this focus on local unmet need within the context of a student's learning environment, the differentiation paradigm is almost the exact opposite of the gifted child model. Rather than defining giftedness as a diagnosed, permanent trait, the differentiation paradigm defines giftedness as a temporary state of unmet need in a specific academic area, ideally for a short period of time.[11] When that need is met, the student can be transitioned out of a particular intervention (assuming the grade-level classroom can then meet his or her needs).

Following implications of the model to their logical conclusion, some advocates of the differentiation paradigm recommend the removal of the age-based grouping structure of the K–12 educational system in favor of a needs-based grouping structure where students are grouped based on their specific learning need. Services offered under this model are hard to outline since, by their very nature, they vary depending on what student needs are not being met. However, in general, they tend to focus on academic areas, involving different pacing of standard classes (such as telescoping and curriculum compacting) and grade acceleration.

In sum, the gifted child paradigm is the broadest, most abstract, restrictive, and distinct from the day-to-day educational needs of students, whereas the differentiation model is the most specific in terms of what its theoretical basis is and also farthest reaching in terms of who would be served under its mandate. All of that said, while the concept of differentiation has existed for decades and research has been conducted on the effects of differentiation in a broader context, there is much less research on the effects of differentiation paradigm models on advanced learners or excellence gaps.

DOES ANY OF IT WORK?

As should be expected, perceptions about whether or not gifted education "works" depend on how we operationalize effectiveness or success.

(As a side note, we continue to be amazed by how rarely K–12 gifted education programs actually have stated goals, which makes evaluating their effectiveness challenging.) In the following sections, we present an overview of the major delivery models that fall under the three paradigms and their respective research bases from the perspective of three primary outcomes: (1) increased student growth and learning, (2) increased learning by disadvantaged groups, and (3) increased performance in those populations at the highest levels of achievement. Table 5.1 at the end of this section summarizes the research on gifted education models and programs.

Part-Time Pull-Out Services

At the elementary level, pull-out or resource-room programs and services are some of the most common forms of intervention for advanced learners.[12] Part-time, often low-frequency or low-dosage, pull-out programs are very common in K–12 gifted education. Yet because of their highly variable nature, they are also difficult to evaluate. What exactly goes on in these resource rooms is inconsistent in content as well as dosage. In a meta-analysis published in 1991, Vaughn, Feldhusen, and Asher found positive effects from pull-out programs as a service for advanced learners.[13] The three studies they found that focused on reading achievement and resulted in an average effect size of .65—this means that those who participated in the programs outperformed their nonparticipating peers by 2/3 of a standard deviation of the outcome measure. The authors also referenced several other studies that were not included for methodological reasons but seemed to be supportive of pull-out models of intervention. An even more-recent study conducted on students from the Netherlands found that gifted education enrichment resulted in higher grades, higher participation rates in science curriculum, and positive long-term effects with regard to university choices and outcomes.[14]

However, what is not clear in most research on such methods is not whether they are beneficial, but rather if they are beneficial *solely* for students who are already advanced. If such pull-out, resource-room, or enrichment programs are, in fact, beneficial for a range of learners, then they should not be restricted solely to advanced learners because to do so would seem unethical—and would also serve to increase excellence gaps. The study based on students in the Netherlands controlled for this using a regression discontinuity design, but this still does not make clear if providing enrichment only to some students and not the others is worthwhile, even from the standpoint of achievement outcomes. Many parents of advanced learners and their advocates are in favor of resource-room type programs and will often defend them with anecdotes about how much particular students enjoyed these services. We don't doubt that students enjoy them. What we are concerned about is that they may be restricted to already-advanced students even though they might benefit many more. If such programs were restricted to identified gifted students, consistent with the gifted child paradigm, and those students happened to be more often from high-income and/or dominant-culture groups, then they could exacerbate excellence gaps.

Within-Class Grouping

One of the two most common methods of instructional grouping involves teachers organizing students within their particular classroom by readiness or ability for a given lesson. Such practices fit within the talent development and differentiation paradigms and are also similar to the full-time, separate interventions often seen under the gifted child paradigm. Students are frequently reassessed and regrouped based on their level of readiness for a particular skill or concept. Several studies, including multiple meta-analyses, have investigated the effects of within-class as well as full-time ability grouping. Adelson and Carpenter, using a nationally representative data set, looked at the reading achievement growth of kindergarten students who, after controlling for a number of factors, were in classes that utilized within-class grouping as opposed to their peers whose teachers did not.[15] They found that students who were grouped made a small but statistically significant increased amount of growth over their non-grouped peers (10.91 points versus 10.29 points over the kindergarten year). Their results also showed that those students who were in a gifted program and whose teacher utilized within-class grouping grew more than 4.3 points more than their gifted peers who did not also experience within-class grouping. For all students, experiencing within-class grouping was beneficial, but the growth was especially strong for those who received both gifted services (not specified in the dataset) and within-class grouping.

In a different study that also focused on first-grade reading, Nomi utilized the same nationally representative data set as Adelson and Carpenter, but used different methods to investigate the reading growth effects of within-class grouping while also disaggregating results by student initial ability and a number of school variables.[16] What she found was that overall, within-class grouping had no statistically significant effect on reading growth. However, when they disaggregated results by school type, they found that those schools most likely to use within-class grouping (diverse, low-income, and high-minority) saw lower growth than similar schools that did not use grouping. Alternatively, the schools least likely to use grouping (high-income, homogenous) saw the greatest benefit—an effect size of .31 for those students who experienced grouping verses those who did not. It's not clear why there was such a strong effect for one group as opposed to the other, though it's possible that even smaller variation in student demographics and starting achievement lead to even more effective grouping.

Nomi's findings contrast with an earlier but seminal meta-analysis on within-class grouping published in 1996.[17] This study found consistent, positive effects for grouping (.17 versus non-grouped students) and also for studies that specifically looked at homogenous as opposed to heterogeneous grouping (.12). The authors found these positive effects held regardless of the initial ability level of students (low, medium, or high), subject area (math/science or reading/language arts), or grade level. When the specific analyses for homogenous verses heterogeneous grouping were done, no significant difference was found for low-ability students, whereas the medium- and high-ability groups both showed significant growth. In this case, results were also much greater for reading/language arts (.36 effect size) than math/science (0 effect). Although the findings were certainly more in favor of grouping, this meta-analysis did not consider the influence of student demographic variables, such as poverty or race, on the achievement outcomes. However, as with much of advanced education, if high-income or dominant-culture groups are more likely to receive a specific intervention, then it could exacerbate excellence gaps unless something is also done to develop the talents of the other students.

Ability Grouping

Ability grouping lends itself to the gifted child paradigm, where some states even have special schools for "gifted" students to be grouped full time, and also to a less extreme degree in the talent development paradigm. Although the differentiation paradigm would also see use from ability grouping, services falling under this paradigm focus more on general grade-level classrooms as a place to start. At the middle and high school levels, classes tend to be sorted or arranged by readiness or ability level.[18] In other words, these students tend to be enrolled with students of similar ability when compared with other classes. Collins and Gan found that this was almost universally positive for all students involved.[19] What was perhaps the most important finding was that high achievers gained additional growth because of sorting, but not at the expense of low achievers. Both groups gained, but if achievement gaps are to close without holding back high achievers, then the lower-achieving group needs to learn even faster or benefit even more than the already high-achieving group.

In what represents the most current summary of the knowledge base on the topic of within- and between-class grouping, Steenbergen-Hu and colleagues conducted a review of all experimental studies related to both forms of grouping as well as a meta-analysis on all grouping studies since 1996.[20] With both between-class or full-time ability grouping, the benefits for high achievers were almost universally positive, with effect sizes ranging from .08 to .49. For average achievers, the results were predominantly negative, with effect sizes ranging from −.45 to .04. For the lowest-achieving students, the results were small but positive (.06 to .18). Although certainly positive for high achievers, the findings for within-class grouping were quite different. In those cases, the benefits for average and high-achieving students were positive, but to differing degrees (.17 to .51 and .09 to .62, respectively) indicating a stark difference for average achievers when compared with between-class grouping. For low-achieving students, the results varied widely (−60 to .65). These findings make clear that grouping is almost universally positive for high achieving students, but the effect on lower-achieving students is more mixed and the exact mechanism for the varied effects is less clear.

What much of this research points to is that whether or not group-ing has an effect on learning gains depends on a variety of factors.[21] Some have been directly measured (such as initial ability of students) and some are harder to quantify, such as what is actually done differ-ently for the student in the various groups. For example, Lou and col-leagues found that extensive teacher training in grouping instructional methods had more than double the positive effect on student learning when compared with teachers who received only basic information.[22] Lou also found that "more or different" curricular designs with regard to grades, materials—that is, modifying the content and format of delivery for the different groups—and teacher training were all more than twice as effective as leaving instruction the same for all groups. This points to successful grouping as more than just a structural intervention, one that requires curricular and pedagogical modifications in order to reap max-imum benefits.

We discuss the role of ability grouping in reducing excellence gaps in chapter 8, but suffice it to say for now that the research in this area is mixed when looking at all students but provides some guidance for future efforts.

Acceleration

Acceleration as a group of methods often includes early entrance to school, early graduation from high school and entrance to college, sub-ject-specific grade skipping, and whole-grade acceleration, just to name a few. All of these methods fit strongly within the talent development paradigm and for the most advanced learners in the differentiation par-adigm—those whose needs are so far from what is typical in their grade level that no differentiation would suffice. It is important to point out from the start that there is no more strongly supported intervention for advanced learners than grade acceleration. Three studies are par-ticularly worth presenting here—two recent studies that involved large data sets and a third that represents the most recent and comprehen-sive meta-analysis ever done on acceleration. McClarty utilized data from the National Educational Longitudinal Study (NELS) to evaluate the high school and college outcomes of students who had skipped an entire grade (the most substantial form of acceleration) compared with same age, non-accelerated peers as well as older age peers.[23] The results are compelling. Students who were accelerated scored higher on PSAT math (.43 effect size) and SAT math (.77 effect size) and on the composite ACT (.91 effect size), as well as the English (.69 effect size) and math (.80 effect size) subscales; earned higher high school GPAs (.64 effect size); and went on to earn higher undergraduate GPAs (.77 effect size). With regard to degree attainment, accelerated students were more than 50 percent more likely to earn a bachelor's degree. Other degree attainment was not statistically different, likely because of small sample sizes. What this all points to is that at least with regard to major high school and college outcomes, accelerated students substantially outperform their similar non-accelerated peers, even after being matched on a wide range of criteria (including race, ethnicity, and socioeconomic status).

Looking beyond school-related outcomes, Park, Lubinski, and Benbow utilized data from more than forty years of research related to the Study of Mathematically Precocious Youth (SMPY) to determine the effects of grade skipping on STEM career outcomes.[24] Looking at three different cohorts, the authors found that those who skipped grade were 50 percent more likely to earn a doctorate than their matched control peers, nearly twice as likely to earn a STEM-related PhD, likely to have received more patents (though this was not statistically significant), and likely to have published more STEM-related publications. Grade skippers were also more likely to do all of this at a younger age, thereby allowing them more years of creative productivity.

Finally, in 2011, Steenbergen-Hu and Moon published findings from an extensive meta-analysis on the effects of acceleration on academic achievement and social-emotional outcomes.[25] This study included thirty-eight studies that had not been included in earlier meta-analyses. After excluding one particularly problematic study, the overall academic achievement effect size was 0.24 and was statistically significant. With regard to social-emotional outcomes, none of the results were statistically significant. However, this is not inherently bad, as it means that accelerated students are no better and no worse when it comes to such outcomes. In other words, they are, on average, just as socially or emotionally well off as their non-accelerated peers—a point that challenges some traditional preconceptions of accelerated students.

Advanced Placement

The AP program has been in existence for more than fifty years. Because of its ubiquity and popularity, it doesn't fit well within a single paradigm—although AP has been criticized by the larger field of gifted education as being insufficient (especially under the gifted child paradigm). Using data for the entire state of Utah and focusing on two graduating cohorts, Warne and colleagues found that those students who were engaged the most in AP English showed scores on the ACT from 1.6 to 5.3 points higher than their peers who did not pass the AP English test.[26] For those who passed the AP calculus test, these differences ranged

TABLE 5.1   Summary of research on various gifted education models and programs

Common practices	Effects on academic excellence	Effects on excellence gaps
Within-class grouping	Convincing evidence of small to moderate positive impact on academic achievement.	Little available research; lack of evidence of positive general effects leads to skepticism regarding excellence gaps.
Differentiation	Little evidence of positive impact on promoting or enhancing academic excellence.	Focus on specific areas of talent/need means students who are talented in one area (versus all or many) receive extra challenge. This could mitigate excellence gaps depending on who is served.
Ability grouping	Convincing evidence of positive impact on student achievement for higher- and lower-ability students. Mixed evidence for average students.	Little available research on use and effectiveness.
Part-time pull-out services	Convincing evidence of positive impact on student achievement; considerable non-experimental evidence of positive impact on other outcomes (e.g., creativity).	Programs tend to serve white, Asian, and upper-income students, therefore exacerbating gaps.
Acceleration	Strong evidence of positive benefits for nearly all forms of acceleration; side effects appear to be sporadic and minor.	Because participating students are likely to be from higher-income families, and from dominant racial/ethnic groups, acceleration could exacerbate excellence gaps.
Advanced placement	Convincing evidence of positive impact on college entrance exam scores.	Limited data suggesting the programs exacerbate gaps; scattered case studies suggest this need not be the case.

from .44 to 3.2 points higher on the various subscales of the ACT. Even when controlling for a range of covariates (including initial achievement), students who passed AP courses performed substantially better on college entrance exams. As we will present in detail in chapter 9, AP and AP-prep programs could have a significant effect on mitigating college-related excellence gaps.

Although according to the Warne study, participation in AP classes may increase scores on college admission exams, traditionally disadvantaged students still take AP classes and score a 3 or better on AP tests at far lower rates than their non-disadvantaged peers.[27] This success gap is particularly large for students from low-income and black families. For example, although in 2013, 48.1 percent of US students were considered low-income, only 21.7 percent of AP exam takers who scored a 3 or better were from a low-income family. Given the strong predictive power of AP exam success on college admission tests, gaps in college attendance and graduation are not a surprise.

The College Board report cited a number of case study districts that have been successful in increasing equity and decreasing excellence gaps through AP. Several of these ideas involve removing financial barriers to students taking the exam, increasing teacher training, alternative identification procedures for locating students who might benefit from AP courses but are not currently enrolled, and better aligning pre-AP curricula at the middle and high school levels so that students are better prepared for AP courses.

IMPLICATIONS FOR EXCELLENCE GAPS

Although we addressed issues of quality and excellence throughout this chapter, there are a few larger themes worth pointing out that cut across paradigms and program models. First, most of the research referenced in the chapter has dealt with "gifted" or "advanced" groups that represent the populations that are too typical in gifted education (more likely to be high-income, white, non-ELL). What this means is the research base on talent development within underrepresented populations is rather sparse.[28] Some studies, such as Card and Giuliano's, did note that effects of certain gifted interventions were even more positive for ELL and low-income students than they were for others, but these findings are rare. What this means is that the larger field doesn't know if the benefits of some of the programs typical to gifted education in K–12, such as acceleration or grouping, would have the same positive effects if applied to a specific population to mitigate excellence gaps. Despite that caveat, an important implication for policy might be to utilize some of the alternative identification methods described in chapter 6 to identify larger numbers of underrepresented students for the programs described above in a proactive effort to develop excellence in these populations and, thereby, close excellence gaps. This assumes that the problem isn't that the programs are ineffective, but just that certain students are not being placed in them. This is a large assumption, as it presumes they would benefit if they were only identified at higher rates, but we cannot know for sure until there is more disaggregated research.

Second, it's important to acknowledge that many of the programs or interventions discussed in this chapter could exacerbate excellence gaps by virtue of the fact that they show positive effects when provided to advanced learners. If an advanced learner is more likely to be from a dominant-culture or high income group (as is often the case) and the same learner is likely to grow at a faster rate because of an intervention she receives, then excellence gaps could widen. That said, the proper policy response is not to eliminate such program so that gaps can be closed. This might satisfy the goal of reducing gaps but it would do so by suppressing the learning of a particular population; a position that is simply unethical. Instead, broader access to these programs must be seen as the first step. Many of the programs we will present in part 3 focus on proactive services to underrepresented programs in order to both develop excellence while also advance the goal of greater equity.

A final implication is that programs, schools, states, and the nation as a whole need to begin considering gaps at the highest levels of achievement when they implement policies or new programs. Far too few studies—even among those that focus on achievement gaps—ever consider what effect a particular intervention will have on excellence gaps. Some projects funded in state education agencies under the most recent Javits Program are just beginning to focus on explicit interventions to address excellence gaps, but this is a metric that should be of concern to all educators—not just those interested in advanced education.[29]

PART THREE

How Do We Shrink Excellence Gaps?

6

Alternative Identification

ANY TIME an assessment is used to gather information about student learning—whether a classroom performance or a standardized achievement test—validity is a primary concern.[1] Just as standardized tests have received increased criticism regarding their validity and narrow focus since the passage of NCLB, some scholars argue that inequality at high levels of achievement stems at least in part from the tests and procedures used to identify high-ability learners. Racial, ethnic, and socioeconomic disparities exist in nearly every area of high achievement: athletics, college graduation, and programs for advanced K–12 students such as AP and gifted and talented programs.[2] For example, one report revealed that the US 2013 graduating class of high school seniors included 48.1 percent students who qualified for free or reduced-price meals. At the same time, only 27.5 percent of AP exam takers were eligible for free or reduced-price meals. The same report also noted that despite making up 14.5 percent of the 2013 graduating class, only 9.2 percent of blacks took an AP exam and only 4.6 percent received a score of 3 or better (against 58.3 percent, 55.9 percent, and 61.3 percent, respectively, for white students). Whether or not these differentials represent some kind of unfair penalization and fault of the tests or bona fide differences in academic achievement continues to be debated.[3]

Gifted and talented programs at the K–12 level have been challenged on the basis of their identification systems as well—and for obvious reasons.[4] Yoon and Gentry analyzed data from the Elementary and Secondary School Survey and the Civil Rights Data Collection from 2002 to 2006 to determine representation rates of different ethnic groups at the state level and in the nation as a whole.[5] They found that among identified gifted students, students of Asian heritage were represented at nearly double the rate of the overall student population. White students were also overrepresented, though at a lower rate—about 1.2 times that of their general population representation. Black, Hispanic, and Native American students were all underrepresented at rates of .55, .70, and .80 times their rate, respectively, in the overall student population, although some states are doing better in this regard than others. This unequal pattern of talent development almost certainly contributes to excellence gaps, as certain groups of students have less access to such programs than others, as we illustrated in the scenarios that opened this book. Even if all students were to begin formalized education in the same place in terms of ability (an assumption that cannot be supported), differential access to talent development will create and exacerbate excellence gaps over time. Since identification and admissions policies often dictate who does and doesn't receive advanced educational services, efforts to improve these measures or the larger processes through which students are identified are an important factor to consider in mitigating excellence gaps.

Identification-focused methods to address excellence gaps, or the general inequality in racial, ethnic, and economic representation rates within high-achieving populations, can be classified into two groups: those that involve the use of different or nontraditional assessments, and those that advocate for using traditional assessments in a different way. Matthews and Peters referred to these categories as the "use different tests" and "use tests differently" perspectives.[6] Both approaches have shown various degrees of effectiveness. Below we present an overview of the methods proposed under both perspectives as well as what promise they have for addressing excellence gaps.

USING DIFFERENT TESTS

Before discussing "different tests" we need to identify the most frequently used tests for identifying talent. Callahan, Moon, and Oh conducted a national survey of gifted programs and found that tests of academic aptitude, ability (including nonverbal ability tests), intelligence, and achievement were reported most often in terms of how students were identified.[7] These methods included individual as well as group-administered tests and national as well as state achievement tests. Similarly, the National Association for Gifted Children's 2014–2015 State of the States report noted "multiple measures"—often achievement and ability tests—as the most commonly reported method of gifted student identification.[8]

Methods under the "use different tests" category stem from the assumption that a major cause of underrepresentation is a deficit in the assessments used to measure advanced achievement, potential, or giftedness. Proponents of different tests methods share the belief that the problem (or at least a large part of it) lies with the tests themselves—they are in some way invalid for assessing advanced ability or achievement in general or within specific populations. The presumption is if a less flawed test were to be developed and used, then the differential rates in representation would shrink. Efforts in this category can be broken down into two specific types: nonverbal ability tests and structured observation protocols.

Nonverbal Testing

Nonverbal ability tests are a type of standardized assessment characterized by the way they are administered to and completed by the test taker.[9] Items or tasks are presented to a student, who can answer those items without the same level of spoken language proficiency that is required on most tests of standard academic achievement. Items on these tests often appear as pattern recognition tasks, where students need to identify trends in shapes or figures and then identify the next figure in the progression. Rather than include any written or spoken instructions, students are presented with a few completed example items in order to see what is expected. The test administrator can also gesture or point to indicate that the student should attempt to identify the next image in the pattern.

Nonverbal tasks have long been used by authors of larger intelligence and aptitude tests as one of several subscales (such as the Wechsler Tests and the Cognitive Abilities Test (CogAT)). They have also been used to create stand-alone nonverbal ability tests such as the Naglieri Nonverbal Abilities Test (NNAT), the Raven's Progressive Matrices, and the Test of Nonverbal Intelligence (TONI). For the most part, it is stand-alone nonverbal ability tests that have been proposed as a solution to underrepresentation.

The reason these types of tests have garnered so much attention is because of their ability to measure general intelligence with less of a language influence. This strength has clear appeal in a nation with a large and growing English language learner (ELL) population, as well as a large population of students who are not grade-level proficient in English. Under these circumstances, such measures would conceivably assess advanced ability more accurately by avoiding cultural or language influences.

There are two challenges with this approach. First, at best, research is rather mixed on the ability of nonverbal tests to identify larger numbers of students from traditionally underrepresented populations. Two different studies examined data where nonverbal tests were used for this purpose, and in both cases, students from dominant cultural groups received higher observed scores and were thus identified at greater rates than were their non-dominant-culture peers.[10] Carman and Taylor found that low-income students received scores that were nearly 30 percent lower than their higher-income peers on the NNAT. Table 6.1 highlights the scope of the problem by showing the score differences reported in Giessman for the CogAT composite (VQN), the CogAT nonverbal subscale (NV), and the NNAT. Both studies suggest that using nonverbal ability tests did not solve the underrepresentation problem, regardless of where the threshold for identification was placed.

Naglieri and Ford have challenged the argument that nonverbal ability tests (specifically the NNAT) will not solve the problem of underrepresentation.[11] Their conclusions center on the logical argument that because these tests involve no language in the directions or items themselves and because there are no images that could be seen as culture-specific (such as a particular kind of tree, verbal analogy, colloquialism, or scenario), these assessments are inherently culturally reduced. If this is correct and by implication the data from the above-referenced studies were flawed and not an accurate representation of the actual effect of using such tests, there is still a serious problem with using such measures as a way to identify students for advanced programs or services. The key criterion for the evaluation of any assessment is the degree to which it is well matched with its purpose. An assessment or identification system should be judged by the degree to which it measures the

TABLE 6.1   Minority subgroup score differences from Giessmann and colleagues*

Group	CogAT-VQN SD-15	CogAT-NV SD-15	NNAT2 SD-15
Black	−1.07	−.81	−1.07
Hispanic	−.69	−.38	−.49
Asian	+.10	+.54	+.61
Native American	−.26	−.04	−.10
White (baseline score)	106.5	106.7	100.5

Source: Jacob A. Giessman, James L. Gambrell, and Molly S. Stebbins, "Minority Performance on the Naglieri Nonverbal Ability Test, Second Edition, Versus the Cognitive Abilities Test, Form 6: One Gifted Program's Experience," *Gifted Child Quarterly* 57, no. 2 (2013): 101–109.

* Scaled to standard deviation units.

SD = score difference; CogAT = Cognitive Abilities Test, Form 7;
NNAT = Naglieri Nonverbal Ability Test composite score; AA = African American;
VQN = Composite score; NV = Nonverbal subscale.

skills and abilities needed to be successful in the particular program into which students will be placed if successfully identified.[12]

Even if nonverbal ability tests are able to identify proportional numbers of underrepresented learners, some of the students identified will not necessarily be successful in the resulting program or intervention because the tests do not include measures of the prerequisite skills for success—assuming that the programs are academic in nature, taught primarily in English, and follow in format of most K–16 courses. If this is the case, then the mismatch between what is measured by the test and what is provided in the program is a fatal flaw of such efforts. For example, if the program will be conducted in English and yet students are identified for the program even if they are unable to learn from instruction delivered in English, then using nonverbal measured for the purpose of reducing excellence gaps is unlikely to work.

Despite these limitations (and every method has limitations), nonverbal ability tests could be used to identify students for non-academic or at least nontraditional advanced learning programs—ones that capitalize on the identified students' strengths in nonverbal areas. Such programs do exist, although they are rare, and are a case where the match between identification system and program is much stronger. Peters and colleagues presented one example of such a program from the Paradise Valley (Arizona) School District.[13] The district wanted to identify greater numbers of students from its large ELL population for advanced interventions. In particular, it wanted more students from this population to take high school AP and honors courses. At the same time, the district knew that these students lacked the English language skills necessary for success in such reading-heavy courses. To address this conflict, the district created what it called the Nonverbal Honors Core Program at the seventh- and eighth-grade levels. Students are identified for participation in this program based on nonverbal ability scores, then teachers who are dual certified in gifted education and bilingual education deliver it. The program thus fosters advanced abilities while meeting students' needs where they are—in this case, language. This is one way that nonverbal ability tests can make sense, as they are strongly aligned with the skills necessary for success in this particular program.

Structured Observation Protocols

A second type of alternative assessment that has shown promise involves structured performance and observation protocols. These protocols include activities designed to elicit behaviors indicative of talent in groups that might not otherwise have to opportunity to manifest those talents to observers. Examples of these systems include the Young Scholars Program and the USTARS Teacher Observation of Potential in Students (TOPS) protocol.[14] In these protocols, the observer (typically the teacher) has both a structured environment (model lessons or activities) and structured observation criteria of what to look for in students while they engage in these tasks. For example, a science lesson might be designed to engage students in tasks requiring critical and creative thinking. Students then work together to complete the activity while the teacher watches for any indicators of talent. In USTARS, teachers engage students in science and literature units and use deep questioning to elicit critical thinking or particularly telling responses from students regarding potential talents.

Structured observation protocols avoid a problem common to most achievement tests and teacher rating scales, which is that each student being observed has differing educational experiences and might not demonstrate the skills the teacher is looking for—he or she might not have learned the skill being looked for because of decreased educational opportunity. In the case of the USTARS and Young Scholars protocols, the content with which the students are interacting is universal—it's presented within the current class—as are the criteria being used to look for gifted behaviors. Thus less of what is being captured by the observers is influenced by educational opportunity. Research on the Young Scholars program has shown a significant increase (565 percent) in the number of black and Hispanic students identified for gifted services. Data from the same source also suggested students are being successful in the programs for which they are identified, likely because of the strong connection between the content of the model lessons and the academic nature of the programs and services provided (this is a critical difference between this method and the nonverbal testing method).[15]

The main district associated with the Young Scholars model is Fairfax County, Virginia.[16] To implement the model, Young Scholar specialists deliver whole-group lessons to students in early primary grades. The specialist and classroom teacher then record any observation of potential in students from underrepresented populations. These data are used alongside standardized test data (including nonverbal assessments), a gifted behavior rating scale, anecdotal records, work samples, and any other relevant material to determine which students might benefit from additional challenge. Students identified can then access a range of services, including cluster grouping, specialized units in math or literacy designed for advanced learners, or simply additional challenges in the regular classroom. Culturally relevant training for classroom teachers is also heavily emphasized so that students' strengths and abilities are affirmed. The Young Scholars program overall places a strong emphasis on being welcoming and inclusive to a wide range of learners.

The greatest potential limitation in structured observation protocols is in scale and practicality. Involving every teacher not only in the completion of an observation protocol but also in the delivery of a standardized set of lessons would be a significant undertaking for most districts. It's also not clear to what degree providing the standardized environment and observation protocol decreases the natural variability that exists between raters. Even with the most highly structured scoring rubric, using so many teachers in the process is certain to increase unreliability. Still, this process of identification shows great potential for locating greater numbers of underrepresented learners for advanced interventions.

USING TESTS DIFFERENTLY

The other category of alternative assessments to locate larger number of underrepresented learners deals with using the achievement, ability, or aptitude tests that are already common in K–12 schools, but in a different way from how they are traditionally applied. The presumption underlying these particular methods is that the way in which assessments are typically used yields low-quality information regarding talent, ability, or achievement, therefore disadvantaging minority or low-income students. Universal screening, local norm comparisons, group-specific comparisons, and doing away with arbitrary classifications entirely are four approaches to correcting this systematic error leading to underrepresentation.

Universal Screening

The simplest application of the "use tests differently" method is universal screening, whereby whatever tests or processes are used to identify talented students are administered to an entire population as opposed to only those students who pass an earlier screening phase. Both McBee and Grissom and colleagues noted that white and Asian students are much more likely to be nominated for gifted programs than their Hispanic or black peers.[17] Thus, putting up a nomination gateway to the processes used to determine giftedness will result in underrepresentation. One possible solution is that the assessment or processes used to determine giftedness could be given to the entire population under consideration. This approach is always preferable with regard to system sensitivity—it will miss the fewest students.[18] On the downside, it comes with cost considerations in terms of time and money.

However, there is a middle ground. McBee and colleagues proposed ways to design systems that balance sensitivity with incorrect identification rates that also have the side effect of costing far less than universal screening.[19] A two-phase identification system—a screening phase followed by a confirmation phase—can be created as to miss as few students as possible in the screening phase while having to test as few as possible with the confirmation assessment. In the example McBee et al. presented, this involved a screening phase threshold of roughly the top 30 percent. Students scoring in the top third are administered the confirmation assessment. In doing this, as opposed to universal screening, nearly all of the benefit was maintained (the fewest students were missed) but for only 30 percent of the cost. Applying such methods allows schools to formally assess as few of students for giftedness as possible while also missing as few students as possible. It is not an easy task or balance but it can be done, and either using universal testing or a well-designed nomination system will result in higher rates of low-income or minority students being identified. Aside from the time and money costs, there is very little downside to universal screening as a method for addressing underrepresentation and excellence gaps.

Local Norm Comparisons

Using local norms is another approach that has gained widespread acceptance in the gifted education research community but has yet to see widespread application in K–12 schools. Many gifted identification criteria use norm-referenced cut-scores such as the ninety-ninth or ninety-fifth percentiles or scores such as 130 or higher on a given test of academic ability, intelligence or achievement, in order to determine eligibility. "Gifted" education is thus operationalized as something only a part of a larger population has need of. But what population? In most cases, these decisions are made relative to the national norm sample that comes with the test. This practice tends to under-identify students in generally low-performing schools, while simultaneously over-identifying students in generally high-performing schools. High-performing schools are likely to have more students who are at or near the upper thresholds used in gifted education identification, and also tend to have larger populations of high-income and dominant-culture group populations, which in turn contributes to the underrepresentation of low-income and minority students. The use of national norms means that talent development programs are more likely to exist and serve more students in schools with fewer numbers of students from traditionally underrepresented populations, as highlighted in the opening to this book.

To combat this problem, several scholars recommend the use of local norms in gifted identification.[20] In this process, students are compared with other students from their local educational setting, ideally using assessments that are universally administered to an entire grade level, as opposed to a national norm group. In most cases, this is the students' school (school-based norms) or district, though district norms are less helpful, especially in large districts, due to the within-district diversity that can exist. The rationale is that if the purpose of gifted education or any kind of advanced academic service is to provide for those who are the most ill-suited and underchallenged in their current educational setting and thus most in need of additional services, then measures of national comparison are not helpful. If a teacher or administrator wants to answer the question "Which of my students is the most advanced in the class?" or "most talented in the school?" or "most likely to be under-challenged?" then a local comparison needs to be made.

A downside to local norms is that they are not often provided to schools as a matter of practice by many test companies, thereby requiring individual schools or districts to compute these norms on their own. Given that this requires little more than sorting students by score, this should not be a major barrier.

There is also the larger problem that being "gifted" or "advanced" within a local comparison does not mean the student will be ready for college or the workplace when he or she finishes K–12 education (and thus leaves the local context). One colleague working at an elite university recently shared the example of students who were among the best students in their high schools, yet struggled in the university, where the local high school context no longer mattered. In other words, when "advanced" is defined as a certain percentage of students within the local context, that status says little about what the student actually knows. If "advanced" or "gifted" is determined at the local level, some students could be labeled as such not because their abilities are especially high but rather just because their peers are, on average, very low achievers. That said, to imply that our universities will be flooded with low-income and minority students who are struggling because, according to local norms, they were successful in high school feels a little far-fetched. If only we could be so fortunate to have that many talented students from those backgrounds excelling in K–12 education, regardless of the norms! Local, norm-referenced comparisons can be effective for locating the most relatively advanced students who might be in need of additional challenge in many school districts, especially given the de facto segregation in American schools. But that is only one step. Once students are identified, attention also needs to be paid to the fact that students need certain levels of knowledge and skills to be successful in higher education and the workplace.[21]

Using local norms also eliminates the problem of the largest number of gifted students being located in the most advanced schools (compared with the nation). Although using national norms has logistical appeal, since the criteria would be identical across the country, it does little to further challenge the students in every school who are currently being underchallenged. When local norms are used, regardless of the actual achievement level of the school or the students within it, the same percentage of students will be identified in every school regardless of their actual level of content mastery. For example, one school's "gifted" eighth graders might be working on geometry and trigonometry while another's are working on pre-algebra—all because of the local comparison group. If the criteria are set at the ninety-fifth percentile of a national norm, some schools will have no gifted kids (often the lowest-income schools), and some will have majority populations of students identified as gifted.

Consider an extracurricular example. If all high schools in the state of Nebraska used national norms to select players for their basketball teams—say, by selecting only those students who were in the top 10 percent nationally in basketball ability—then some schools would have full rosters (with some having more qualified players than available slots), and other schools, probably the majority, would not have enough players to field a team. We would never do that for extracurricular or cocurricular activities, but we often do not question the same strategy applied to academics.[22]

Consider instead the situation if the ninety-fifth percentile were applied to a local norm. Each school would have about 5 percent of students identified as needing additional services due to ill-suited grade-level instruction. Although still an arbitrary number, it at least acknowledges that all schools have students who could be doing more and are currently underchallenged. This would have the effect of identifying far more low-income and racial ethnic minority students than would national norms because, students from underrepresented populations tend to receive lower average scores than do their non-underrepresented peers. By changing the process so that disadvantaged kids are not being compared with advantaged kids, we can reach a better metric of relative talent and ideally close excellence gaps.

In researching the use of local norms, we came across another, quite reasonable concern about their use (in addition to the problem noted above that being identified as gifted in a local comparison does not mean the student will be ready for college or the workplace): What happens when a student qualifies for and receives advanced education services in one school then moves to a new district with higher local norms (that is, where the student no longer qualifies for or can receive services)? That's a great question and an unfortunate scenario, because students who move often tend to struggle, and gifted students are not exempt from these effects.[23] But we have been unable to find any data on how often this situation would happen. Poor students and their families certainly relocate a lot more than average, but the data suggest that they move to similar communities, which would probably obviate any major problems with local norms. But until we have solid research in this area, this remains an open question.[24]

Group-Specific Comparisons

As good as the use of local norms might sound (and we do recommend that all K–12 programs use local norms any time a norm-referenced criterion is used to identify academic talent), it would not completely eliminate underrepresentation and would still leave certain populations underrepresented in advanced academic programs. Instead, even within low-performing schools, the highest-income—and often non-minority—students will be the most likely to be identified. Part of this stems from the fact that educational opportunity is strongly related to academic achievement and economic opportunity is not equally distributed across all racial/ethnic groups. If the goal is to eliminate or at least substantially mitigate gaps in identification rates, additional steps are required.

A more invasive way to modify the manner in which assessments are used to identify students for advanced educational interventions is to go beyond using local norms and also make comparisons on the basis of group-specific norms, which compare given students only to others in their closest or most similar peer group. Lohman makes this point very clearly by arguing, "Always, the preferred comparison group would be those who have had roughly similar opportunities to acquire the abilities sampled by the test."[25] He further suggests that talented ELLs would be best assessed by comparing those students to other ELLs, the idea being that such students have had more similar opportunities to develop the kinds of skills required for performance on most academic tests (specifically English language skills) and therefore represent a more accurate and fair comparison group for other ELL students.

The other grouping variable that would make the most sense relates to family income. Comparing students on one particular income group only to those of a similar income group would allow for a more accurate identification of those students who are most talented given a somewhat comparable set of past educational opportunities.

Peters and Gentry applied this method to a diverse urban school's data.[26] Looking at a single school, they applied local norms, taking state achievement test scores from a single building and then comparing rates of identification under a single, general norm comparison and a group-specific norm comparison. When they applied a general, whole-school norm in this fashion (for example, the top 10 percent) they found that low-income students remained underrepresented by approximately fifteen percentage points compared with their representation in the overall population. However, when a group-specific norm was applied (the top 10 percent was identified both for the low-income and high-income group) this underrepresentation disappeared. Of course, in this application, low-income students were given a kind of preference within the identification system on the premise that they had been exposed to fewer educational opportunities to learn the skills needed to pass the state achievement test. In a sense, the identification decision was made only after controlling for some degree of educational opportunity.

We introduced this method as more invasive than several others we've discussed because it would involve applying different criteria for gifted program admittance based solely on a student's income group and with much less consideration for the student's actual level of readiness. This could harm the validity of the identification procedure or the larger nature of advanced programs as being needs-based. This could also strike some people as strange or even inappropriate since some kids would receive a preference based on some demographic variable such as family income and it would mean a more diverse range of needs would now be identified for services. Applying group-specific norms could also result in a paradoxical situation where two students with identical achievement scores in a content area (say, math) might not both be identified as gifted—that the level of performance for one student indicates a talent or high level of ability given her educational opportunity whereas that same level of performance does not indicate talent for the other student (because his opportunity has been greater). That said, if the goal is to ameliorate underrepresentation in gifted education with an eye toward the longer-term goal of closing excellence gaps, this method has been shown to work.

Another study, conducted on a much larger scale, evaluated efforts by one of the largest school districts in the nation to address underrepresentation in a similar fashion.[27] The Broward County (Florida) School District implemented a universal screening system in 2005 (discussed below), to combat the low rate of representation of students from black, Hispanic, low-income, and ELL families in its gifted population. Instead of relying on parent or teacher referrals in deciding to whom to administer an intelligence test to identify students for gifted services (as had been done in the past), the district began screening all second graders, first by administering a nonverbal ability test to each, then administering intelligence tests to those who passed through this screening phase with a score two standard deviations above the norm. Although this might not seem ideal, given the cautions about screening phases described above, the district had more than 265,000 total students, which made universal screening with individually administered intelligence tests impractical. The addition of a universal screening phase to replace nominations was done because substantial underrepresentation had been observed for years, and the district hoped that testing everyone, even in a screening process, might help close these gaps.

What is perhaps most important to note is that the district had tried group-specific norms in the past, allowing low-income or ELL students to be identified as gifted with an IQ score of 116, while other students needed a 130. On its own, this modification to the confirmation phase did not work to eliminate underrepresentation because so few low-income or ELL students ever received a parent or teacher recommendation for testing—they never had the chance to use the group-specific norm because they never passed through the nomination phase. It was only when universal screening (using group-specific norms on the screening phase) was combined with group-specific norms that the district was able to boast increased representation rates of 80 percent, 130 percent, and 180 percent for black, Hispanic, and low-income students, respectively. Universal screening plus group-specific norms for students from ELL and low-income families was found to dramatically decrease the differential identification rates without any significant decrease in the newly identified students' success in gifted programs.

In the case of Broward County, as with any application of group-specific norms, students from one or more subgroups were given a preference to compensate for the fact that they had been exposed to fewer educational opportunities. Although there are certainty ways to rationalize this both from the perspectives of equity and assessment, they are not without controversy, which is why we suggest both universal screening and local norms be tried before more invasive methods are implemented.

Losing the Arbitrary Classifications

Consider an even simpler application of using tests differently: using them to plan targeted instruction instead of classifying students. Much of the discussion up to this point has focused on how to better locate advanced learners or advanced potential in learners from underrepresented populations so that they can then be identified and then provided with an appropriate service. But is the middle step of identification really necessary? Much of the time and effort in gifted education at the K–12 level is spent on identifying students—making 100 percent sure that the students who are provided with some kind of advanced intervention are for sure, truly, 100 percent gifted (whatever that means) and not just bright or the beneficiaries of lots of practice. But even if this works to assure advanced learners are challenged (a presumption there is reason to doubt), is it necessary? Could there be a more efficient and less work-intensive process to talent development? We believe this is worth considering.

The hypothetical question becomes: Is there a way to move directly from observing a need (through data, such as the observation that a child was entering kindergarten far behind his or her classmates in skills) to providing a necessary intervention to address that need while bypassing any requirement to formally identify the student as "at risk" (or "gifted" if the student showed exceptional ability)? In the response to intervention (RTI) framework, a similar process was designed to be more responsive and seamless so that kids would not fall behind. A hoped-for side effect was that fewer students would need special education labels as their needs were able to be met outside of the formalized special education system. Applying such a model to advanced learners could also be viewed as a way to "use tests differently" to locate and provide for larger numbers of advanced learners from traditionally underrepresented groups. It is worth emphasizing that although RTI has largely focused on low-performing or special education students, it was originally supposed to be an "all student" model whereby all students, including those who were already advanced, were helped to grow and develop. Although little research has been done on whether or not such a philosophy of instruction could close excellence gaps, it seems to contain all of the right ingredients.

Using local or even group-specific norms as described above, a school could identify those students who are seen as most talented (compared with others having similar educational opportunity) and then devote additional resources to their further development. If proactive effort were put toward identifying members of traditionally underrepresented groups, such as through Young Scholars or group-specific norms, then this could help combat excellence gaps, especially in the early grades before they grow too large. If as much attention were paid to closing early excellence gaps in this fashion as is paid to remedial achievement gaps, then gaps in AP test rates, college attendance, gifted identification, and college completion might be smaller as student progress through their educational career.

7

Poverty Reduction

IF YOU WANT to get people involved with education or public policy riled up, say something about poverty in the United States. The topic elicits strong reactions across the political and ideological spectrums, and conversations can quickly become heated. Jonathan spent a couple of months dealing with the fallout, both positive and negative, from a blog post in which he stated that serious education reform cannot take place in the absence of poverty reduction, and later, that serious poverty reduction cannot take place in the absence of education reform.[1]

Disappointingly, the reactions in both directions were lacking in nuance. People who loved the idea focused on the fact that education reform should be primarily about addressing poverty; critics (and there were mostly critics) focused on the fact that reform already focuses a great deal on poverty reduction.[2] To borrow a term from Stephen Colbert, the available research suggests both facts are more "truthy" than true.

We see sufficient evidence to question whether alleviating poverty leads to the elimination of excellence gaps, and we strongly disagree with the notion that any meaningful, large-scale attempts have been made to reduce childhood poverty in the United States for a long time. For example, consider this thought experiment we often share with our students: Think of as many major education reforms as you can, at the national and state levels, from the past twenty years. It's likely a pretty long list! Now think of as many major childhood poverty reduction programs as you can from that same period. That's a much shorter list (although you can make it longer by adding poverty reduction programs that have been scaled back or eliminated). The fact is that the United States spends a large amount of money on basic supports for low-income families (though we note that this amount isn't large when compared with the rest of the federal budget), but there is very little focus on actually eliminating or reducing poverty itself.

In this chapter, we explore the role of interventions designed to address aspects of economic vulnerability that may help shrink excellence gaps. The first section looks at the nature of the country's poverty problem; the second explores what we know about the effects of growing up economically vulnerable in this country. The meat of the chapter then explores interventions that made help with our excellence gap problems.

HOW POOR ARE WE?

One of the paradoxes of the United States in the twenty-first century is that the country is among the richest in the world, yet has one of the poorest populations. The US Census from 2013 shows that over 45 million Americans live in poverty, representing 14.5 percent of the population.[3] Although this poverty rate is not exceptional (similar rates were experienced in the early 1980s and 1990s and rates were historically much higher before the implementation of Social Security and Great Society social programs in the 1930s and 1960s, respectively), population growth has led to more Americans living in poverty today than at least since the 1950s.[4]

Poverty rates for children eighteen years old or younger have dropped slightly during the current economic recovery, currently standing at 21.1 percent, representing over 15 million children.[5] According to a 2012 UNICEF report, the rate is one of the highest in the developed world.[6] Nearly 10 percent of households (3.8 million households) experience some degree of food insecurity, defined as "access to adequate food is limited by a lack of money and other resources"; these household data translate to over 8.5 million children experiencing some degree of food insecurity in 2013.[7] It's important to note all of these different terms: low-income, poverty, food-insecure, and many others are often used interchangeably, even though they are operationalized and defined differently. They also assume that people not classified as being in any of these groups do not experiences the challenges related to financial or economic challenges—assumptions that are not as safe as they might seem.

Over the past generation, the number of K–12 students qualifying for free or reduced-price lunch programs, one of the most widely used metrics of low-income status, has substantially increased (see figure 7.1). For the 2012–2013 school year (the latest available data), 51.3 percent of students qualified for these programs, meaning that over half of our public school students live in households whose income is 1.85 times the poverty level or less. For a family of four, this means an income of slightly less than $50,000 a year. That rate is up from 49.6 percent in 2011–2012, continuing the trend since the last economic crisis from 2007–2009 of a roughly 1.5 percent annual increase. In twenty-two states (plus the District of Columbia), over half of the student population qualifies for lunch assistance (up from eighteen the year before), with over 60 percent qualifying in nine of those states and the District of Columbia (up from five the previous year).[8] It's unquestionable that childhood poverty and economic insecurity are on the rise.

However, these statistics mask a number of important complexities related to measuring poverty and determining its impact on children and families. Poverty is not easy to define, and measuring it is not without

FIGURE 7.1   Percentage of public school students eligible for the National School Lunch Program

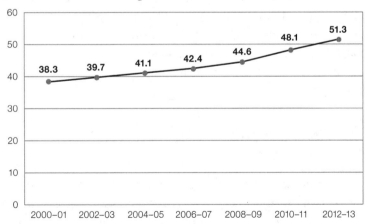

Source: Data from various NCES databases and reports. Data from 2002–2005 were puzzlingly hard to locate, so data points in that range are estimated based solely on 2000–2001 and 2006–2007 data.

considerable controversy.[9] Some US databases rely on whether students are qualified to participate in free or reduced-price lunch programs, but the issues around using this data point as a measure of poverty are well documented (e.g., some urban schools do not offer lunch programs and therefore don't attempt to qualify children for this program; some students do not want to stand out and thus do not apply for the program).[10]

Other databases simply do not have any indicators of family economic well-being, further complicating matters. After all, some students who qualify for free or reduced-price meals do not experience the factors associated with poverty for a variety of reasons, and even some seemingly wealthy people might still face financial challenges. The picture is not as clear as it might seem.[11]

For example, 25.2 percent of children living in households at or below the poverty line are estimated to experience food insecurity. In households with income-to-poverty ratios of 1.85 or lower (the cutoff for free or reduced-price lunch), food insecurity rates are not terribly dissimilar, at 21.5 percent.[12] For these reasons, we prefer to use the term *economically vulnerable* to describe students who deal with the myriad issues faced by individuals who lack socioeconomic security in the United States.[13] In the data provided below, we use lunch program qualification as a proxy for economic vulnerability, as it is the only relevant indicator available in the data sets of interest. It's worth noting that in our experience, schools are becoming more and more reluctant to share data related to free or reduced-lunch status owing to student privacy issues. Although this caution may be warranted, making economic data even harder to access is not going to help address the challenges associated with family poverty.

RACE AND POVERTY AREN'T THE SAME THING

Another complication that is relevant to the current analysis is that much education policy—and many related policy debates—focus primarily on race/ethnicity at the expense of economic vulnerability. This focus is understandable given the country's long, troubled history of racial and ethnic discrimination, but although some racial/ethnic groups are more likely to experience poverty than others, economic vulnerability is experienced by all racial and ethnic groups.[14] In other words, socio-economic insecurity is often correlated with other demographic charac-teristics, but those correlations do not explain all of the variance, and correlation should not be inferred to represent causation. Instead, pov-erty and race tend to co-vary with other factors that do influence educa-tional achievement such as school quality and access to supplementary educational resources.

At the same time, we need to acknowledge the substantial overlap between race/ethnicity and socioeconomic status. This correlation has important and somewhat severe implications for public schools, as can be seen in figure 7.2 (the data are a few years old, but they almost cer-tainly haven't changed much, at least in a positive way, since 2009, given that rates of economic vulnerability and poverty have risen since that time). This figure illustrates how black, Hispanic, and Native American students are concentrated in high-poverty schools. For example, very few black, Hispanic, or Native American fourth graders attend public schools where 10 percent or less of the student body qualifies for lunch assistance; rather, these students overwhelmingly attend public schools

FIGURE 7.2   Distribution of public school fourth graders, by school free or reduced-price lunch rate, 2009

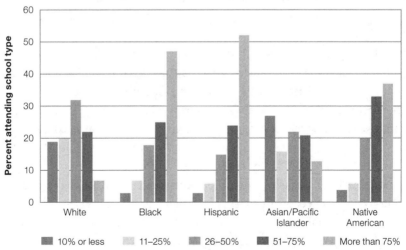

Source: National Center for Education Statistics, "Status and Trends in the Education of Racial and Ethnic Minorities," https://nces.ed.gov/pubs2010/2010015/tables/table_7_5b.asp.

with more than half of the study body qualifying. Over half of Hispanic students attend schools where more than 75 percent of the students receive lunch assistance. The pattern for white and Asian students
is very different, with 71 and 65 percent, respectively, attending schools
with 50 percent or fewer of the students qualifying for lunch aid.

ARE AMERICAN CHILDREN REALLY THAT POOR?

It's worth noting that the topic of childhood poverty in the United States
has become even more controversial lately. The impetus for the heated
discussions was an article by Mike Petrilli and Brandon Wright in Education Next, expanded on in a *National Review Online* piece, in which
they argued that research suggesting that the United States has a very
high childhood poverty rate compared with other countries, such as the
UNICEF report cited earlier, greatly exaggerate the depth of US child
poverty.[15] They sharply criticize the use of a relative poverty definition
when calculating these rates (poverty often defined in such approaches
as earning less than half the median salary in a given country). From
their perspective, when comparing countries, "Many of the US households that are counted as poor on a relative measure would be considered middle class on an absolute measure." They provide data suggesting
that US poverty, when estimated in absolute terms, is fairly typical for a
developed country.

The response to these arguments, and especially the *NRO* article, was
intense, with many counterarguments that Petrilli and Wright's original analysis had itself made too many assumptions about the distinc-
tion between relative and absolute poverty. For example, Matt Bruening
noted that the local economic context matters. If you use absolute poverty estimates, he noted, you have to factor in the cost of goods within
each economy. And many countries have social services for the poor
that don't involve cash transfers or other direct benefits (which Petrilli
and Wright relied on in their calculations), such as free health clinics
and other social services that are not as widely available to economically vulnerable children and their families in the Unites States. Using
an approach that accounts for purchasing power within each country,
Bruening found that disposable income for households with children,

even when using the absolute poverty approach, was among the lowest in the developed world.[16] By way of illustration, at the fifth percentile of per capita income, children in poor Norwegian families have 97 percent more per capita disposable income than children in similar American families, in large part because of a wide array of public social safety supports that families do not have to purchase on their own.

This isn't a book on the intricacies of defining and measuring poverty, and we will resist the temptation to jump further into the weeds in this debate. Our take on the situation is that the United States clearly has a lot of economically vulnerable children (probably more than other rich countries, in both relative and absolute terms), and those children rarely excel academically. That said, one aspect of the Petrilli-Wright argument that was largely lost in the heated debate is that they argued that relative poverty rates are a better indicator of income inequality than absolute poverty, and that we need to focus on income inequality just as much as poverty. We can't disagree that income inequality needs more attention in American public policy, but we are also in agreement with the critics who have demonstrated that American childhood poverty rates are indeed among the worst in the developed world. Both of these conclusions have an impact on how we design educational and social experiences to address excellence gaps.

EFFECTS OF POVERTY

As discussed in chapter 3 (see figure 3.2), socioeconomic excellence gaps are pronounced and growing, at least based on the indicator of the percentage of students scoring advanced.[17] However, some researchers have noted that the "percent scoring advanced" measure may mask progress being made by the lower-performing groups (that is, a group's performance may be increasing, but the average performance level may not have reached the cut-off for the advanced achievement level). As a result, researchers often use ninetieth percentile scores for subgroups. Figure 7.3 depicts ninetieth percentile scores for NAEP grade 4 mathematics. Using this metric, which is not without its own strengths and weaknesses, excellence gaps are at best stagnant. After thirteen years of significant improvement in scores, assistance-eligible students' scores in 2013 are still significantly below those of non-eligible students in 2000.[18] All

FIGURE 7.3   NAEP grade 4 mathematics, 90th percentile scores by lunch status

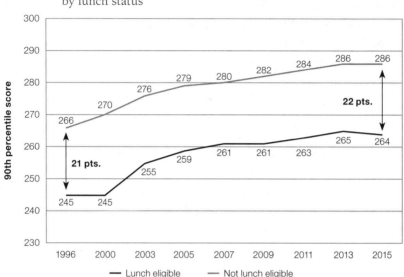

of the excellence gap gains on this measure from 1996 to 2007 have disappeared over the past few years.

Whether economic vulnerability is a cause of excellence gaps or merely correlational (and we find it hard to argue it isn't causal at least in part), socioeconomic excellence gaps definitely exist. Scholars have noted a wide range of other effects of poverty and low income on students, their families, and their communities, and for our purposes we don't need to go into any great depth about them. But they include most aspects of children's physical, cognitive, and affective health and development, primarily due to the effects of deleterious environments, lack of access to quality education and other human services, and lack of resources.[19] Research has also shown that childhood poverty leads to a host of problems when the child moves into adulthood, including negative effects on economic productivity, health, personality, and even cognition.[20]

For example, in one particularly interesting recent study, researchers found that childhood socioeconomic status (SES) was related to adult desire to eat when needed; people who grew up in relatively high socioeconomic status tended to eat more often when they had high energy needs and less often when they had low energy needs; participants who grew up in lower socioeconomic circumstances tended to eat at high levels regardless of energy need.[21] Regardless of the specific outcomes, the research literature provides ample evidence that growing up economically vulnerable has lasting effects into adulthood, *even if the adult is no longer economically insecure*. These myriad, negative influences result in large socioeconomic differences in achievement, including excellence gaps.

DOING SOMETHING ABOUT IT

We see two broad sets of approaches to addressing this type of excellence gap: poverty reduction programs and interventions to shrink socioeconomic excellence gaps by improving the performance of economically vulnerable students. These approaches are not mutually exclusive, of course, but they operate on different scales and therefore involve different levels of resources.

Poverty Reduction

Compared with other developed countries, the United States spends far less as a percentage of GDP on aid for the poor.[22] In an analysis of the influence of tax and transfer policies on income inequality and growth, the OECD grouped the United States with Chile, Israel, Mexico, Portugal, and Turkey as countries "characterised by above average inequality originating from the labour market . . . Capital and self-employment income also tend to benefit a small group of households. Cash transfers have little redistributive impact because they are small in size and often largely insurance-based . . . Overall, for these nations both inequality in household disposable income and the poverty rate are well above the OECD average."[23] Indeed, in our research for this book, we find few people arguing that our high poverty rates have not been a function of our economic and social policies.

Growing income inequality and high childhood poverty rates are not an inevitable part of the American experience. And one doesn't have to look far to see that poverty can be directly addressed (and largely defeated) in a big segment of the US population. Without Social Security, nearly half of seniors would live in poverty, versus the reality of 10 percent today.[24] Growing old in America used to mean a pretty good chance of dying in poverty, but Social Security, along with other aid programs, has greatly improved the lives of Americans as they age. Similar progress has not been made, especially over the past few decades, in reducing child poverty. Compare the sharp reduction in senior poverty from the mid-1960s to today (from about 28 percent to 10 percent) with the lack of change in the childhood poverty rate over the same time period (from about 20 percent to 21 percent today).[25] Poverty reduction among seniors is unquestionably one of the country's biggest public policy accomplishments; lack of poverty reduction among children is one of our biggest public policy failures.[26]

Our review of this literature leads to several observations:

- Multipronged efforts, involving a range of public- and private-sector policy changes and interventions, are likely to be most effective.
- Considerable empirical evidence is available to guide these comprehensive efforts.
- Education is a key part of any effort, but it must be part of a broader approach.[27]

Not surprisingly, there is little evidence that reducing poverty will shrink excellence gaps, but it feels self-evident. Even if reducing poverty does not share a one-to-one relationship with decreasing excellence gaps, we can't see excellence gaps decreasing without some broader effort to mitigate the effects of poverty.

Addressing Socioeconomic Excellence Gaps

Despite the controversies mentioned above, acknowledging the role of poverty in causing excellence gaps is fairly straightforward—other than armed conflict, poverty is arguably the most severe of human conditions, and its effects are harsh, all-encompassing, and long-lasting. Finding promising strategies for shrinking poverty-based excellence gaps, however, is a much more difficult task, in large part because recommendations abound, but research support for various strategies is remarkably thin.

As a case in point, Plucker and Harris recently reviewed research on the use of acceleration strategies with economically vulnerable students.[28] They found the literature to be full of suggestions that acceleration *could* be an effective intervention for closing socioeconomic excellence gaps.

For example, they concluded that acceleration strategies involving distance education technology could be effective, assuming the interventions do not rely on resources in the students' schools, which are often poorly resourced and provide little programming for high-ability students. Other preliminary research suggests that extracurricular activities and mentoring programs may promote the engagement and achievement of gifted students in high-poverty schools.[29]

In 2012, the Jack Kent Cooke Foundation and NAGC held a symposium on low-income, high-ability students, accompanied by the publication of the report Unlocking Emergent Talent: Supporting High Achievement of Low-Income, High-Ability Students.[30] Among the recommendations was providing a range of academic and social supports for low-income students, removing barriers to gifted education services, and conducting more extensive research on targeted interventions. A preK–20 approach to service delivery for talented, economically vulnerable students would appear to be a wise strategy, given the potential for these students to get "lost in the cracks" during transitions between educational levels.[31]

We find the removal of barriers to be especially important, but we also caution that removing barriers to participation may be more difficult than expected. For example, some acceleration options may involve a need for transportation, yet economically vulnerable students may not have access to easy or reliable transportation beyond their neighborhood.[32] An economically secure family may be able to jump into one of the family cars and make a quick fifteen-minute trip to participate in a special program, but a student living in poverty may need to make a much longer, perhaps unchaperoned, trip via public transportation taking an hour or more each way (if public transportation is even available in their community; see Kneebone's research on the increasing concentration of suburban poverty[33]).

But Plucker and Harris also cautioned that there are legitimate questions about whether certain strategies can work with this population of talented students. Recent research provides evidence that many students attending high-poverty schools do not have many of the technological skills necessary to benefit from internet-delivered programs.[34] And much of the research on the effects of poverty reduction on student outcomes has been conducted with mixed-ability populations, making it difficult to determine the extent to which the many debilitating correlates of poverty (e.g., lack of access to reliable transportation, health care, well-resourced schools, and technology) impact the use of acceleration and other interventions with economically vulnerable students.[35] In general, little empirical work has focused on the efficacy of most traditional talent development strategies when used with poor students.

A THIRD WAY

There is a third set of interventions that combines both poverty reduction and addressing socioeconomic excellence gaps. They aren't exactly invisible—if anything, they are becoming ubiquitous—but they are rarely discussed in the context of shrinking excellence gaps because they operate outside of both the K–12 sphere and public policy. We will introduce them by way of a couple of anecdotes.

We once attended a conference session that involved a panel of high-tech, defense, and aerospace companies. The industry representatives were all concerned about the lack of high-performing students in general, but they were especially concerned about the shallow talent pool of minority and low-income students. One of their major concerns was that many of the best jobs require security clearances given the sensitive technology involved, and only US citizens can get security clearances. Too few talented US students, largely a consequence of too few high-performing minority and low-income students, equals too few candidates for key positions. We are still surprised that this issue has not caused more educational change. The companies' short-term solutions were expanded internship and summer experiences for high school students.

But such programs may start too late. A few years ago, Jonathan was at lunch with the provost of a very large research university. As we discussed the university's efforts to get bright minority and economically vulnerable students on campus and ultimately into graduate school and the workforce, the provost noted that waiting until students got to high school was far too late, as many of the most talented students had already dropped out or were severely underperforming by that time. His solution was to "grow our own," meaning that the university would partner with elementary schools to identify promising minority and poor students, then put in place a range of (vaguely specified) activities and supports to raise the quality of each student's educational experience and increase the odds that they would still be high-performing by high school graduation.

In general, we think of this type of program as being a "fund-and-support-the-child" initiative. Some are heavier on the support than the funding and vice versa, but the intent is the same: to provide poor students with resources and experiences they otherwise would not have access to or be able to take advantage of (these programs are similar to the "front-loading" efforts we will discuss in chapter 9). For example, sometimes they can be narrowly focused, such as the Kalamazoo (Michigan) Promise program, effective for students graduating in 2006, in which anonymous donors guaranteed 65 percent or more of college tuition for any graduates from Kalamazoo high schools, with up to 100 percent of tuition covered for students attending district schools from kindergarten through high school.[36] We have little data on whether the program helped shrink excellence gaps, and getting these data should be a priority, given the expansion of such programs (e.g., the Kalamazoo Promise program became the basis for the greatly expanded Michigan Promise Zone Authority, which expands the program around the state).

Among the best examples of this type of program are the scholarships provided by the Jack Kent Cooke Foundation. When Jack Kent Cooke died in 1997, he left much of his wealth to form the Foundation, which is dedicated to helping support talented students growing up in poverty, as he did. The Foundation offers three scholarships: The Young Scholars Program, which provides support from grade 8 through high school (up to sixty-five recipients selected each year); the College Scholarship Program for graduating seniors (up to forty recipients); and the Undergraduate Transfer Scholarship for community college students who are transferring to four-year colleges (up to eighty-five recipients). Students can receive more than one of the scholarships, resulting in up to ten years of support.

The scholarships, which at up to $40,000 per year are among the most generous in the country, come with additional financial support for some of the other "nice to haves" that wealthier students don't think twice about (travel costs for parents to attend family weekends, summer internship funding so students can participate in unpaid internships). In addition, the Foundation has advisers who not only monitor academics and provide additional support as needed, but also guide the scholarship recipients to other campus resources. One of their staff told us that one of their mantras is, "You're not stupid to ask for help—you're stupid not to."

Research and evaluation data on the Young Scholars (and similar) programs is becoming convincing: 94 percent attend four-year schools versus 54 percent of non-selected applicants and 44 percent of high-ability, high-poverty students nationally; only 3 percent of Young Scholars don't enroll in any type of higher education versus 19 percent for non-selected applicants and 31 percent of similar students nationally.[37] Of the College Scholars, 96 percent graduate and 93 percent do so debt-free (the Foundation also offers a forgivable loan program), and 37 percent move on to graduate school. The Undergraduate Transfer Scholars, when compared with non-selected applicants, are more likely to attend selective colleges, earn their degree more quickly, and enroll in graduate school at nearly 2.5 times the rate of non-selected applicants. These evaluation data aren't the result of carefully controlled experimental studies, and the programs aren't old enough yet to allow for the analysis of outcomes at various points after the Scholars enter the workforce. But there is little question that such programs provide the financial support, counseling and advice, and implicit knowledge of the educational game that poor students and their families lack.

CONCLUSIONS ABOUT ADDRESSING POVERTY EXCELLENCE GAPS

We are hardly idealists on the topic of poverty reduction policies. Living in an age of fiscal conservatism, arguing for large federal and state programs to alleviate poverty feels quixotic. But in our mind, fiscal conservatism is not about not spending; it's about spending wisely, making smart long-term investments, and backing financial decisions up with data. From this perspective, childhood poverty reduction will be expensive, but childhood poverty and growing income inequality are hardly bargains!

A fiscally conservative approach involves weighing costs against benefits. If poverty reduction programs can save money, then how is that any different from arguing that expensive tax cuts lead to growth? The only difference in our minds is that the benefits of social welfare programs tend to be felt decades later, making them a long-term investment—which feels like a fiscally conservative and prudent approach to us.[38]

Government programs to reduce childhood poverty are almost certainly necessary. But nearly every large-scale poverty reduction effort around the world has and does involve education. It's not an either-or: in order to shrink and eventually eliminate socioeconomic excellence gaps, we need to reduce poverty and do a better job of educating bright poor students so they can take advantage of their talents.

But we also have concluded that there aren't a ton of great educational interventions at hand, at least ones supported by empirical evidence. Shockingly few, in fact. And that's where fund-and-support-the-child programs become important. Indeed, if we were advising a private foundation or philanthropist on how to shrink socioeconomic excellence gaps, we would strongly recommend (1) more research on interventions and (2) in the meantime, fund-and-support-the-child programs. The former is an investment in future interventions, and the second is a way to start helping some advanced students while government poverty reduction efforts and intervention research catch up to where they need to be.

THE COMPLEXITIES OF PROVIDING OPPORTUNITY

One common theme in the literature on economically vulnerable students, both for all students and specifically for gifted students, is the need to provide equitable opportunities for a rigorous education and talent development.[39] This is obviously hard to argue against, and we strongly endorse equality of opportunity for all children. But, based on our personal experiences, we worry that opportunity is being conceptualized too narrowly.

For example, if an opportunity is provided to poor, talented students, (1) the students and their caregivers need to know the opportunity exists, (2) they need to believe they should be taking advantage of the opportunity, and (3) they need a realistic chance of accessing the opportunity. We think of these conditions as successful communication, belief and acceptance, and low barriers to access. If any of those three conditions aren't met, then the opportunity is meaningless.

Regarding communication, as our colleague Julia Link Roberts often notes, "An opportunity isn't an opportunity if people don't know about it." Sending a note home with a student may not be adequate for communicating the various opportunities available to him or her. Strategies that prioritize face-to-face communication and multiple communication strategies may be most effective. One recent example of how opportunities for talent development can be communicated is the study conducted by Lu and Weinberg, which provides evidence that participating in New York City's public preschool programs led to greater participation in the identification process for the city schools' gifted education programs.[40] The authors hypothesize that participation in the preschool program allowed for better information sharing about the gifted program identification process, resulting in a test-taking rate nearly five times higher for full-time preschool participants and three times higher for part-time participants compared with students who did not participate in the preschool program. Students must have a clear understanding of the availability of programs designed to help them.[41]

Regarding belief and acceptance, our colleagues at the Center for Talented Youth at Johns Hopkins University recently observed that parents of high-ability students living in poverty often believe that their children do not deserve an opportunity, voicing their concerns that their children were identified as talented by mistake. The CTY researchers have yet to unpack these observations, and research on parents of advanced students, especially poor and minority advanced students, is woefully thin (although there are a few exceptions that prove the rule[42]). But the anecdotal evidence suggests that some economically vulnerable students may be further hampered by families that do not understand or accept the opportunities being offered to them.

Regarding access, the logistical difficulties caused by economic insecurity are well documented.[43] Transportation is an especially big issue. If a family doesn't have a car and other transportation is not provided, how will a student attend an afterschool or weekend program (especially in rural areas)? Even if the program in question is within walking distance, is it safe for the student to walk unaccompanied to and from the location where the opportunity is being provided? If the opportunity is technology-based and occurs outside of school hours, does the student have adequate technology to participate fully at home? For a typical upper-income family, with two or more cars, safe neighborhoods, and more-than-adequate tech and bandwidth in the home, these questions are irrelevant; for lower-income families, these questions are mission-critical. Without low barriers to access, equal opportunity can be a well-disguised myth.

8

Ability Grouping

ANOTHER POTENTIAL SET of interventions that have implications for advanced education and excellence gaps—and a controversial set, at that—is that of ability grouping. The extent to which the word grouping raises strong emotions is illustrated by the following situation in which Jonathan once found himself when interviewing middle school principals in a large, urban school district about their programming for advanced students. The principals were asked to describe the one thing that seemed to be working best across all of their instructional efforts. Without hesitation, several mentioned their math program. When asked to elaborate, one principal described that the school formed different levels of instruction based on previous student achievement and interest level, trained teachers specifically to work with a given level, and adapted curriculum, instruction, and assessment in ways that best met the needs of students at each level. On top of that, the staff reassessed students at regular levels so they could be moved among the levels as necessary.

The principals were then asked to describe their least successful program, and there was again almost unanimity in their concerns about English/language arts. It became clear during the ensuing discussion that the innovations being used in math were not being used in English, and Jonathan asked, somewhat naively, "Why aren't you ability grouping in English like you are in math?"

The reaction could not have been much more severe, other than if they had thrown things at the interviewer. "We would *never* ability group our students," said one principal, as he clutched his chest. Another accused, "I can't believe you think we would do that!" Jonathan considered a bit of sarcasm: "Well, I guess you're right. You're assigning students to math classes based on prior achievement, focusing teaching and resources to maximize learning within each group, and regularly assessing whether students should be moved to different groups. That could never be confused with grouping." But instead, he said, "Oh, OK, my bad."

As silly as this example may sound, we have heard many similar stories over the years—the "strategy that must not be named" elicits strong, often emotional reactions from educators, and it has for many years. As a result, any examination of the potential role of ability grouping in reducing excellence gaps needs to start with a little history about why it became such an emotional raw nerve for many people.

One caveat before we begin: Because we often work in gifted education, some will assume we are both biased in favor of ability grouping. We understand where that assumptions comes from, but it is incorrect. The field of gifted education has a very mixed history with grouping, to an extent those outside of the field probably don't realize. When grouping became a political hot potato roughly twenty-five years ago (more on this below), experts within gifted education moved in two very different directions: one group advocated for ability grouping, noting the largely favorable meta-analytic work and questioning the efficacy of heterogeneous grouping options for gifted students[1]; the second acknowledged case studies and smaller-scale studies showing where ability grouping had gone wrong, and suggested alternative reactions to this finding aside from the complete abandonment of the method. Of course, the distinctions between these two "camps" are slightly exaggerated here, but these differences in attitude toward grouping have existed within the field of gifted education for over a generation. For example, see the recent—and pointed—back-and-forth between Delisle and Tomlinson, both highly influential figures within the field, on the usefulness of differentiation, in which both scholars address grouping issues.[2]

More to the point, we have each vacillated over the years about the extent to which ability grouping should be used with advanced students, let alone all students. From this perspective, we understand fully the angst that grouping often creates. But the fog surrounding efficacy research has begun to lift, and the preponderance of evidence leads us to believe that grouping, in general, is a good thing. But (and this is a significant *but*) like any other pedagogical method, it can go wrong and especially in regard to the topic addressed in this book, it may not be great for addressing excellence gaps.

WHY GROUPING IS CONTROVERSIAL

We don't have great data on the historical use of grouping by ability in American schools, but the conventional wisdom is that the practice was widespread through at least the 1980s. The tide began to turn against grouping around that time, probably beginning in the 1970s, based on the belief that low-income, black, and Hispanic students were disproportionately placed in the low-achieving groups, where they received poor-quality instruction and insufficient resources to promote their learning. This belief is largely supported by research from that time, although many of the critiques were aimed at both between-class grouping and within-class grouping.[3] Perhaps the most widely known critique of between-class grouping was Oakes's Keeping Track, a scathing indictment of how such practices systematically (and systemically) discriminated against poor and minority students by placing them in the lowest tracks with the least-experienced teachers.[4]

The result was a considerable backlash against both between- and within-class grouping. Generally, any acknowledgment that students might have different educational needs and therefore might not be best suited in completely heterogeneously grouped classes was seen as heresy. Loveless noted that political and cultural pressure to reduce between-class grouping was remarkable, with major national organizations advocating the elimination of the practice, and several states pushing hard to get their schools to move away from it.[5] For example, the National Education Association to this day "supports the elimination of [between- or within-class] groupings. NEA believes that the use of discriminatory academic tracking based on economic status, ethnicity, race, or gender must be eliminated in all public school settings."[6]

The move away from ability grouping was rapid, with a steep decline in the amount of between-class grouping throughout the United States.[7] Interestingly, some of the literature from this period acknowledged that high-performing students tended to benefit from some forms of grouping, while other scholars either glossed over this fact or maintained that no students benefit.[8] For example, Wheelock, in an interview on her book *Crossing the Tracks*, was asked, "Does ability grouping—or tracking—enhance academic achievement?" to which she responded, "No, and research tells us that it is not a neutral or benign practice, either. Although it is widespread and widely accepted, ability grouping generally depresses student achievement and is harmful to kids."[9] We can't help but wonder if such an unequivocal statement is true of any educational intervention, let alone one with as complicated and nuanced research base as ability grouping.

However, the elimination of grouping may not have been as absolute as many of us believed. And it is certainly becoming more acceptable to broach the topic. In fact, while many people (such as the principal we quoted at the beginning of the chapter) seem to abhor any kind of grouping, data show its practice is on the rise. Perhaps this indicates that the term is the problem, not necessarily the practice—something we will discuss next.

Terminology Matters When It Comes to Grouping

One recent education policy trend that largely appears to ignore this history is think tank advocacy that speaks about the virtues of "tracking." To many people, the term tracking reflects the historical practice of putting students in mostly permanent tracks—in other words, ability groups they can't get out of. This practice tended to result in sharp distinctions between the haves and have-nots, between white and Asian American students on the one hand and students of other racial/ethnic backgrounds on the other. As Jonathan likes to tell teachers when speaking on this topic, there is a really easy mental device to use when trying to differentiate the two terms: tracking is evil, flexible grouping is good (we're not kidding about that).[10]

We used to feel, when advising people to stop advocating for tracking, that we were charging windmills. But over the past couple years, we have noticed a slowly building trend of thinkers and policy experts advising people to talk of *ability grouping* rather than *tracking*. We know that may come across as a semantic quibble, but it is a small yet important victory for educational excellence because there really are substantial differences. Whereas most anti-grouping advocates tend to see grouping as bad and only completely heterogeneous grouping and class assignment as good, we believe there is a vast continuum between the two wherein best practice lies.

Many of the arguments raised in objection to grouping are largely the-oretical or, more accurately, ideological and political.[11] The reader should note that there are theoretical, ideological, and political arguments in favor of grouping, too. This is not the place to get into a deep, philo-sophical argument about grouping, but much of the pro-grouping mes-sage is summed up in the oft-quoted line attributed to Thomas Jefferson, "There is nothing more unequal than the equal treatment of unequals." Putting aside the fact that Jefferson almost certainly never said that, the quote makes a good point: treating students who are achieving at differ-ent levels with very similar instructional strategies is a strange measure of equality.[12] And, from a practical perspective, many educators, fami-lies, policymakers—and yes, even students—are coming to an import-ant revelation. Differentiation in an age-based classroom is hard! It is difficult to learn, it is difficult to implement, and it is difficult to master.[13] Ability grouping, in principle, narrows the range of required differentia-tion, theoretically making it easier to provide appropriate levels of chal-lenge for each student. Nothing is guaranteed, of course, but if skillful and successfully implemented differentiation is expected of classroom teachers, then they need to be given classrooms of students where this is actually possible.

CURRENT PREVALENCE OF GROUPING

By far the most comprehensive review of the use of ability grouping in the United States was conducted by Tom Loveless in 2013.[14] Using NAEP data, he found that 28 percent of fourth-grade students received read-ing instruction via within-class grouping in 1998, with the percentage steadily increasing to 71 percent in 2009; in math, the percent was 48 percent in 1992, dipping into the mid-1990s then increasing to 61 per-cent in 2011. Even while many were stating their opposition to grouping, it was gaining popularity on the ground in schools.

The ability grouping figures were also interesting. In grade 8 math, the percentage of students receiving instruction in classes grouped by ability was 75 percent in 1990, dipped slightly in the mid-1990s to 71 percent, then slowly and steadily increased to 76 percent in 2011. Although data for other subjects is spotty in the NAEP database, it appears that ability grouping was less common in all other subjects in the early 1990s and has receded or plateaued since that time. Clearly there are a number of educators who believe in the actual practice of educating students based on what they already know, even if they are uncomfortable with any reference to the term "grouping."

These data suggest that the death of grouping has been greatly exaggerated, with considerable within-class grouping in reading and ability grouping in math, although other subjects appear to be grouped far less frequently. There seems to be something about math that makes homogenous classes more palatable than in other content areas.

RESEARCH ON GROUPING AS AN EXCELLENCE GAP INTERVENTION

There is little question that grouping by prior achievement is, on balance, an effective strategy for promoting educational excellence. The simple fact is that some students are so different in their learning needs that asking one teacher to hit on topics such as addition while simultaneously challenging students who need geometry is, in our view, unreasonable and likely to be ineffective.

The research reviewed in chapter 5 makes it clear that ability grouping benefits high achievers over a wide range of settings, content areas, and studies. Although racial/ethnic and socioeconomic variables were included in some of the studies referenced by Lou and colleagues and Steenbergen-Hu and colleagues, no research on grouping has looked at closing excellence gaps as a direct outcome.[15] That said, there are some important logical connections as well as some studies that looked at differential effects by language proficiency and starting proficiency in the academic area being studied (for example, reading). First, on the positive side, the data presented so far strongly suggest grouping benefits high achievers in the form of allowing increased growth and achievement. Second, and less encouraging, if students from low-income and racial/ethnic minority families are less likely to be identified as high-achieving, then it stands to reason that grouping could make achievement gaps worse—including excellence gaps. This could be part of why Plucker and colleagues found increasing excellence gaps at the same time as Loveless found resurgence in the use of grouped classes nationwide.[16] In essence, the intervention of grouping appears to work, but it is not being made available to advanced achievers from all racial, ethnic, and income groups. This alone could exacerbate excellence gaps.

In a substantial literature review that included a range of international studies and comparisons, Schofield, in support of several previous studies, showed that ability grouping tends to benefit the initially high achievers the most and as such exacerbates achievement gaps as those students grow faster than do their initially low-achieving peers.[17] This finding was further supported by research on the German secondary school system (which applies strict grouping methods) where students in the highest-achievement schools showed the greatest growth. Although Steenbergen-Hu and colleagues find the benefit of grouping on low- or average-achieving students to be mixed, they also find that students who are initially high-achieving nearly always benefit from grouping.[18] This is a good thing. Yes, gaps are widened when some students learn more and faster, but the solution to these gaps is not to eliminate all grouping in order to slow those students down. Rather, the focus should be on how to improve the educational experiences of the low- and average-achieving students so that they too can experience an appropriately challenging education and grow in their learning. This should not be seen as a zero-sum game.

In a study that seemed to turn conventional wisdom on its head, Robinson found that ELLs actually benefited more from grouping than did their white peers.[19] This came out to an effect size of .53 (half a standard deviation of additional growth) for limited-English-proficient Hispanic students who were grouped compared with similar students who were not thus grouped. These same students also grew more than white ability-grouped students (.12 effect size). The author made the specific point that ability grouping would helped close achievement gaps as limited-English-proficiency students grew at a faster rate than their white, English-proficient peers. By first grade, the achievement gap for non-grouped students had grown by 3.6 points, while for the ability-grouped students it had shrunk by 3.9 points. Unfortunately, as is true with students from many disadvantaged groups, most of these gains were lost over the summer months and the overall benefit faded by the end of first grade when grouping was not continued. However, those students who were grouped for both kindergarten and first grade saw even greater benefits than those described above. In the end, achievement gaps were reduced the most when students were grouped for both grade levels, suggesting that at least with regard to reading gaps for language proficiency groups, ability grouping does show promise in closing gaps and doing so in a way that still increases the learning of all students.

Ability grouping can be used when the focus is on developing the talents of underrepresented learners as well as closing excellence gaps. In a large urban school district in Florida, Card and Giuliano sought to determine which groups of students benefited from full-time ability grouped "gifted" classrooms.[20] They focused on advantaged students who were admitted based on high IQ scores (130+), disadvantaged students (ELL or low-income) who were admitted under a lower threshold IQ score (116+) or students who were not administered an IQ test but instead were identified based on having received the highest academic achievement scores in their school and grade. What the authors found was that of the three groups, the only one to benefit from the separate courses were those admitted on the basis of academic achievement (as opposed to intelligence). Further, high achievers from low-income or minority background benefited the most, with math and reading gains of .4 to .5 standard deviations. As with the Robinson study, this study supports applications of ability grouping both in terms of developing advanced abilities and in closing excellence gaps.

THE BIG TAKEAWAYS FOR ABILITY GROUPING

At the end of the day, we have to group students in some way—choosing "not to group" doesn't mean you are not grouping, just that you have somewhat arbitrarily chosen to use age-based/heterogeneous grouping. This may be done for ideological reasons, or because the research isn't convincing enough for you, or maybe because it simply feels safer. Indeed, one of the benefits of grouping solely based on age is that it takes the drastic differences and inequalities that exist across and within schools and grade levels and removes them from sight as everyone learns the same things regardless of prior knowledge. This choice feels safe, blocks an uncomfortable reality from view, and is now the perceived cultural norm. But cultural norms can and do change.

Critics of grouping generally lump between-class grouping and within-class grouping together. In other words, when grouping is frowned upon, teachers can't even put their highest-achieving students together within their own classroom for certain activities. This feels extreme to us, and it has the flavor of social engineering. Technically, it probably reduces excellence gaps, but only by bringing the top down. That is a poor solution to our excellence gap problems. Closing gaps is a moral action only if in doing so we build up and support the students who are behind; not if we slow down those who are ahead. Bringing the top down may help shrink excellence gaps but is morally repugnant and ultimately self-defeating.

Part of the resurgence of grouping may be that heterogeneous grouping (or what many call "not grouping") was less of a concern in the NCLB era because, as noted in chapter 1, growth for all students was not a priority in federal and state education policy. Now that growth is being considered in addition to measures of minimum proficiency as mechanisms behind education accountability systems, the performance of all students matters; including that of both students well below proficiency and well above proficiency. A teacher who has many advanced students in her class might get lots of points or credit on the achievement category, but will be hard-pressed to earn many growth points as many of these students have already topped out the test.

What's even more challenging about a heterogeneously grouped class is the wide diversity of learning needs. A fifth-grade teacher is likely to have students who are basic readers as well as those who are ready for high school math. This is an incredibly challenging task for any teacher, let alone one facing all of the other challenges of contemporary K–12 education. Some level of thoughtful grouping is necessary if a given teacher is expected to show growth with a class of twenty-five students with diverse learning needs.

What concerns us even more with the anti-grouping policies is that they are likely to force families who have the means to open enroll into more accommodating districts or leave the public educational system altogether in order to find a better fit. In an age where school choices (whether public or private) abound, parents who feel their students are not being challenged often have a lot of flexibility with alternatives. Not only is this bad because it further segregates student populations, but it also exacerbates excellence gaps. Those parents who must rely on services provided through public education are likely to be left wanting when it comes to advanced options, whereas parents who have the money and the savvy to search out other options are likely to see their students continue to grow. As we have noted, this unequal access to talent development is a major cause of excellence gaps.

In no way are we saying that parents who do seek advanced options for their children are in the wrong. Parents can and should do whatever they think is in the best interest of their children. But we can hold that belief and still lament that the lack of grouping and other appropriate interventions in many public school classrooms denies opportunities to students whose families are not able to go above and beyond.

Will ability grouping help advanced students grow academically? The research suggests that it will, and the available participation data suggest that, at least in math, most educators implicitly agree. But, oddly, they do not appear to feel that grouping is beneficial in other subject areas. This phenomenon brings us back to the opening anecdote in this chapter: It may not be acceptable to say you are grouping, but most students are grouped in math. Yet that "stealth" grouping doesn't carry over to other content areas, and implementing between-class grouping may help promote student achievement in those other areas.

All of that said, what happens in groups is more important than the grouping itself as a structural or organizational change. If high-quality instruction and ample resources for learning are provided to students in all levels, then there is little reason to suspect that the grouping wouldn't work for all students. But if the neediest students are provided with the newest, least-experienced teachers, then the familiar, past patterns of racial and socioeconomic discrimination will rear their ugly heads and exacerbate excellence gaps.

9

Targeted Programs

MOST OF THE ATTENTION paid to students from underrepresented populations in advanced academic programs has focused on their identification or broader concepts such as culturally responsive pedagogy. Such foci have intuitive appeal—compared with changing entire educational systems, mitigating the inequality that exists in the United States, or offering specialized programs such as Head Start to every child who might need greater educational support, they are intuitive, logistically straightforward, and involve fewer disruptions to the existing educational paradigm. If, for instance, your talent development program has far too few black, economically vulnerable boys, then it makes sense to ask if there are better ways to identify academic talent among those specific students.

What has received far less attention is the conception of targeted, culture-specific talent development. What we mean by *culture-specific* talent development are programs or policies that proactively seek to develop the skills and abilities of a particular student subgroup, typically one that has been underserved or has average lower levels of academic achievement. At first, this idea might seem a little strange. Why would gifted education or any advanced educational program look for students who, by their very nature of not meeting traditional criteria, will not benefit from the advanced services a school seeks to provide? The answer is both moral and practical. From the moral or social justice perspective, most organizations and institutions have goals to develop the skills and abilities of *all* students—not just those whose skills are, on average, the highest. Within the field of K–12 gifted education, there is also a concern that if certain populations are not included in gifted education programs, then those very programs could exacerbate (and probably *are* exacerbating) excellence gaps.

Second, many of the populations of students who would be targeted by such programs—black, Native American, Hispanic, and low-income students—represent the fastest-growing student populations in the country (for example, the number of public K–12 students qualifying for free or reduced-price lunch has increased by 1.25–1.5 percent annually for several years and now stands at over 51 percent). If educational systems cannot figure out the best way to develop the skills and talents of students in these populations, then huge amounts of personal and societal potential will be lost. Part of culturally responsive teaching is the idea that all students are valued for their strengths and, in our minds, this should include the proactive development of their talents, regardless of how those talents compare to students' peers.

Fortunately, we were able to find a number of programs that provide support to specific groups of students, and we found them at both the K–12 and higher education levels. In this chapter, we describe some typical programs and explore the extent to which they shrink excellence gaps.

CULTURE-SPECIFIC TALENT DEVELOPMENT: K–12

Culture-specific programs for advanced learners exist in the K–12 realm, though there seem to be far fewer and they receive far less attention than programs targeted at remediation or the reduction of minimum-proficiency gaps.[1] But we did find some promising programs, and we provide some examples below. Such programs are especially important if the goal is the reduction of excellence gaps.

Front-Loading —

More a strategy than a program, within gifted education front-loading means preparing students for advanced programs before they even have the chance to be identified or enroll.[2] Such programs are almost like advanced education boot camps. They take students who are not on the typical trajectory to need, benefit from, or be identified for advanced programs and help them explicitly prepare. Front-loading efforts mitigate excellence gaps by potentially offsetting the negative effect of decreased educational opportunity and access on the need for or placement in advanced educational interventions.

A good example of front-loading is the College Board's SpringBoard program. Because of the ubiquity of AP courses, they are often a focus of efforts to reduce disproportionality and, therefore, excellence gaps. Black students in particular are still highly underrepresented among AP examinees as well as among the population of students who score at least a three 3 on their AP exams. In 2013, black students represented 14.5 percent of the class cohort population but only 9.2 percent of the AP examinee population and 4.6 percent of the population that scored at least a 3. On a more positive note, Hispanic students exam taking and performance are approaching the percentage of those students in the total K–12 student population.[3]

Partially in response to lower rates of AP course participation by some student groups, the College Board developed the SpringBoard program to front-load rigorous curriculum in the middle grades to better prepare students for high school AP courses. In research conducted by the College Board on 106 schools that had purchased and used the SpringBoard curriculum in the previous four years, the results were compelling.[4] Black students saw a 109 percent increase in AP exam participation between 2004 and 2008, compared with a 37 percent increase in non-SpringBoard schools. The success rate (score of 3 or higher) on the AP exam was only slightly better for SpringBoard students—34 percent increase versus a 27 percent increase for non-SpringBoard schools. What's especially salient for excellence gaps is that black students saw the greatest gains in exam participation for any group, which would contribute to decreased excellence gaps in exam participation. However, gaps regarding AP exam success would show less change as black students' growth was in the middle of the pack compared to other racial/ethnic groups. Overall districts that used SpringBoard for at least three years saw 50 percent greater growth in the number of students scoring at least a 3 on an AP test, as did districts that only implemented for one or two years, suggesting that student performance benefits increased as the program became established in a school.

A second evaluation of the SpringBoard curriculum provided evidence that exposure to its English language arts curriculum resulted in statistically significant increased growth for students at all quartiles. Exposure to the SpringBoard curriculum accounted for 2.5 months to a full year of additional growth in student learning. The report also noted that this is the yearly growth estimate and that further participation would be additive. The results for math were more modest but still statistically and practically significant, suggesting additional growth ranging from .4 to 4.5 months for each year of exposure.[5]

Although much of the research on SpringBoard showed gains across the proficiency and racial/ethnic spectrum, it's important to note that including such a program in the first place would likely decrease excellence gaps. That's because the advantage held by some students of having greater educational opportunity would be lessened as the public educational system attempted to match that advantage with SpringBoard; instead of some students receiving informal "pre-AP" curriculum outside of school, it would be provided as standard to everyone as part of a public education. The initial research and evaluation studies of SpringBoard appear to back that up, at least partially. Gaps in AP test participation are closing, but gaps in test performance are narrowing at much slower rates.

Culture-Specific Programs

Project EXCITE. Project EXCITE began, like so many culture-specific initiatives, with an observation of significant underrepresentation of students from certain populations in the Evanston (Illinois) School District's gifted program. The district served approximately seventy-five hundred students, with roughly equal proportions coming from white and black families, but the program had an more specific goal than many gifted programs in that is was targeted at getting minority students ready to benefit from advanced math and science courses in high school.[6] Students were identified for Project EXCITE early—in third grade—to make sure any potential talent wasn't lost as students progressed through school.

In this particular program, front-loading took the form of parental education and support, peer support, academic enrichment, and additional student support as needed. The parental support component was focused on engaging parents and families as partners. Speakers were brought in to help parents learn how to create an encouraging home environment for their children and how to work with the school to help their children achieve at high levels. Families also received a home computer in order to support home-based learning and engagement. For peer support, high school students served as tutors and mentors. The EXCITE students themselves were also cluster grouped in their regular school day to form a community focused on advanced achievement. By the time these students entered high school, they had been learning together for up to six years.

Enrichment programs also took place after school and during the summer. The summer enrichment programs were especially helpful as they allowed the EXCITE students from the different elementary buildings to build friendships so that they would know each other when they moved to middle and high school. In a way, all of these supports and additional interventions were designed to prevent students who showed potential from falling out of the ranks of high achievers.

The outcomes of the program can only be described as impressive. For example, in four of the middle schools, 50–80 percent of the minority students enrolled in algebra had participated in Project EXCITE. The district also saw a 300 percent increase in the number of minority students enrolling in pre-algebra in sixth grade. Even those who did not continue to succeed in the advanced tracks still far outperformed other minority students, with 88–100 percent of each cohort scoring at the proficient level in reading and math. Even if these students were not as advanced as some of their peers, this was still a substantial achievement and represented a decreased excellence gap.

Although the findings are impressive, Project EXCITE is not a panacea. Some students did not succeed, some had discipline problems, and some moved away and did not complete the program. That said, looking for a silver bullet for the problem of excellence gaps and underrepresentation is not the goal. Instead, the goal is to seek out programs or interventions that might help mitigate excellence gaps and better develop talent in those populations that tend to not have their talents developed. The higher rates of advanced achievement among Project Excite's black students should help close excellence gaps.

Mentoring Mathematical Minds. Taking a similar yet distinct approach, the Mentoring Mathematical Minds (M^3) curriculum was originally developed in response to America's lackluster performance in math on international assessments—particularly with regard to the proportion of students scoring at advanced levels.[7] Unlike Project EXCITE, this curriculum was not targeted originally for a specific racial, ethnic, or income group. However, it has since been applied for the purpose of developing math talents in mathematically promising English language learners (MPELLs) in a similar fashion.[8] In a project funded by the Jacob K. Javits Gifted and Talented Students Education grant program, the researchers implemented the M^3 curriculum with third-grade MPELLs in an after school environment.

The M^3 curriculum involves both enriched and accelerated math content in which students are encouraged to act like mathematicians. Each grade level (third, fourth, and fifth) includes four units covering numbers and operations, data analysis or probability, and algebra. On average, the content is accelerated by two grade levels with an emphasis on problem solving, real-world connections, and communication. There is also a significant focus on communicating results. Lessons are differentiated and include "hint" cards" and "think beyond" cards, which are extra support or challenge activities designed to differentiate the curriculum up or down for those students who need it.

In Cho, Yang, and Mandracchia's evaluation of the project, the authors focused on 171 MPELLs from six elementary schools who were randomly assigned to treatment or control conditions.[9] Nearly all participants qualified for free or reduced-price meals. Treatment classes met after school for roughly forty-five minutes three times per week. Students significantly increased their math test performance compared to the control group (effect size of .64). No significant differences were found in reading achievement, though the authors suggest this may have been due to ceiling effects.[10] The authors also noted math achievement gains varied across classrooms and that fidelity of implementation is a key factor of program success.

As with Project EXCITE, the M^3 curriculum could be used to close excellence gaps (when targeted at a particular underrepresented population) as well as close readiness gaps for advanced programs later in participants' K–12 career. Just as schools may implement specific programs to help close minimum proficiency gaps, they could also implement either program to help mitigate excellence gaps. A district with a persistently low percentage of low-income or ELL students enrolled in middle school honors or high school AP classes could implement curriculum such as M^3 at the elementary level in order to prepare students for these later options.

Nonverbal Honors Core—Paradise Valley Unified School District. English language learners are often a particular challenge in the field of gifted or advanced education because even though they often have advanced talents, their lack of English language proficiency may be a barrier to their benefiting from typical kinds of advanced programming options (such as AP) because those programs are typically taught in English. The Paradise Valley Unified School District (PVUSD) in Arizona served approximately thirty-two thousand students in the greater Phoenix area, including 30 percent Hispanic and 37 percent receiving free or reduced-price meals.[11] The district is known for its gifted program, which ranges from self-contained programs for profoundly gifted students to cluster grouping in every one of its thirty elementary school buildings. Such is its renown for advanced learning options that the district takes in a number of gifted students through open enrollment from other districts.

Because of its substantial ELL population, the district recognized that it needed to think differently about identification and programming. Worthy of special note is the nonverbal honors core program that is offered at the middle school with the highest ELL enrollment. After blanket testing all sixth-grade students from the school's feeder elementary buildings, those identified are placed in the nonverbal honors core for seventh and eight grades. Program teachers are certified in gifted education as well as bilingual or English as a second language. Thematic units, specialized field trips, and a variety of other hands-on experiences are used to prepare students to traditional advanced learning options once they get to high school. In one way, the program can be seen as designed (if not explicitly) to close excellence gaps as measured by student readiness for advanced program options once the students enter high school.

Location, Location, Location

In 2011, the US Department of Justice and US Department of Education co-published guidelines on how to "achieve diversity and reduce cultural isolation" in elementary and secondary schools.[12] Although not targeted at advanced learners specifically, several of these recommendations could mitigate excellence gaps. For example, one of the cases presented dealt with the strategic siting of programs within a district. As with the Paradise Valley nonverbal honors program, gifted programs could be sited within buildings with large populations of underrepresented learners so that greater attention could be paid to their particular needs while at the same time increasing the diversity of students served in identified gifted populations. A study by Briggs, Reis, and Sullivan referenced the Euclid Avenue Gifted/High Ability Magnet program outside of Los Angeles.[13] The school population was 98 percent Hispanic, and all were eligible for free or reduced-price meals. There was also a large bilingual student population with most students transitioning from classifications as Spanish speakers to English speakers by the end of the program in fifth grade.

One important component of the program is that it was dual language. Perhaps more importantly, the program was located in a school and neighborhood that was almost completely attended by Hispanic students. This way, any advanced learners from this area did not need to travel to a community where their cultural group was less represented in order to be appropriately served. As we've noted, this an important consideration, since although higher-income families may be willing and able to travel to a building where advanced services are available, other groups may be less able, may live farther away, or may feel less comfortable sending their children to a school where they will not look like most of the other students.

This program and the USDOJ guidelines point to the idea that districts should be proactive in where they place programs or services as a way of mitigating excellence gaps. For example, although a Title I school with a large population of low-income students might have few high-scoring students, a lack of access to advanced programs could exacerbate excellence gaps, as students who are even just above average could be underchallenged. One way to be proactive in addressing excellence gaps would be to devote additional resources or staffing to buildings where the students don't initially appear to require advanced services. This could also take the form of magnet schools, specialized programs that include culture-specific mentors in addition to the academic curricula, or even components that include families. Much of this parallels efforts focused on remediation and retention in schools but is instead focused on advanced achievement.

In our discussion in chapter 6 of identification-related interventions, we referenced the example of Broward County's efforts to address gifted education disproportionality, emphasizing the alternative identification system used to locate more ELL and low-income students. What's also important is that the district was proactive about addressing this problem. For example, it noticed that only 28 percent of its identified gifted students were black or Hispanic, compared with 60 percent of the total student population. It also noticed that thirteen schools had *no* identified gifted students, whereas those with the lowest numbers of low-income students had almost 10 percent of their students identified. If gifted education programs work to increase achievement among students who are already high-performing, than this differential access almost certainly enlarges excellence gaps.

Not only did the district modify its identification system in order to locate more talented students from low-income and ELL families, but gifted services were expanded and offered in more buildings. After the alternative identification system, which used universal screening, was implemented, every one of the 140 largest elementary schools had at least one third-grade student identified as gifted. In their study of the effects of this modification, Card and Giuliano noted that the newly identified students benefited more from participation in the district's gifted program than did the students who would have been identified under the original criteria. Given that the newly identified students were more likely to be economically vulnerable, ELL, and/or black or Hispanic, the Broward County efforts appear to be shrinking excellence gaps.[14]

CULTURE-SPECIFIC TALENT DEVELOPMENT: HIGHER EDUCATION

As we mentioned at the start of this chapter, interventions focused on eliminating excellence gaps are fairly new at the K–12 level. However, one place where they have received much more attention over the last thirty years is in colleges and universities (institutions of higher education, or IHEs). The following examples are instructive for the development of excellence and reducing excellence gaps.

Dartmouth Native American Initiative

A 2015 report from the Jack Kent Cooke Foundation found that because of complex application procedures and perceived high cost (before scholarships and aid), many students from low-income families never even apply to highly selective IHEs. The researchers noted that "there is significant evidence that most low-income students lack the information to navigate admissions practices effectively and that many top low-income students, because of 'sticker shock,' are deterred from even applying to highly selective schools."[15] In many cases, services or programs that fall under the label of "advanced" (for example, highly selective IHEs, gifted education, AP courses) tend to be undersubscribed by certain students even when all of the data suggest those students would be successful in the particular program. As recently as the fall of 2015, the federal government has tried to mitigate one of these barriers—the financial aid application process—by simplifying the Federal Application for Federal Student Aid (FAFSA). One study found that a simplified FAFSA process, along with some support in completing the application, increased the college matriculation rate of low-income students by eight percentage points.[16]

Although supports such as streamlined aid applications or simplified admissions applications can help address enrollment gaps, certain students remain underrepresented in IHEs even when some of those IHEs have an explicit mission to enroll and educate specific student populations. One such IHE that was referenced in the Jack Kent Cooke Report was Dartmouth College in New Hampshire.

Since its founding, Dartmouth College has had as one of its missions the education and instruction of Native American youth. In the 1970s, under the direction of a new president, Dartmouth renewed this emphasis with the creation of several programs targeted at increasing the admission and graduation rates of Native American students. This process begins with the Native American Community Program for high school seniors. Seniors who are interested in the Native American Studies program or are interested in any program but want to understand the community that is in place for Native American students can apply for a specially structured campus visit. Students attend sessions with current Native American students, meet over meals in the Native American House community building, and receive targeted counseling on the admissions and financial aid process to mitigate barriers that might exist for students who are unfamiliar with the process. These efforts are aimed at eliminating the financial, logistical, and cultural barriers that might prevent students from applying or enrolling in the college. For Native American students, many of whom come from the opposite end of the country from Dartmouth, the geographic, cultural, and logistical challenges of applying can seem daunting. The takeaway here is that if universities wish to close gaps in application to, enrollment at, and graduation from an IHE, then these barriers need to be eliminated.

Providing financial support for students to visit campus and extra counseling on the admissions process is only part of the solution. As Garrod and Larimore note in their book about the Native American Program at Dartmouth, the university also had to confront its culture of using stereotypes in campus murals and traditions. Importantly, simply getting students to campus isn't enough.[17] As was pointed out in chapter 6, locating students is important, but additional programs and services are also needed to assure success. For the cohort of students beginning college in 2007, Native American students were second only to black students as the least likely of any group of college enrollees to graduate in six years, with a 23 percent graduation rate.[18] Attacking this more stubborn excellence gap requires an increased feeling of belonging and acceptance over which institutions often feel as if they have little control.

Call Me MISTER

The Eugene T. Moore School of Education at Clemson University, like many other IHEs and K–12 schools around the country, began to notice a shrinking pool of teacher education candidates who came from underserved, socioeconomically disadvantaged, and educationally at-risk communities. Started in 2000 at Clemson but now expanded to twenty other IHEs, the Call Me MISTER (Mentors Instructing Students Toward Effective Role Models) program (CMMP) was designed to increase the number of black males in the teaching force. What's particularly interesting is that the program, which is focused on mitigating a kind of excellence gap, was itself designed to address K–12 achievement gaps. The overarching idea is that increasing the supply of black male teachers who can serve as role models and mentors to K–12 students might spur larger numbers of black male K–12 students to perform at advanced levels.

CMMP itself is relatively simple. Once accepted to the IHE where the program is offered, an interested student completes a second application explaining why he wants to be a teacher and how the program will benefit him as a student. Other background and personal information is collected, and applicants are then interviewed. Students who are accepted into the program receive financial and academic support, mentoring, and targeted professional development—targeted in that the students must themselves be from an underserved or underrepresented population. Support includes seminars ranging from leadership skills to test-taking strategies. In exchange, participants undertake community service, mentor other students, recruit potential participants, and commit to teaching in an elementary school in their state for one year for each year they received the scholarship.

An article by the W. K. Kellogg Foundation noted that since its inception, the program has graduated 150 certified black male teachers, all of whom are still working in K–12 schools.[19] That level of retention is impressive, as the turnover among beginning teachers tends to be much higher. The same article noted 164 current program participants. In a way, this program represents a small case study in closing a very particular type of excellence gap—that of black males as certified teachers. Surprisingly, what it took to accomplish this small victory was nothing earth-shattering in its input or implications, though the outcome was impressive. Students were mentored to provide a feeling of belonging, they were proactively recruited, and they were supported academically when and if they needed help with certification exams. Yes, this meant additional resources in terms of money and time, but these expenditures resulted in small reductions in this particular excellence gap. More to the point, closing this gap should lead to greater success at closing excellence gaps for K–12 black students, especially males. A small investment at one level of education should prove to be effective in closing excellence gaps at both the higher education *and* K–12 levels.

IMPLICATIONS

We see a number of themes and commonalities across the types of programs discussed in this chapter. Front-loading is a strong piece of many of these initiatives, as is providing and encouraging access via strategic location of services and universal screening. And higher education clearly has a big role to play. From streamlining financial aid and admissions to providing support to complete those documents and processes, higher education personnel have implemented a range of reforms to promote access to higher education. We also found examples of programs that may be doubly effective, such as recruiting and graduating black and Hispanic teachers, which helps shrink excellence gaps, then the teachers help to shrink gaps in the K–12 populations they are teaching.

A major takeaway from the programs described in this chapter is that representation gaps and excellence gaps can be addressed if educational institutions see the closure of such gaps as a priority worthy of investment. Peters and Engerrand described the tension between equity and excellence that exists within advanced educational programs.[20] In one sense, these programs don't exist to address equity—they exist to challenge students who need more challenge. However, this singular focus has left most institutions with large and growing excellence gaps. If these institutions do indeed have goals related to greater equity in their programs and services, then specialized, group-specific interventions designed to mitigate these achievement gaps may be needed. American educational institutions seem to have implicit, and sometimes explicit, dual goals. They want to challenge all learners (achievement focus) but they also want to close gaps, especially between racial/ethnic groups. Too often, reaching the second goal is approached via sacrificing part of the first: if challenging all learners means increasing gaps, then the system will just focus on challenging some learners. There must be a way to have it both ways. Much of what we discussed in this chapter is how educational institutions can challenge advanced learners while simultaneously closing advanced performance gaps. We believe it is possible.

10

Personalization and Psychosocial Interventions

PERSONALIZED LEARNING and psychosocial interventions may come across as a strange combination for a single chapter, and in some ways they are. We could have just as easily titled this chapter, "Things that sound sexy but may not really work," but that would have been a little pessimistic. However, that is indeed what we're dealing with here: topics that have been written about extensively, with growing and intriguing research bases, but little research on how they impact excellence and excellence gaps. And there are reasons to believe these movements either do not hold much promise for promoting excellence and shrinking excellence gaps—or may even have the opposite effect. Despite the scant research base, the potential harm of these increasingly popular interventions leads us to review what we know about their potential role in closing excellence gaps. In theory or concept, they should work. But the honest truth is we just don't know yet.

PERSONALIZATION

When discussing excellence gaps, people often point to technology as the panacea for our educational and talent development ills. They note that rapidly advancing tech allows educators to personalize learning for each student, achieving the goal of individualization that educators, parents, and students have sought for decades. In an age when a huge portion of our waking hours is spent on technological devices that facilitate highly personalized experiences, the extension of this aspect of our lives to education seems not only obvious but inevitable. It makes perfect sense. Individualized education plans (IEPs) lead to response to intervention and an expansion of differentiated instruction for a larger number of students. This has now morphed into Multi-Tier Systems of Support (MTSS) and personalized learning—all aimed at better matching student needs with services. There's little here to find illogical or objectionable, and yet very little of it has been researched with regard to increasing achievement in general, let alone increasing rates of advanced achievement or closing excellence gaps.

The *potential* for such personalization to shrink excellence gaps is considerable. If a talented student is learning below his or her capabilities, then a truly personalized education system would determine the level of underachievement, identify and implement strategies to not only catch the student up but push the student beyond grade-level expectations, and provide the flexible pacing that could allow all of this to happen in a relatively short period of time. Although we suspect such systems would allow a jump in advanced achievement for all students—raising excellence rates but not shrinking excellence gaps—we still believe the possible effects of personalization are worth considering.

Such a focus fits well with recent theoretical developments exploring the interrelated nature of talent development and the student's environment. For example, Barab and Plucker argued that any activity that is considered "talent" is essentially transactional in nature: it is the product of an individual within a context that offers opportunities (including but not limited to tech access) for him or her to act in ways that can be appreciated as exceptional.[1] The authors believed that ability and talent "arise in the dynamic transaction among the individual, the physical environment, and the sociocultural context."[2] This conceptualization of situated talent points directly to the empowering role of technology to personalize a student's learning experience within a given social context.[3] If technology can expand the richness and capacity of a student's learning environment, then there should be potential for increasing the amount of talent.

Schools are increasingly technology-rich learning environments, so in theory they should be great places to individualize student learning to promote excellence and shrink excellence gaps. Increasing numbers of teachers and students have reliable, high-speed internet access; available laptops, tablets, and other smart devices and technology specialists who help integrate technology throughout the school and curriculum—not to mention a student population that is increasingly technology literate (but that literacy is unevenly spread among the haves and the have-nots[4]). Yet research suggests that the sharply increased access to technology has not led to greater tech integration in the classroom, especially in urban schools.[5] Even when integrated, the types of technology used tend to be narrow, focusing on test preparation and library research rather than tools that allow students to create and share content or develop twenty-first-century skills like collaboration and communication that increasingly lead to and characterize success in educational and workplace contexts.[6]

Benjamin Riley recently shared this observation about tech-focused approaches to personalization, which strikes us as pretty accurate: "Sprinkle the phrase 'personalized learning' into virtually any conversation or speech regarding education, and you'll see heads nodding in happy agreement. Although some might view this as evidence of merit, I suspect that the personalization concept has become an empty vessel into which one may pour any number of competing theories or policies."[7] Couple this amorphous personalization craze with a lack of research on the effectiveness of personalization strategies with advanced learners, especially research on how those myriad strategies can help shrink excellence gaps, and our enthusiasm for personalization as a possible solution for closing gaps becomes tepid. Indeed, the "promise" of personalization can make excellence gaps worse, as the use of technology to individualize education may be limited to certain groups of students.[8]

We do not find this to be terribly surprising. Previous efforts to personalize education, from differentiation to learning styles to RTI models, have all been promising but, in the end, are associated with little data regarding effectiveness to promote the learning of high-ability students or shrink excellence gaps.[9] These interventions *feel* brilliant, and anyone who has children or interacts with them in any way, shape, or form—ourselves included—intuitively understands the need to value and treat each child as an individual. But the research is not convincing that personalization strategies promote advanced achievement appreciably better than "non-personalized" efforts, and the strategies are associated with no evidence whatsoever regarding excellence gaps (although we acknowledge it is early yet for some of these interventions).

PSYCHOSOCIAL INTERVENTIONS

One of the hottest areas of intervention work across the social sciences—including but not limited to education—involves psychosocial interventions. Simply put, can human performance and behavior be improved with relatively straightforward strategies that address not the symptomatic behaviors but rather the individual's psychology? Psychologists have long known that motivation, attitude, and the social context of the learning environment are all strongly predictive of success.[10] Based on this, it seems reasonable to investigate excellence gap remediation interventions that are based not on cognitive tutoring or front-loading, but rather that focus on these psychosocial variables. For example, can excellence gaps in science be closed not by changing science instruction but by interventions affecting student identity and personality? In particular, interventions involving constructs such as grit, mind-set, and self-affirmations are currently receiving a lot of attention in education.

We find the concept of *stereotype threat* to be an especially promising area of inquiry. In essence, stereotype threat occurs when individuals within a group begin to believe stereotypes about its abilities and characteristics.[11] Such stereotypes may limit the academic success of, for instance, a poor Hispanic student if she internalizes any stereotypes about the ability of poor Hispanic females to perform at advanced levels of achievement. If this student doesn't see advanced achievement as something that Hispanic students "do" or "are," then closing excellence gaps will be nearly impossible.

This parallels work to help women overcome stereotype threat related to achievement in science and mathematics. For a quarter century or more, researchers have pointed to negative gender role stereotypes as a possible cause of female underachievement in STEM areas.[12] Interventions have been designed to address these issues, but these interventions took a big step forward when they focused tightly on stereotype threat as the causal mechanism.[13]

The potential role of grit, growth mind-sets, and positive self-beliefs and other constructs in mediating and shrinking excellence gaps is enticing, which is probably one reason why they continue to be discussed with such enthusiasm in the educational excellence research community.[14] And there is little debate that students who exhibit grit, growth mind-sets, and positive self-beliefs are more likely to perform at advanced levels than students who lack grit, have fixed mind-sets, and hold self-limiting beliefs; these constructs also differentiate between high-ability individuals and various levels of success.[15] The potential overlap of all of these psychosocial constructs is still subject to debate, but noncognitive factors clearly matter in the development of talent.[16]

But despite the potential of psychosocial interventions, these research areas do not yet provide very helpful information for shrinking excellence gaps. A great case in point is the research on self-affirmation interventions. These relatively brief interventions usually involve students reflecting on positive aspects of their lives and themselves, usually in writing, with the hope that these self-affirmations, by forcing students to present themselves with evidence of hardiness, resilience, and success, will help them move past stereotype threat and other psychological roadblocks to achievement.[17] It is also reasonable to expect these interventions to carry over to other students in a particular class. In other words, if the poor or minority students benefited from such an intervention, then the class environment would improve and all students would benefit from the spillover effects. If targeted at particular populations, then this intervention could help mitigate excellence gaps.

If this type of intervention were to work, it would essentially be the holy grail for excellence gaps: something easy and inexpensive to implement that benefits underperforming students but still has at least a limited benefit for everyone in the class. Furthermore, these effects may be recursive, in that students with increased performance as a result of these strategies will presumably have their greater performance rewarded in some way (e.g., placement in higher level courses), which should lead to additional positive feedback and attributions of success.[18] Psychosocial interventions would also help tackle the internal psychological processes that almost certainly play a role in the formation and staying power of excellence gaps. To be frank, as we have followed this research over the years, we have often been heard to utter the phrase, "This could be awesome."

Except it may not be awesome. In one of the better, more exhaustive research programs to date, researchers studied the effects of a brief self-affirmation in several cohorts of students in a diverse school, beginning in seventh grade.[19] In the original study and some follow-up research, they found convincing evidence that such interventions closed racial achievement gaps (as measured by student GPA), with African American students benefiting from the intervention much more than white students. The researchers also found evidence that starting the intervention earlier in the school year yielded significant benefits. But the academic benefits were largely experienced by low-performing and moderate-performing students, not high-performing students. This suggests that such an intervention could help close minimal-proficiency gaps, but not excellence gaps, at least not in such a form. That said, it does leave us wondering if there isn't some kind of self-affirming curriculum that could help low-income or minority students of potential to perform at advanced levels.

In another follow-up study, the researchers took this work further, investigating the extent to which the intervention influenced the achievement of students who did not receive it. They hypothesized that the greater the "treatment density" within each classroom, the greater the spillover effects for all students in the class.[20] And that is pretty much what they found, although treatment density for African American students appeared to be the primary driver of any positive effects. But again, low-performing students appeared to benefit significantly more than high-performing students. This research and related studies lead us to question whether brief psychosocial interventions are promising approaches to addressing excellence gaps, partly because stereotype threat may be less of an issue for high-potential students.[21]

But then here's where it gets tricky. A few studies suggest this type of interventions may indeed help shrink excellence gaps. For example, Walton and Cohen used a clever intervention designed to help college students deal with the often-difficult transition to college.[22] Students in the treatment group read a fictitious report about a survey of upper-class students at their university in which the students reported feelings of lack of belongingness early in college, but that those feelings dissipated as the students moved toward graduation. As the authors noted, "Concerns about belonging were thus represented as common at first, as temporary, and as due to the challenging nature of the college transition."[23] To drive these points home, students were then required to write essays about their similar experiences, which they then turned into a visual recording to be shown to future students. Walton and Cohen essentially turned any student perceptions of themselves as victims into perceptions of being successful role models for other students, and they did it in roughly an hour per student. In contrast to the K–12 research, the researchers found evidence that high-ability African American students appeared to benefit academically more than low-performing African American students and both high- and low-performing white students (substantially more, in fact). Clearly, there is some nugget of potential in this area.

Good, Aronson, and Harder found similar evidence that psychosocial interventions increase the performance of women in advanced math classes at the college level.[24] In a study of students in an advanced, fast-paced calculus course, students in the treatment group were told the test they were about to take had been extensively piloted with no evidence of any gender differences in the results. Not only did the women in the treatment group outperform the women presumably exposed to stereotype threat, they outscored men in both the treatment and control groups. This is an especially relevant study because (1) the researchers took a number of steps to replicate real-world conditions under which stereotype threat would be experienced (an important change from previous work in this area) and (2) these were high-ability students majoring in STEM disciplines, taking an advanced mathematics course. All of this work tells us that it is possible to positively influence students' self-perception in ways that can improve academic achievement. What's more, it appears that this work could be implemented at relatively low cost, given the potential outcomes.

CONCLUSION

In this chapter, we tackled interventions that we would classify as promising, but largely unproven, related to better aligning learning environments to each student. It just makes sense that highly personalized learning via all the great tech now available would help—but we're not sure. And it just makes sense that some of these psychosocial interventions would also help, and they are generally so inexpensive and quick! But the results are thin or mixed there, too.

In regard to personalization, with its heavy emphasis and reliance on technology, the exponential increase in tech availability within schools has not been met by a parallel increase in how teachers use technology to foster student learning, let alone foster excellence and shrink gaps. Improvements in how we prepare educators to use technology may help over the long term, but in general this area of activity is long on potential and short on evidence of effectiveness.[25]

Psychosocial factors such as stereotype threat, low conscientiousness (a term used by personality psychologists to refer to range of skills including but not limited to task commitment, time management, and problem solving), and fixed mind-sets create artificial ceilings on student achievement, and interventions designed to address these self-limiting beliefs appear to increase the academic success of low- and moderate-performing K–12 students. However, such interventions do not appear to shrink excellence gaps appreciably, at least in middle and high school. Research is more promising at the college level, but a great deal more is needed to determine the extent to which psychosocial interventions can be effective tools in our struggle to eliminate excellence gaps.

In an earlier paper, Scott and his coauthors adapted Freedman's comments on regression in an analysis of the identification of talent.[26] Adapting Freedman's categories of potential conclusions about an area of research, we offer the following four possibilities for psychosocial or personalization interventions with regard to excellence gaps:

1. These interventions usually work, although they are (like anything else) imperfect and may sometimes go wrong.
2. These interventions sometimes work in the hands of skillful practitioners, but aren't suitable for routine use in schools.
3. Psychosocial or personalized learning interventions might work, but they haven't yet.
4. Psychosocial or personalized learning interventions can't work.

At this point in the life and research base of psychosocial or personalized learning interventions, we are inclined to think the truth lies somewhere between items 2 and 3. The truth is, applying psychology and using psychological principles to influence a person's behavior is very difficult, even in a one-on-one environment, let alone in a classroom. Such methods could be used to shrink excellence gaps, but to do so would take more dosage and creative application of psychology and technology than has so far been implemented in schools. This does not mean this isn't an area that could be fruitful for future research, but we are hesitant to recommend these types of interventions to educators and policymakers seeking to address excellence gaps, although the research base is more convincing for college students than K–12 students.

11

College Attendance and Success

AS WE NOTED in chapter 9, in many ways, colleges and universities were the first institutions to notice, become concerned about, and attempt to do something to address excellence gaps. Three factors—differential rates of attendance at, performance in, and graduation from institutions of higher education—are as good a set of indicators of excellence gaps as are those based on academic achievement at the K–12 level. They are also an important measure of the long-term outcome of K–12 excellence gaps, as years of neglecting advanced learners at the pre-college level are likely to yield fewer students who are college-ready. What makes higher education gaps different is that IHEs have been working to close such gaps for more than forty years.

MEASURES AND METRICS

College Enrollment

It will come as no surprise that from 1967 to 2012, the overall enrollment in higher education by eighteen- to twenty-four-year-olds has increased substantially: from 26 percent to 41 percent.[1] The same federal statistics show an even greater increase for black students (13 percent to 36 percent) and Hispanic students (13 percent to 38 percent) compared with their white peers (27 percent to 42 percent), indicating some of the gap measured by college enrollment has narrowed (figure 11.1). These data

FIGURE 11.1   College enrollment by race/ethnicity, 1967–2012

Source: "Percentage of 18- to 24-Year-Olds Enrolled in Degree-Granting Institutions, by Level of Institution and Sex and Race/Ethnicity of Student: 1967 Through 2012," (Washington, DC: National Center for Education Statistics, n.d.), accessed November 15, 2015, http://nces.ed.gov/programs/digest/d13/tables/dt13_302.60.asp.

show that the IHE enrollment gap is about the smallest it has been since the 1960s, with Hispanic and black enrollment at all-time highs.

Unfortunately, the same trend has not been observed for students from high-, middle-, and low-income families, as illustrated by figure 11.2, which shows college enrollment data by family income from 1967 to 2013.

To be sure, some of the income-related gap has shrunk (see figure 11.2). However, part of this may be due to the fact that starting in the early 1990s, three-quarters of all high-income students were already attending college, suggesting they may have been hitting a natural enrollment ceiling. The gap between low- and middle-income families has shown some shrinkage but in general has hovered between 10 and

FIGURE 11.2   College enrollment by family income, 1975–2015

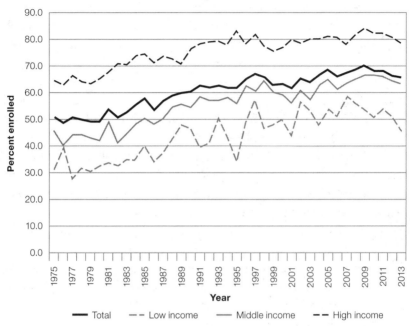

Source: "Percentage of Recent High School Completers Enrolled in 2-Year and 4-Year Colleges, by Income Level: 1975 Through 2013," National Center for Education Statistics, http://nces.ed .gov/programs/digest/d14/tables/dt14_302.30.asp.

20 percentage points since 1975, with the current gap at about 19 percentage points (46 percent versus 64 percent). The high-low gap has fluctuated between 25 and 35 percentage points, with the current gap at about 33 points (46 percent versus 79 percent). Although this could be seen as a negative (that large gaps in attendance still exist across income groups) it could also be seen as a positive (the gap has not grown despite increasing costs for higher education).

At the same time as college attendance has grown for all three income groups, the cost of higher education has grown much faster. An analysis by the College Board found that from 2003 to 2013, the consumer price index increase for higher education tuition increased more than 79 percent. This is nearly twice as much of an increase as the next most expensive component of the consumer price index—medical care. Translated into dollars, in 1975 the cost of a four-year degree was just over $10,000. In 2015–2016, that amount was more than $32,000, with most high-ranked universities costing well more than that for a single year of schooling.[2] Since the financial crisis in 2008–2009, attendance has decreased for every income group. Of course, measuring the cost of college against family income is a complicated comparison, given that the increase in both college cost and enrollment concurred with increases in financial aid and student loans making policy implications regarding the effect of income on attendance even less clear.

One factor that facilitated the increase in enrollment to tolerate and even flourish despite the increasing cost was the simultaneous increase in federal student aid. In the twenty-year period from 1994 to 2015, average per-student financial aid increased by roughly $6,000.[3] Although this came nowhere close to keeping up with the growth of out-of-pocket costs, this increase in aid availability certainly helped counteract the negative effect higher costs might have had on enrollment. As we've discussed throughout this book, financial resources heavily influence attainment of high levels of achievement. Although the data in figure 11.2 are far from causational, they do make clear that some greater degree of access to higher education comes with greater levels of financial resources. This could, and has at the federal level, point to one particular intervention when it comes to excellence gaps—decrease financial barriers to the programs and services that develop advanced potential.

College Performance

Part of the lower rate of college attendance of black and Hispanic students could be explained by the fact that, on average, these students have lower GPAs, just as these students receive lower scores on tests of educational achievement in K–12 education. However, Culpepper and Davenport noted that even after controlling for high school grades, Hispanic and black students still received lower first-semester college grades.[4] Clearly there are more factors than just differential levels in college readiness that predict these differences in performance. Some of these differences, such as differences in average family income or feelings of belonging on campus, could point to some of the potential interventions described in chapter 9, such as front-loading, or the psychosocial interventions described in chapter 11, as ways to mitigate these gaps.

Some scholars have suggest that proactive affirmative action policies may contribute to the relationship that exists whereby minority graduation rates have decreased despite an increase in enrollment (discussed below).[5] As will be addressed in more detail below, affirmative action policies explicitly modify the entrance or admission criteria for a particular group so that students from that group become increasingly represented on campus. These policies are proactive and inherently modify the level of academic readiness required for entrance (though possibly to a negligible degree). A side effect of such policies is that while they do increase the diversity of the students on campus, they also decrease the level of academic readiness on campus within the particular demographic groups they support, possibly leading to the lower rate of success than might otherwise be expected if only the members of those groups with sufficient levels of academic readiness were admitted. This argument suggests that part of the reason for fairly flat levels of academic performance of racial/ethnic minority students is that they are increasingly being admitted to a program (higher education) not because they are ready or have a need for it, but rather in order to reach the institution's goal of increased diversity. However, that goal of increased diversity (with a secondary goal of closing excellence gaps) can be realized only if the students admitted are then successful as measured by grades and graduation rates. Otherwise one excellence gap (enrollment; see figure 11.1) is closed while another is widened or remains stagnant (graduation; see figure 11.3).

Degree Attainment

Arguably, the most important outcome of higher education is degree attainment or graduation. Although performance in college is a complicated metric (since not all students enroll in degree programs at equal rates), graduation rates are a cleaner measure of gaps. Further, graduation rate tends to be a popular metric of college success, such as on the federal college scorecard.[6] A 2012 study by the National Center on Educational Statistics found that after accounting for various student, high school, family, and postsecondary institutional factors, black students still had 32 percent lower chance of receiving an associate's or bachelor's degree. Hispanic students had a 25 percent lower chance of attaining the same degrees.[7] In their reasons for leaving their postsecondary

FIGURE 11.3   Six-year graduation rates by race/ethnicity and cohort

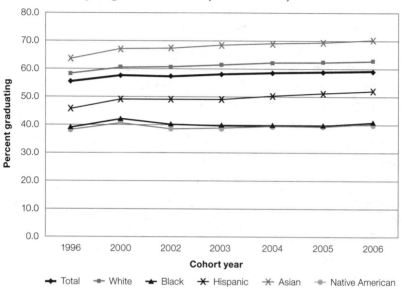

program before graduating, Hispanic students were more than twice as likely to report academic problems than their white peers (26 percent versus 11 percent) and even more likely than their black peers (10 percent reported that problem). Financial and personal reasons were the most common reason for leaving, but these reasons were reported at similar rates for all racial/ethnic groups (within 5–9 percentage points). As increasingly diverse students are entering IHEs, their lower graduation rates point to either a lack of readiness on their part, a lack of appropriate support on the part of the IHEs, or some combination of the two.

Figure 11.3 presents the six-year graduation rate by racial/ethnic group for students starting college in each of seven cohort years.[8] What is immediately clear when comparing figures 11.1 and 11.3 is that IHEs have been much more successful in enrolling students from underprivileged backgrounds (specifically racial/ethnic minority groups) than they have in successfully moving them through degree programs. Looking at figure 11.1, we can see that from 1996 onward (the dates corresponding to those in figure 11.3), Hispanic enrollment went from 20 percent in 1996 to 38 percent in 2012. For these same students (those in the 1996 and 2006 starting cohorts) we can see graduation rates of 46 percent and 52 percent, with the long-term graduation trend being fairly flat.

Part of this outcome is to be expected. Any new group of students entering a higher education program is likely to include some students who need additional remediation and support beyond what the IHE already has in place. A wider range of diversity within a college-attending population also means there is a wider diversity of readiness and need. Thus these flat graduation statistics could be seen as less of a negative, if not quite a positive; that is, despite an influx of new students from more diverse backgrounds, colleges and universities were actually able to increase six-year graduation rates, even if only by a few percentage points. Certainly, there is still much more to be done, but IHEs appear to have been able to at least maintain and slightly increase graduation rates despite enrolling an increasingly diverse student body.

There is another reason to focus on graduation rates with regard to excellence gaps. Unlike enrolling in an IHE, actually graduating from college requires a far wider range of academic and non-academic dispositions. For example, the grit, or persistence, required to complete a college application is relatively low (though it must be noted some would have been required to earn sufficient test scores and grades to be admitted). But actually attending and graduating from college requires a much higher level of conscientiousness and much higher levels of dedication and persistence. This is important for excellence gaps because even high-performing students can lack in these critical dispositional areas. Students must be challenged in order to develop these skills and as the K–12 educational system has focused less on advanced learners in favor of proficiency, advanced students have fewer pre-college opportunities to develop these skills.

As was discussed in chapter 6, the data from figure 11.3 could be seen as indicating a level of mismatch between what the entering students need and what is provided as part of the standard program. IHEs have been successful in applying nontraditional or alternative identification systems to locate larger numbers of students from disadvantaged backgrounds to enroll in higher education. The question then becomes what this larger and more diverse student body means for the programs themselves. How do they need to change or adapt in order to increase success rates and thereby close excellence gaps?

In the following section we detail some of these proactive efforts to address differential performance gaps on some of the variables discussed so far (rates of enrollment, performance metrics, and graduation rates) with a specific focus on what implications they might have for the goal of increasing the rate of high performance among students from disadvantaged groups.

ADDRESSING HIGHER EDUCATION EXCELLENCE GAPS

Affirmative Action

No topic in this book is more nuanced, complicated, or controversial than is the class of methods known as affirmative action, particularly when applied to assist racial/ethnic minorities access advanced educational opportunities. It is fortunate, if not also somewhat politicized, that the federal judiciary has devoted substantial attention to affirmative action programs in such a way as to give educational practitioners some clear guidance on what is and is not acceptable regarding preferential treatment of some students groups in admission. Although most of these cases deal with higher education, some have spilled over to K–12 education and even into K–12 gifted education. In the following sections we outline multiple examples (in chronological order) of when IHEs have attempted to use various types of affirmative action in order to close excellence gaps as measured by college enrollment. We emphasize legal issues in this section because whether or not a policy is seen as permissible depends on small details that are important to consider.

The University of California Medical School

One of the earliest examples of an IHE's affirmative action program was the process of admission to the University of California—Davis (UC Davis) medical school.[9] In a direct effort to increase the diversity of its student body and therefore increase the diversity of the physician work force in the United States, UC Davis instituted an explicit preference for racial minority students. This took the form of reserving a fixed number of spaces in each entering class for students from minority populations. As a result of this policy, Allen Bakke, a white student, was denied to UC Davis because there was insufficient space, even though his scores on the Medical College Admission Test placed him higher in readiness for medical school that several of the students who were admitted through the university's racial preference program. His suit eventually led to the Supreme Court case *Regents of the University of California v. Bakke*.

After lengthy legal proceedings, the Supreme Court issued a plurality ruling stating that while race-based affirmative action was permissible, certain practices of how the UC Davis policy was implemented were not. The most salient point for this discussion is that the justices were most concerned about the university's heavy-handed and explicit reservation of a fixed number of seats for certain student populations regardless of their academic readiness or the readiness of their non-minority peers. In their view, this amounted to a quota imposed solely for the purpose of racial balancing, and this was deemed unconstitutional (addressed in more detail below). The quota did, for obvious reasons, serve to diversify the enrolled student body of the program because seats were quite literally reserved to make it so. This is similar to the idea of group-specific norms discussed in chapter 6, but less subtly done with regard to a variable that is less correlated with opportunity to learn—race.

The directions and lessons learned from *Bakke* were clear and are still being applied. First, in attempting to reduce or eliminate excellence gaps as measured by enrollment, IHEs cannot eliminate these gaps simply for their own sake, nor can they eliminate them by explicit consideration of race absent a compelling government interest. However, as Justice William J. Brennan, in his separate opinion in *Bakke*, argued, race can be used to remedy past racial discrimination or injustice and that addressing this injustice represents a compelling government interest. However, as we will discuss next, the devil is in the details.

The University of Michigan Law School and Undergraduate Program

Roughly twenty years after *Bakke*, the University of Michigan Law School sought to apply the lessons learned from the *Bakke* decision to diversify its enrolled populations and the resulting college-educated workforce.[10] Having witnessed what happened in *Bakke*, the law school avoided setting aside a certain number of spaces and instead implemented a policy that considered a student's race, ethnicity, or other factors related to diversity as a subjective and unquantifiable "plus" when making admission decisions. The idea was that if two otherwise equally qualified students applied to the law school, the student who came from a diverse background would receive this subjective plus and thus be admitted over his or her peer.

In 1996, Barbara Grutter, a white student from Michigan, applied to the University of Michigan Law School. After being placed on the wait list, she was eventually denied acceptance. In 1997, she filed suit against the university and several individuals who represented it, claiming that she had been discriminated against on the basis of her race. Although the university did not hide the fact that race was included as a factor in its admission decisions, Grutter claimed that the school had no compelling interest to do so, thereby violating her Fourteenth Amendment rights as interpreted by the Supreme Court (primarily *Bakke*).

The key question throughout the initial district court and eventually Supreme Court considerations related to whether or not the law school's stated position that having a diverse student body (including a wide variety of diversity beyond simple racial diversity) fulfilled a compelling government interest by contributing to an increased educational experience. Although this was the position of the university, it had not set a number of diverse students to be admitted (no quota) nor was there a set number of points added for these students to their application simply for being from a diverse background. Instead, as noted, coming from an underrepresented group was seen as a kind of subjective "plus" to an application. Erica Munzel, the dean of admissions at the time, emphasized that this practice was necessary because a "critical mass" of minority students could not be reached if admission decisions were based solely on traditional criteria of GPAs and LSAT scores. She argued that the school's affirmative action program was necessary in order to achieve their goal of a reduced excellence gap in law school enrollment.

An expert witness for the university, educational researcher Stephen Raudenbush, analyzed the acceptance data from the year 2000. Raudenbush found that by taking race into account when making admission decisions, the university was able to boast a class made up of 35 percent minority students. He testified that had minority status not been considered, only 10 percent of those would have been admitted, shrinking the total minority student population to 4 percent (a much larger excellence gap). In this sense, the effect of relying solely on test scores (such as the MCAT in *Bakke* or the LSAT in *Grutter*) parallels what happens frequently in K–12 gifted education programs: Students are identified in a "color blind" fashion relying solely on a test, and drastic underrepresentation is the result.

The purpose of the university's affirmative action policy was to include students with a broader range of life experience who might be able to contribute a wider perspective to the profession than those students who were not minorities. The belief was that a population of legal program graduates who were all from similar backgrounds would be weaker than if their perspectives and previous life experiences were more diverse. and that the wider the perspectives brought to bear on any given problem or case, the better the outcome. A "critical mass" of such students was required so that the minority students did not feel isolated and because a certain size population was required in order for the benefits to be realized. The policy also had the effect of significantly decreasing enrollment excellence gaps.

In the end, the district court ruled that the law school's practice was unlawful, primarily because the inclusion of race as a factor in admission had not been carefully tailored and was too subjective. A court of appeals disagreed and reversed this decision, ruling that the use had in fact been sufficiently tailored. In 2003, the Supreme Court agreed with the appellate court by a 5-4 majority that the University of Michigan Law School did in fact have a compelling interest in attaining a diverse student body and therefore was justified in its practice of including minority factors (specifically race) in its admission policy. However, the majority opinion included an important caveat from *Bakke*: "The Law School's interest is not simply 'to assure within its student body some specified percentage of a particular group merely because of its race or ethnic origin.' That would amount to outright racial balancing, which is blatantly unconstitutional."[11]

The majority opinion, written by Justice Sandra Day O'Connor, further argued, "A race-conscious admissions program cannot use a quota system."[12] Instead, racial information can be used to weight a decision about an applicant without in any way insulating this applicant from comparison to others. Applicants must be evaluated as individuals in such a way that avoids making race or ethnicity the defining feature in the decision to admit them. In other words, reducing excellence gaps can involve the direct consideration of a student's race or ethnicity if that consideration is not the defining criterion for admission and if reducing such a gap can be justified as a compelling government interest.

It is important to note that this case differed in an important way from *Gratz v. Bollinger*, a related case considered by the Supreme Court, in which a white student was denied undergraduate acceptance to the University of Michigan. In a 6-3 decision, the court found that the undergraduate program, which awarded a fixed number of points to an applicant if he or she was from a minority population, was, in fact, unconstitutional. This practice violated the requirement discussed in the *Grutter* decision in which the court found that race may not insulate an applicant from being compared to other, potentially more qualified applicants. The court found that assigning fixed points served as this insulation. This system also essentially reserved a fixed number of spaces (quotas) in the university for ethnically diverse applicants, which stands in clear violation of law. Automatically assigning a fixed number of points or reserving set number of seats was also found to fail the test of narrow tailoring and created a situation in which race was the predominant factor in an individual's application.

In the end, the lesson from the two Michigan cases seems clear. If closing excellence gaps in student enrollment is a goal for an institution, it cannot do so in a way that directly reserves a set number of spaces or allocates an arbitrary number of points to students based directly on their race or ethnicity. Instead, student diversity must be considered much more broadly and among a wide range of factors.

Percentage Plans

In 1996, four white plaintiffs filed suit against the University of Texas at Austin's law school over its practice of admitting Hispanic and black students who received lower Law School Admission Test scores.[13] After much shorter proceedings than were seen in *Grutter* or *Bakke*, the Fifth Circuit Court of Appeals found in favor of the petitioners and ruled UT's practice of affirmative action unconstitutional. Up until this lawsuit, the University of Texas at Austin had relied on an affirmative action program to increase diversity whereby racial or ethnic minority students were given a subjective preference (other factors being more or less equal) in admission. With this program no longer allowed, the Texas state legislature developed an alternative method to achieve the same goal of increased diversity (reduced excellence gap measured by enrollment) at its flagship campus. First passed in 1997 and implemented the following year, the new policy, termed the "Top 10 Percent Rule," automatically granted admission to UT-Austin to any high school student who graduated in the top 10 percent of his or her class. Under the new law, the percentage of the university's student body admitted rose from 41 percent in 1998 to 81 percent in 2008.

In an analysis of the effect of the Top 10 Percent Rule, Tienda, Alon, and Niu found no significant difference in the diversity of the enrolled populations admitted under the racial/ethnic affirmative action (1992–1996) and the Top 10 Percent policies (1998–2002), suggesting the policy was a success in terms of at least maintaining the levels of diversity present under affirmative action.[14] Because of the strong correlation between family income and racial/ethnic minority status, providing a preference to those students from low-income schools (which was the major effect of the program, since the students in the top 10 percent of the high- and middle-income schools were already likely to have been admitted) avoided the direct consideration of race while also maintaining a diverse population. Income was perceived as a less controversial measure of diversity than race or ethnicity.

Although the university was able to maintain its decreased enrollment excellence gap after the end of racial/ethnic affirmative action, the policy on its own might not have been likely to support the larger goal—decreasing excellence gaps as measured by educational attainment or graduation rates. In effect, the university was able to close the gap in attendance, but if the same thing happened at UT-Austin as happened nationwide as described in figures 11.1 and 11.3 above, then more students would have been enrolled only to not be as successful as their peers. Luckily, this is not what happened. A report from UT-Austin found that even as the percentage of the students admitted under the Top 10 Percent Rule increased (and therefore diversity of need increased), so did freshmen retention rate (87.7 percent to 91.9 percent), four-year graduation rate (30.2 percent to 51 percent), and six-year graduation rate

(64.6 percent to 77.4 percent).[15] These students also had higher graduation rates than did their non-Top 10 Percent peers. The university was able to reach its goal of increased diversity without setting students up for failure. This outcome flies in the face of our concern, based on national enrollment and graduation data that increased enrollment is too rarely followed up with student success. With the Top 10 Percent Rule, UT-Austin seemed to accomplish both goals.

In a way, UT-Austin's effort mirror those described in chapter 6 regarding group-specific norms as an identification-focused intervention. Instead of making decisions based on standardized tests using national norms, UT-Austin began admitting students if they were the most talented in their local high schools. Because of the natural diversity that exists in high schools and the populations that they serve, this had the effect of maintaining the diversity that UT-Austin had previously achieved through direct (and controversial) affirmative action. As the level of racial/ethnic diversity increased in Texas high schools, more of these students began qualifying for admission under the new Top 10 Percent law, thereby maintaining diversity at UT-Austin without directly relying on race.

Texas was not the only state or university system to implement such a geographic or school-based percentage plan in order to increase student diversity. Florida implemented a similar procedure, called the Talented Twenty program, to guarantee admission to a Florida state university to any student who placed within the top 20 percent of his or her graduating high school class.[16] As with Texas, this was implemented after more traditional race-based affirmative action programs were struck down in 1999. Talented Twenty students are also given a preference when it comes to applying for state financial aid in an attempt to further remove barriers (and, in theory, close excellence gaps). However, as there is no single application nor single institution or office overseeing this program, much responsibility falls on the student for its success, including applying to multiple universities and being rejected under traditional criteria, working with a school's guidance counselor, and even returning to a campus that previously rejected him or her and asking for reconsideration under the Talented Twenty program. The student may still not be accepted to that campus as the program only guarantees admittance to a state university—not necessarily the one that is most convenient or best

suited for the student.[17] Unfortunately, the move away from more traditional affirmative action to the Talented Twenty program has not resulted
in the kind of increased diversity that was its goal. Instead, Marin and
Lee noted that the program admitted mostly students who would have
been admitted anyway.[18] This, coupled with decreasing rates of applications from black and Hispanic students to state universities, has resulted
in an overall decrease in the diversity of the enrolled student population. Whereas UT-Austin's program was designed and implemented by a
single campus, Florida's was controlled at the state level with much less
involvement by individual campus. This left individual Florida IHEs out
of the loop regarding which students would be attending, when, and
what support they would need to assure success.

The University of California system has a system similar to the Florida model. As of 2011 (though first implemented in 2000), students who
graduate within the top 9 percent of their class receive admission to
one of the system campuses.[19] As with Florida, this program was implemented in response to a legal restriction on traditional affirmative action
programs based on race[20]; but some version of this program has been
in place for decades, most often in addition to traditional affirmative
action. Although in the first few years after the restriction on affirmative action was implemented, enrollment of racial/ethnic minority students decreased, it has since risen for black and Hispanic students while
decreasing for white students.[21] Although these are positive trends from
the standpoint of excellence gaps, much of the decrease is likely attrib-
utable to larger demographic changes in addition to larger recruitment
efforts for disadvantaged students.

Unfortunately, the general sense is that such *percentage plans*, as the
Texas, Florida, and California efforts are often termed, is that they do
not serve to decrease enrollment gaps to the same degree as does race-
based affirmative action.[22] Simply maintaining an existing level of racial
or ethnic diversity within a program (such as in Texas) is not often a
stated goal. Rather, with regard to closing gaps, the goal is to increase
the enrollment of a certain group. Although demographic changes are,
in part, serving to close gaps, enrollment in higher education is still far
lower for racial/ethnic minority students than is their representation in
the larger US population.

LESSONS LEARNED FROM HIGHER EDUCATION

There are two clear lessons to be taken from our discussion of IHE efforts to address excellence gaps. First, such efforts need avoid the explicit use of student race or ethnicity as much as possible because it is very challenging to implement in a way that will not be subject to legal challenges. In the one case where it was deemed appropriate (*Grutter*), it was allowed only with a number of caveats—ones that were not satisfied when a similar effort was applied to K–12 schools.[23] Second, eliminating racial or ethnic excellence gaps in enrollment should not be the end goal. Rather, the goal should be increased learning, not simply proportionality. Of course, IHE performance and graduation gaps cannot be closed until the enrollment and attendance gap is closed. But if students are enrolled in order to decrease excellence gaps but then not provided with sufficient support and end up not being successful, then the increase in enrollment was an empty gesture.

In a direct effort to help K–12 schools and IHEs apply the lessons learned from the various cases described above, the US Departments of Justice and Education issued two memoranda. The first provided guidance on how IHEs might increase the diversity on their campuses; the second related to efforts to increase diversity in K–12 schools.[24] In both cases, the federal government emphasized the use of family income, geographic residence, neighborhood, or other race-neutral factors as factors to take into consideration when an institution tries to increase diversity in its programs. Based on this and the more nuanced discussion of the legal cases and enrollment data discussed above, it seems clear that when institutions are seeking to close enrollment excellence gaps, utilizing race-neutral measures of diversity is preferred (as in percentage plans such as the Top 10 Percent Rule) and can also result in the selection of those students who are most likely to benefit from the intervention to be provided.

It is unfortunate that the reason percentage plans can be effective is because schools in the United States are so segregated. As Sheryll Cashin put it, percentage plans such as those in Texas and Florida "rely on racial segregation to achieve diversity by ostensibly race-neutral means. They are a beginning, and rare among diversity policies in that they account, albeit indirectly and incompletely, for the fact of residential segregation and its attendant disadvantages."[25] Making local comparisons within a school district works to increase diversity because neighborhoods and schools tend to be more homogenous than society at large. In Texas, the simplicity of the program allowed it to be more successful than its California or Florida peers. In the latter two cases, states guaranteed admission to some state school, but not necessarily the flagship campus. They also included a range of other requirements that often raised barriers. Unfortunately, UT-Austin's success may also be its downfall as an ever larger percentage students are admitted through the Top 10 Percent Program and the campus still struggles to close admissions excellence gaps in the post affirmative action era.

The University of Texas at Austin is not unaware of the lingering excellence gap. In fact, the *Grutter* decision in 2003 led the university to augment the Top 10 Percent Rule with the reinstatement of affirmative action utilizing race or ethnicity as one factor in order to, once again, try and close enrollment excellence gaps. Specifically, the university included race, ethnicity, or family income as one of several factors in it holistic review process. Unfortunately, with such a small number of seats remaining after those who qualify for the plan are admitted, even an open door for racial/ethnic minority students via holistic review would not close the gap. What's worse, holistic review actually makes the enrollment excellence gap *worse* by admitting proportionally more white students than are in the larger population. As of 2008, approximately 81 percent of admitted students were Top 10 Percent students. Of the remaining 19 percent who were admitted through holistic review, the vast majority (approximately 13 percent) were white. At this point, the evidence seems to suggest that ignoring race or ethnicity will only get an institution so far when it comes to decreasing excellence gaps in higher education. If the second goal of decreasing excellence gaps while simultaneously challenging advanced learners and fostering excellence is to be achieved, more direct and explicit support may be needed both before and during the college years.

PART FOUR

Taking a Big Swing at It

12

A Plan for Addressing Excellence Gaps

CURRENTLY, TALENT development and educational excellence come with opportunity, psychological, and financial price tags. Because advanced education has generally been either an afterthought or a very low priority of K–12 public education, families that seek to challenge their academically talented students have to pursue options outside of the public system—private schools, afterschool and weekend programs, summer experiences, and more recently, internet-based options. If families are aware of the other resources (opportunity), believe their children are worthy of them (psychological), and can afford them (financial), then their children are in pretty good shape.

And there are other, hidden costs. But they are "hidden" only in the sense that the affordability of options for talent development is taken for granted by some families, but the accessibility of these options are either very limited for many students or students and their families are simply unaware of them. For example, if the single parent of a talented student does not own a car, taking the student on public transportation to a distant afterschool or weekend enrichment program may mean working fewer hours or simply missing an entire shift of work. Other families wouldn't think twice about jumping in the car on the weekend and driving a half hour to a cool afternoon program at the local science center. Or consider the role of unpaid internships for high school and college students—students in economically secure families can afford to take an unpaid (or poorly paid) internship, and they often have the professional connections to make such internships happen. But a poor, loan-strapped college student may not be able to learn about internship opportunities, and even if they do, the lost income from not having a summer job may be too high a cost to bear. And if we layer geographical concerns on top of all these other factors (How many good unpaid internships are located in low-income urban and rural communities?) something that seems like an afterthought to many families and students becomes a wedge that drives either end of the excellence gap further apart.

But as we have discussed throughout this book, the portion of the American population that can pay those price tags is slowly declining. Our back-of-the-envelope estimate is that these costs are now beyond the reach of at least 60 percent of the K–12 student population, based on the percent of economically vulnerable students and those in rural areas without access to plentiful talent development opportunities—a 60 percent that is not the same in terms of race or ethnicity as the other 40 percent. As a result, excellence gaps are at best stagnant, and by some measures they are growing. Given the importance of talent to the American economy and culture, shrinking excellence gaps and thereby raising overall levels of excellence needs to be a national priority.

REFRAMING THE DISCUSSION

Deliberations about whether and how to address excellence gaps occur within the current political and education policy context, which has both plusses and minuses. It's no secret that equity and inequality are major topics of discussion both in American education and society more broadly. This has led to a range of policy priorities and proposals both within public K–16 education and in public policy related to housing, taxation, and insurance, among others. As of mid-2015, the percentage of Americans believing that income and wealth should be more evenly distributed stood at 63 percent.[1] A search for "educational inequality" in Google returned more than 1.7 million responses. Within this context, as we have noted, despite the ubiquity of issues related to educational and opportunistic inequality, excellence gaps have grown dramatically. The data in figures 3.1 and 3.2 can only be described as shocking—3 percent of low-income fourth graders scored advanced in reading, compared with 15 percent of their higher-income peers; 21 percent of Asian fourth graders scored advanced in math, compared with 1.3 percent of their black peers. Yet what may be even more shocking than the size of these excellence gaps is the lack of attention they have received from equity-minded policy makers.

We don't believe most people would disagree that this is a problem. American education has no shortage of challenges. Where reasonable people seems to disagree is whether or not this issue of large and growing excellence gaps is a problem that warrants school, state, and national attention, or whether it is simply too low of a priority compared to minimal proficiency gaps, crumbling infrastructure, or higher education student debt. In chapter 1, we noted that public policy toward advanced education and excellence gaps has changed in recent years. The Every Student Succeeds Act now includes some provisions meant to counter decades of neglect regarding advanced education, including explicit language allowing Title I funds to be used to promote advanced learning, the Title II requirement of professional development including material on advanced learners, and the reporting requirements with respect to advanced performer assessment data. Several states have begun to consider how they might tackle excellence gaps, and researchers now widely acknowledge the problems caused by disparate levels of advanced achievement in different groups of students.

The point of this book is to explore ways to tackle these gaps, and we have generally found lots of possibilities and promising avenues but few empirically supported interventions. In other words, we see plentiful room for optimism but not quite the level of supporting research that we had hoped for.

In the balance of this chapter, we highlight areas where attention to advanced education—and the racial, ethnic, and income inequality that often comes with it—appear to be on the verge of some positive change. We then conclude the book with several recommendations that we believe could have a positive effect on the number of advanced achievers who come from low-income or racial/ethnic minority families. If educators, policymakers, families, and communities want to take a big swing at excellence gaps, here are our best suggestions.

RECENT INITIATIVES

The following five areas are good omens for an increased focus on advanced education and eliminating excellence gaps: growth-focused accountability and educator evaluation; out-of-level testing; the Javits Act; Response to Intervention; and wider attention to these issues by national thought leaders. We approach them all individually from a glass-half-full perspective in order to suggest some places where recent efforts and reforms might result in positive change for advanced learners.

Growth-Focused Accountability and Educator Evaluation

The evaluation of teacher, principal, and school effectiveness received increased attention with the implementation of the Race to the Top competitions in 2009. Whereas under NCLB, most schools were evaluated based on the number of students who were at or above grade-level performance, Race to the Top encouraged states to adopt teacher evaluation systems that relied, in part, on the amount of growth students experienced each year. These variables were often called value added and referred to how much content mastery a given teacher contributed toward student test scores. In the Race to the Top proposals, teachers were expected to add at least a year of growth to all of the students in their classes.

Although certainly controversial and problematic to implement, as a policy, evaluating educators based on growth has one major benefit for advanced learners: it meant schools had to think about them. Whereas in the past, students who were already grade-level proficient could learn nothing and still contribute toward a positive evaluation for a school or teacher because they were already proficient, under growth-focused models of evaluation, all students need to show growth regardless of their starting level of proficiency. Imagine an average classroom with half of its students above and half below grade-level proficiency in math. Under the old system a teacher needed to worry only about getting half of these students to grade level (not that this was easy or that teachers purposively ignored the other students). Under the new, growth-focused system, teachers were expected to show growth in everyone. Although states are still struggling with how to implement such systems in a fair and valid way, they do carry great potential for focusing more attention on advanced learners, especially those in schools where large percent-ages of students are below grade level and advanced learners tend to receive little, if any. attention.

Going forward, it seems many states are pulling back on value-added evaluation systems or that they are realizing the statistical and assess-ment challenges they entail. In their place, states could simply add components to school report cards or data reporting systems such that schools are made aware of how advanced learners are doing. Report cards could be augmented to include data related to excellence gaps or the performance of those students who are already grade-level proficient. When "achievement" performance is boiled down to a single number on a school report card, it's not clear to policy makers or parents if all students came in proficient and thus not much had to change in order to receive a high score, nor is it clear if all students "achieved" at sim-ilar rates or similar rates of growth. Simple disaggregation could go a long way even if teacher, principal, and school evaluation systems don't include variables related to growth for all students.

Out-of-Level Testing

Another component coming directly from ESSA that shows potential for supporting advanced learners is that states may use computer adaptive tests as part of their mandated achievement testing. This class of assess-ments allow an individual student to complete items that are based on how she or he answered prior questions on the test, allowing for the abil-ity to test students below or above grade level as appropriate. In the past, under ESEA and NCLB, students had to be tested using grade-level con-tent in order to assess whether or not they were learning above or below grade level. This requirement led to the development and use of tests with extremely narrow ranges. The tests could tell if a student was below or above a certain cut score, but then became much less accurate for students who were farther from that cut score. For the most part, states were not allowed to use more accurate computer adaptive assessments for the purposes of accountability because they could result in students completing below or above grade-level items. In other words, the stu-dent who was ready for geometry and trigonometry was not allowed to be tested at that level because she was only in fifth grade and therefore had to be tested on multiplication and division. With ESSA, states are allowed (but not required) to assess students using adaptive tests, which would yield much more useful data on the current level of understanding as well as growth of advanced learners.

The major Common Core assessments are a good example of the limited progress educators have been able to make in this area.[2] Those assessments are indeed adaptive, but only about a grade level in each direction, and some states, such as Wisconsin, never even got around to utilizing the adaptive component before dropping the assessment altogether. That's not much in the way of adaptability, but the developers point to federal restrictions on grade-level testing. Whether NCLB and related regulations actually prevent a state from testing above grade level is a discussion for another day, and probably a pointless one. The reality is that the vast majority of educators and education officials across the country believe that testing out of grade level is prohibited, resulting in our current situation. The reason for the federal emphasis is clear and logical: under NCLB, elected officials didn't want a state to test fifth graders at a third-grade level, thereby producing more positive estimates of student learning than were actually occurring. But to translate that logic to the avoidance or outright prohibition on above-grade-level testing was silly. With the passage of ESSA, this has the potential to change (although given that the draft ESSA testing regulations do not mention above-grade-level testing, we are concerned that states will not emphasize this aspect of the tests).

The good news is that there are several other tests that have adaptive frameworks. In addition to the Common Core–aligned Smarter Balanced assessment, two of the most common are the Northwest Evaluation Association's Measure of Academic Progress (MAP) and Renaissance Learning's STAR assessments. In these tests, when students answer an item correctly, they are presented with a harder item. If they answer an item incorrectly, they are presented with an easier item. All of this yields an accurate understanding of what students actually know and can do. This data can allow teachers to place students in classes and employ interventions that are the most likely to yield growth and can also be used to evaluate progress. Although all new assessments have their challenges, there are few downsides to computer adaptive assessments, as they are almost always more accurate for all students but have even more significant implications for advanced learners. It's possible that as more states and district choose to use such tests, that they will become aware of just how high some of their students are performing. When parents, district personnel, and policy makers notice the diversity of need that exists in a given grade level of classroom, this could spur additional consideration for how and where these advanced learners are most likely to be challenged.

The Javits Gifted and Talented Students Education Program

Although the federal Javits grant program has existed for roughly twenty-five years, its inclusion in ESSA in 2015 codified it as a more permanent program than it was in the past, when it needed to be constantly reauthorized. ESSA also solidified the focus of the Javits program on building and enhancing the capacity of schools to support high-ability learners. What is even more relevant for excellence gaps is that ESSA put particular focus on low-income students, those who were limited English proficient, and those with disabilities. For fiscal year 2016, the Javits program received $12 million in funding to support schools in the identification of talented students from underrepresented populations and the design and implementation of programs to develop their abilities. This targeted emphasis on underrepresented learners means the Javits program in general can be seen as an excellence gap mitigation effort. In fiscal year 2015, more than one of the funded projects focused on closing excellence gaps as a goal.[3] Especially if used in tandem with some of the state and local policy efforts described at the end of this chapter, the Javits program could have a significant impact on mitigating excellence gaps. But if nothing else, it stands as the sole federal program that directly addresses efforts to reduce excellence gaps.

Response to Intervention

As of 2014–2015, nine states responding to a survey of gifted education practices reported that their state permitted local school districts to include gifted and talented students in their response to intervention (RTI) models or frameworks.[4] We see this as a positive for two main reasons. First, it's likely to bring additional attention to advanced learners in general. Whereas additional services are often provided for special education or remediation students, schools seeing advanced learners on parallel to those in need of remediation could result in more teachers tiring lessons, compacting curriculum, and otherwise proactively planning their curriculum for advanced learners. Secondly, including advanced learners in RTI models might also help educators move away from any lingering deficit models of thinking where they are only on the lookout for behavior problems or students in need of remediation. If advanced learners receive attention, educators may proactively look for signs of talent as well. As noted in chapter 10, we still want to see data on the effectiveness of RTI models with advanced students and regarding the closing of excellence gaps, but the inclusion of high-potential students in RTI models is a philosophical victory.

Wider Interest in Advanced Education

Finally, thought leaders in the education policy community, including think tanks such as the Thomas B. Fordham Institute and federal agencies such as the National Science Foundation, have recently begun to emphasize the need to focus on educational excellence and the elimination of excellence gaps.[5] Even groups that traditionally have not found these issues to be important have slowly come around.[6] Sure, it drives us crazy that some of these groups act like they are the first people to discover the topic, but at the end of the day, all that matters is that influential people and groups are coming around to the long-term harm done to the country when excellence and excellence gaps are ignored.

A PATH FORWARD FOR ADDRESSING EXCELLENCE GAPS

After reviewing the available research and model programs around the country, we strongly believe that the following approach, depicted visually in figure 12.1, reflects the current state of the art for addressing and eventually eliminating excellence gaps. These six sets of interventions, which cross levels of education and policy and are not meant to be exhaustive, are the best bet for shrinking excellence gaps while educators wait for comprehensive childhood poverty measures to be put in place. Note that we are not saying that we need either childhood poverty reduction or the following educational and policy interventions, but rather that we need both. Most educators can't tackle the poverty

FIGURE 12.1   A foundation for addressing excellence gaps

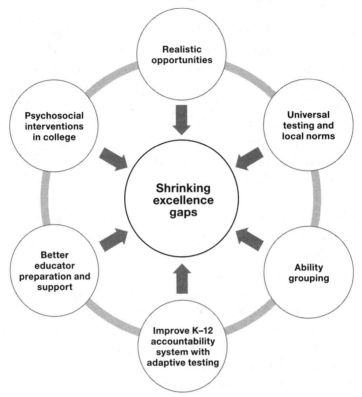

reduction part of the equation by themselves, but we believe they can affect the following issues directly in their own schools districts or indirectly by working with state-level policymakers.

We also believe that the foundation of all excellence gap interventions should be front loading. The research on front-loading provides ample evidence that taking talented students who are not on a trajectory to perform at advanced levels can benefit significantly from programs that help these students "catch up." Programs such as the College Board's SpringBoard and the Center for Talent Development's Project EXCITE are helping students become better prepared to take advantage of advanced learning opportunities, which will eventually lead to shrinking excellence gaps.

Realistic Opportunities

Opportunities Can Be Complicated. The three keys to opportunity for advanced learning are successful communication, belief and acceptance, and low barriers to access. If an opportunity for developing the talents of students exists, students and their caregivers need (1) to know the opportunity exists, (2) to believe they should be taking advantage of the opportunity, and (3) a realistic chance of accessing the opportunity. Each of these three criteria are necessary but not sufficient for an opportunity to move options for advanced learners from being a nice idea to a real benefit for a talented student.

Don't Be Afraid to Use Title I Funds for Advanced Learners. ESSA also opened up Title I funds as being eligible for use for the identification and education of advanced learners. A state could bring together a virtual library of interventions that a district could use to target a specific subgroup of advanced learners. For example, it could use part of the load of one of its Title I staff to focus on supporting teachers in how to tier lessons to a higher level for advanced learners or how to modify advanced options to appeal more to underrepresented populations. Without proactive support of this new flexibility in Title I, districts are likely to continue to use the funds solely for struggling learners. If, instead, a state takes on the issue of encouraging districts to include attention to advanced learners and providing ideas and suggestions for what that might look like, these efforts could be used to address excellence gaps. State education agencies can also modify their application processes for Title I funds in order to make it clear that such funds can be used for advanced learners, especially those from underrepresented populations.

Universal Testing and Local Norms

One of the clearest takeaways from chapter 6 is that non-universal screening for talent will leave many students out, and those students will be disproportionately from underrepresented populations. A clear implication is that whenever possible, assessments or systems used to identify talent should be administered universally to all students under consideration. This could take the form of testing or observing all second-grade students instead of only those who received a teacher recommendation.

This will involve some increased time and money, but it will also mean the best chance for students from low-income or minority families to be identified. This is one of the clearest action steps that gifted or advanced programs should take. If addressing underrepresentation is truly a goal, then moving toward universal assessment is a must.

A benefit to universal screening is that it would make the application of local norms very easy, since data would be available on all students. Implementing local norms would increase the number of identified advanced learners in the schools with the largest numbers of low-income and minority students. Of course, simply identifying them isn't likely to have much of an effect on their learning, but if they are identified and then provided with additional support, local norms could have an effect on excellence gaps.

Proactive Identification and Support. If districts want to close excellence gaps, other measures must be taken. District staff will need to proactively seek out students of potential who also come from low-income or racial/ethnic minority families. Additional efforts such as group-specific comparisons and allowing teachers to recommend students into certain programs even if their test scores aren't particularly high. And such proactive identification can't be implemented in isolation. Students who are identified via alternative criteria need to be provided additional support in order to be successful. Mentoring, tutoring by older peers from similar communities, or additional support from school staff all need to be considered. The standard rule is that for any modified or proactive identification system to be successful, curriculum supports need to be modified or expanded as well.

Ability Grouping

Although often unpopular because of its association with tracking, ability grouping has been shown to increase the number of underrepresented students identified as high-achieving over time.[7] What can be said for sure is that grouping is a very general term that can be used to refer to a range of options. What can also be said is that some applications of grouping have been shown to be very effective at both increasing student achievement and increasing the number of students from minority populations identified as high achieving over time. We see great promise in trying to narrow the range of achievement that any single teacher is expected to instruct in a general classroom setting. We also believe there are ways to do this that are flexible and do not set up students for low expectations. All of that said, any district looking to implement grouping should do so with care and with an eye toward what effects such a practice will have on excellence gaps.

K–12 Accountability Systems

Most states will be rethinking their K–12 school accountability systems over the next one to two years. They generally tinker with their systems routinely, but ESSA has important implications for those systems that will encourage and allow for major retooling. Accountability systems have a demonstrable effect on education policy and student outcomes, yet few states have much in the way of excellence indicators in their systems' data points.[8] Adding such indicators would send an important message that advanced learning and growth is important and obtainable for all K–12 public school students.

Some states, such as Wisconsin, now include points derived from schools' ability to close gaps on their school report cards. Unfortunately, in no cases that we know of can schools earn these points by closing excellence gaps. Instead, only minimal proficiency gaps allow schools to earn credit for their efforts toward equity. Changing state policies to allow for excellence gap closure to be included on school report cards would allow schools to devote resources (such as the Title I funds now allowed to be used for advanced learners thanks to ESSA) to receive credit for their work toward achieving greater equity in this area. As we mentioned in the preface, it isn't clear to us why any one "gap" closure would be preferred over another. If a local school community sees talents in their low-income, black, Native American, or Hispanic students going underdeveloped, it should not be penalized for devoting money and effort to this goal.

As an example, figure 12.2 presents part of a Wisconsin school district's report card. This is a district that was labeled as "significantly exceeding expectations"—the highest of five ratings of quality—in large part because of its high numbers of proficient and advanced learners. At the same time, notice that its growth and gap closure categories are

FIGURE 12.2   Example of Wisconsin district report card

Priority areas	District score	Max score	State score	Max score
Student achievement	**90.9/100**		**66.4/100**	
Reading achievement	42.5/50		29.8/50	
Mathematics achievement	48.4/50		36.7/50	
Student growth	**75.1/100**		**62.4/100**	
Reading growth	36.3/50		31.5/50	
Mathematics growth	38.8/50		30.9/50	
Closing gaps	**75.6/100**		**66.3/100**	
Reading achievement gaps	15.0/25		17.0/25	
Mathematics achievement gaps	17.6/25		16.3/25	
Graduation rate gaps	43.0/50		33.0/50	
On-track and postsecondary readiness	**92.8/100**		**85.3/100**	
Graduation rate	39.0/40		36.0/40	
Attendance rate	37.5/40		37.2/40	
3rd grade reading achievement	4.1/5		2.8/5	
8th grade mathematics achievement	4.7/5		3.5/5	
ACT participation and performance	7.5/10		5.8/10	

Source: Wisconsin school and district report cards are available at http://dpi.wi.gov/accountability/report-cards.

its lowest scores. Such systems are becoming the norm under twenty-first-century models of school, district, and teacher evaluation.

Of course, districts could create district-level or school-level goals for closing excellence gaps on their own. Many teachers now craft Student Learning Outcomes/Objectives (SLOs) as a form of goal setting and personal evaluation. District or building leadership could encourage or mandate that these goals include the closing of excellence gaps, the identification of larger numbers of advanced learners from underrepresented populations, or the growth of advanced learners beyond grade-level proficiency. In addition to crafting a plan for how a building will close minimal proficiency gaps, administration could also be required to include a plan for how they will close excellence gaps related to target populations.

Better Educator Preparation and Support

Mandate Greater Attention to Advanced Learners in State Teacher Preparation Programs. The federal Higher Education Opportunity Act (HEOA) was signed into law in the summer of 2008.[9] This law made three substantive changes regarding teacher training. First, it required teacher training programs to instruct their students in the identification of student learning needs that included the needs of advanced learners. Second, it required that teacher training programs instruct their students in how to differentiate instruction for advanced learners and otherwise meet their learning needs. And third, it required that the state report cards on the quality of teacher training programs include criteria on how the first two requirements were being addressed and evaluated. This would have meant that every teacher completing a training program over the last five to eight years would have received some training regarding how to challenge advanced learners. Unfortunately, we have little reason to think that states followed the intent of HEOA with regard to advanced learners. Most state reporting that we know of makes very little reference with regard to how teacher-training programs are evaluated to assure their candidates are being appropriately training with regard to the identification and instruction of advanced learners.

This state of affairs points to a relatively easy recommendation for states to implement: enforce the HEOA requirements related to advanced learners. Teacher training with regard to students who are already at proficiency is embarrassingly weak. Few states require specific coursework in teacher training programs, and only Kentucky requires such material be included in both teacher *and* administrator preparation programs.[10] And even so, as a group of administrators in Kentucky recently told one of us, "requiring" this content is very different from ensuring that all educators are exposed to this material.

If states want to address the low overall rates of advanced achievement or specifically excellence gaps, they should require teacher preparation programs within their state to follow the lead of the Javits Program at the federal level. This would involve requiring teacher training programs to include content on how to identify when students are being underchallenged, how to differentiate curriculum in order to better meet their needs, how to implement student acceleration processes, and how to support underrepresented learners in their work toward advanced achievement. In our experience in teacher education, advanced learners tend to receive one or two lessons of attention, *at most*, within a larger class about special education. With this as the state of affairs, it should be no surprise that teachers focus more of remediation than on developing excellence.

Be Proactive in Enforcing Title II Requirements. As was mentioned in chapter 1, ESSA requires that any state and district that accepts Title II money must report on how those funds were used to increase the capacity of teachers to reach all students. Importantly, the definition of "all students" specifically includes gifted and talented students. If states want to address excellence gaps, they could proactively enforce this requirement or even focus a state priority on the closure of excellence gaps through staff professional development. Unlike with HEOA, where the mandates were weakly enforced (at best), states could implement extensive oversight of Title II funds to make sure that they are being used to develop educator ability to reach all students. Many of the programs and examples included in part 3 could be implemented as part of Title II. For example, a district could train its teachers in the use of the Mentoring Mathematical Minds curriculum for high-potential English language learners.[11] Similarly, a district could seek to expand the pre-AP programs for low-income students to close excellence gaps and increase overall rates of achievement. A range of options is possible if a state takes on this issue as a priority with its Title II funds. Since most states are just beginning to determine how the ESSA rules and requirements will be implemented, this seems like the perfect time.

Provide Proactive Professional Development. Because K–12 educators learn almost nothing about advanced learners in teacher training programs, schools need to take on this task on their own. Now that Title II funds can be used for this purpose, even fewer barriers remain. We don't mean to suggest that schools begin putting their teaching staffs through license or master's degree programs in gifted education. Instead, they should seek out support or teacher training that will help general educators increase their capacity to challenge a wider range of students. Questions to be answered include: How do I differentiate for an elementary student who is reading at the high school level? What materials are best for a middle school student who is ready for trigonometry? How can we decide how and whether or not to accelerate a child to the next grade level without missing important content? What does supporting black students look like in advanced education? All of these questions and many more can be addressed via proactive attention to advanced learners within a single district. Districts tend to have extensive control over what in-services they put on and what conferences their staff attend and topics related to advanced learning should be in the rotation just like any other topic of need.

Psychosocial Interventions in College

Although we struck a cautionary note in our review of psychosocial interventions in chapter 10, and are generally pessimistic about their potential to shrink excellence gaps at the K–12 level, the research on the impact of stereotype threat interventions on college excellence gaps is convincing. These interventions are also cost-effective and rarely time-intensive, suggesting that they can be applied widely. Any comprehensive approach to addressing excellence gaps needs to consider the role of psychosocial interventions at the college level.

TAKING A BIG SWING AT IT

The National Academy of Engineering recently compiled a list of the "Grand Challenges for Engineering in the Twenty-first Century." Although the fourteen challenges have a strong science and engineering flavor, they cut across almost all aspects of human activity and well-being, from making cost-efficient solar energy and sequestering atmospheric carbon to providing access to clean water, improving infrastructure, and securing cyberspace.[12] The United Nations' 2030 Agenda for Sustainable Development contains similar items, in addition to goals to eliminate poverty and hunger, strengthen innovation, and create just and peaceful societies through rule of law, among many others.[13] Despite the diversity of these challenges, they have one clear, common thread: a great deal of talent will need to be brought to bear if we are to address any of them successfully.

One of the goals of this book is to encourage people to ask where this talent is going to come from. Within the United States, can we continue to produce a mediocre percentage of talented individuals and supplement our talent deficit by importing the best and brightest from other countries? As we argued in part 1, this is a shortsighted strategy for two reasons. First, our country's thirst for talent outstrips our ability to import our way out of the talent shortfall via immigration, especially given that the fastest-growing segments of our K–12 student population are generally the groups on the bottom of the excellence gap. Second, in solving the world's major problems, we need to increase our global pool of talent, not move a small group of talented individuals from country to country in a game of musical chairs.

Based on our analyses presented in parts 2 and 3, as well our recommendations in this chapter, we believe there is a path forward for increasing the number of talented students in the United States and, perhaps more importantly, shrinking excellence gaps and eliminating, once and for all, the country's talent underclass. In this concluding chapter, we have reviewed and summarized what we've learned and proposed a set of steps for state policy makers and school districts. Some of these recommendations, from our perspective, are low-hanging fruit; other items are somewhat idealistic. But all would help, and we strongly believe that all are attainable.

The recommendations in this chapter and indeed all of the analyses in part 2 and example programs in part 3 stem from a larger philosophy that must be adopted before these ideas can be considered valid or important: Every child deserves the opportunity to be challenged. Being challenged and learning new things in school should be seen as the overarching philosophy of K–12 education. The pressing challenges facing the world will not be solved by armies of minimally proficient students who were able to coast through formal education. Instead, every child deserves to learn something new every day, and the economic future of the United States depends on the embracing of this belief. Second, as schools move to implement needs-based, personalized learning for all students, additional consideration should be paid to excellence gaps.

Instead of eliminating or cutting back programs so some students don't learn too quickly, consideration of excellence gaps should take the form of providing additional supports and resources, such that lack of educational opportunity and access do not prevent low-income or racial/ethnic minority students from achieving at advanced levels.

NOTES

CHAPTER 1

1. Chester E. Finn and Brandon L. Wright, *Failing Our Brightest Kids: The Global Challenge of Educating High-Ability Students* (Cambridge, MA: Harvard Education Press, 2015), 69–76.

2. Paul E. Peterson, Saving Schools: From Horace Mann to Virtual Learning (Cambridge, MA: Harvard University Press, 2010); Diane Ravitch, The Death and Life of the American School System, (New York: Basic Books, 2011); Joel Spring, American Education, 17th ed. (New York: Routledge, 2015).

3. Richard B. Russell National School Lunch Act, 79 PL 396, 60 Stat. 230 (1946); "History of Head Start," US Department of Health and Human Services, 2015, www.acf.hhs.gov/programs/ohs/about/history-of-head-start; "Title I—Improving the Academic Achievement of the Disadvantaged," US Department of Education, 2004, www2.ed.gov/policy/elsec/leg/esea02/pg1.html.

4. Civil Rights Act of 1964, PL 88–352, 78 Stat. 241.

5. Ibid., p. 7

6. James S. Coleman et al., *Equality of Educational Opportunity,* (Washington, DC: National Center for Educational Statistics, 1966).

7. Elementary and Secondary Education Act of 1965, PL 89-10 (1965), p. 14.

8. Ibid., p. 466.

9. Jonathan Plucker, *Advanced Academic Performance: Exploring Country-Level Differences in the Pursuit of Educational Excellence* (Policy Brief 7) (Amsterdam: International Association for the Evaluation of Educational Achievement, 2015), http://www.iea.nl/fileadmin/user_upload/Policy_Briefs/IEA_policy_brief_Aug 2015.pdf.

10. Elementary and Secondary Education Act of 1965, p. 14

11. An Act to Close the Achievement Gap with Accountability, Flexibility, and Choice, So That No Child Is Left Behind, PL 107-110 (2001).

12. Thomas S. Dee and Brian Jacob, "The Impact of No Child Left Behind on Student Achievement," *Journal of Policy Analysis and Management* 30, no. 3 (2011): 418–446.

13. Jack Jennings and Diane Stark Rentner, "Ten Big Effects of the No Child Left Behind Act on Public Schools," *Phi Delta Kappan* 88, no 2 (2006): 110–113; Thomas S. Dee, Brian Jacob, and Nathaniel L. Schwartz, "The Effects of NCLB on School Resources and Practices," *Educational Evaluation and Policy Analysis* 35, no. 2 (2013): 252–279.

14. Every Student Succeeds Act, PL 114-95 2015.

15. The High Cost of Low Educational Performance: The Long-Run Economic Impact of Improving PISA Outcomes (Paris: Organisation for Economic Cooperation and Development, 2010), http://www.oecd.org/pisa/44417824.pdf.

16. Mapping State Proficiency Standards onto the NAEP Scales: Variation and Change in State Standards for Reading and Mathematics, 2005–2009 (Washington, DC: National Center for Education Statistics, 2011), http://nces.ed.gov/nationsreportcard/pdf/studies/2011458.pdf

17. Betty Hart and Todd D. Risley, "The Early Catastrophe: The 30 Million Word Gap by Age 3," American Educator Spring (2003): 4–9.

18. Sabino Kornrich and Frank Furstenberg, "Investing in Children: Changes in Parental Spending on Children, 1972–2007," Demography 50, no. 1 (2013): 1–23.

19. Mimi Engel, Amy Claessens and Maida A. Finch, "Teaching Students What They Already Know? The (Mis)Alignment Between Mathematics Instructional Content and Student Knowledge in Kindergarten," Educational Evaluation and Policy Analysis 35, no.2 (2013): 157–178.

20. Derek Neal and Diane Whitmore Schanzenbach, "Left Behind by Design: Proficiency Counts and Test-Based Accountability," Review of Economics and Statistics 92, no. 2 (2010): 263–283.

21. Ron Haskins, Richard J. Murnane, Isabel V. Sawhill, and Catherine Snow, Can Academic Standards Boost Literacy and Close the Achievement Gap? (Washington, DC: Brookings Institution, The Future of Children, 2012): 2013; David. H., Frank Levy, and Richard J. Murnane, "The Skill Content of Recent Technological Change: An Empirical Exploration," Quarterly Journal of Economics 118 (2003): 4.

CHAPTER 2

1. Marni Bromberg and Christina Theokas, Falling out of the Lead: Following High Achievers Through High School and Beyond (Washington, DC: The Education Trust, 2014), https://edtrust.org/resource/falling-out-of-the-lead-following-high-achievers-through-high-school-and-beyond/.

2. Nathan Burroughs and Jonathan Plucker, "Excellence Gaps," in Critical Issues and Practices in Gifted Education, ed. Carolyn M. Callahan and Jonathan Plucker (Waco, TX: Prufrock Press, 2014), 255–265.

3. Hal Salzman and Lindsay Lowell, "Making the Grade," Nature 453 (2008): 28–30.

4. "Education Statistics Digest 2014" (Singapore: Singapore Ministry of Education, 2014), http://www.moe.gov.sg/education/education-statistics-digest/files/esd-2014.pdf; the United States has approximately 65 million K–12 students, with 15 percent scoring advanced on the Grade 4 TIMSS Science assessment and 10 percent on the grade 8 science assessment. Assuming a 12.5 percent advanced rate for the entire K–12 population produces an estimate greater than 8 million students performing at advanced levels in science.

5. Based on data from the IMF (2015), US GDP by purchasing power parity is $17,419 billion versus Singapore's GDP of $453 billion.

6. We acknowledge that countries such as Singapore, with very limited natural resources, often need to put a premium on human capital development in order to grow their economies. But our broader point in this section still stands. To say the United States advanced performance is adequate is ludicrous.

7. Data from the 2015 TIMSS administration is not scheduled for release until late 2016/early 2017.

8. David Rutkowski and Ellen Prusinsi, *The Limits and Possibilities of International Large-Scale Assessments* (Bloomington, IN: Center for Evaluation and Education Policy Analysis, 2011), http://eric.ed.gov/?id=ED531823.

9. See also arguments in favor of the predictive validity of these tests, such as Nathan R. Kuncel, Deniz S. Ones, and Paul R. Sackett, "Individual Differences as Predictors of Work, Educational, and Broad Life Outcomes," *Personality and Individual Differences* 49, no. 4 (2010): 331–336; Paul R. Sackett, Matthew J. Borneman, and Brian S. Connelly, "High Stakes Testing in Higher Education and Employment: Appraising the Evidence for Validity and Fairness," *American Psychologist* 63, no. 4 (2008): 215–227.

10. Jonathan A. Plucker, *Advanced Academic Performance: Exploring Country-Level Differences in the Pursuit of Educational Excellence* (Amsterdam: International Association for the Evaluation of Educational Achievement, 2015), http://www.iea.nl/fileadmin/user_upload/Policy_Briefs/IEA_policy_brief_Aug2015.pdf.

11. See Tom Loveless, "Lessons from the PISA-Shanghai Controversy" (Washington, DC: Brookings Institution, Brown Center Chalkboard, March 18, 2015).

12. Compare, for example, the perspectives in Jaekyung Lee, "Review of *Do High Flyers Maintain Their Altitude?*" (Boulder, CO: National Education Policy Center, 2011), and Yun Xiang, Michael Dahlin, John Cronin, Robert Theaker, and Sarah Durant, *Do High Flyers Maintain Their Altitude? Performance Trends of Top Students* (Washington, DC: Thomas B. Fordham Institute, 2011).

13. Jae Yup Jung, Marie Young, and Miraca U. M. Gross, "Early College Entrance in Australia," *Roeper Review* 37, no. 1 (2015): 19–28; Ketty M. Sarouphim, "Slowly but Surely: Small Steps Toward Establishing Gifted Education Programs in Lebanon," *Journal for the Education of the Gifted* 38, no. 2 (2015): 196–211; Kirsi Tirri and Elina Kuusisto, "How Finland Serves Gifted and Talented Pupils," *Journal for the Education of the Gifted* 36, no. 1 (2013): 84–96.

14. Jonathan A. Plucker, Jennifer Giancola, Grace Healey, Daniel Arndt, and Chen Wang, *Equal Talents, Unequal Opportunities: A Report Card on State Support for Academically Talented Low-Income Students* (Lansdowne, VA: Jack Kent Cooke Foundation, 2015), http://www.excellencegap.org/.

15. Greg J. Duncan and Richard J. Murnane, "Growing Income Inequality Threatens American Education," *Phi Delta Kappan* 95, no. 6 (2014): 8–14.

16. Cengiz Alacaci and Ayhan Kursat Erbas, "Unpacking the Inequality Among Turkish Schools: Findings from PISA 2006," *International Journal of Educational Development* 30, no. 2 (2010): 182–192; Heidi Knipprath, "What PISA Tells Us About the Quality and Inequality of Japanese Education in Mathematics and

Science," International Journal of Science and Mathematics Education 8, no. 3 (2010): 389–408.

17. Robert Dorfman, "A Formula for the Gini Coefficient," *Review of Economics and Statistics* 61, no. 1 (1979): 146–149; Branko Milanovic, "A Simple Way to Calculate the Gini Coefficient, and Some Implications," *Economics Letters* 56, no. 1 (1997): 45–49.

18. Much of the controversy surrounding Gini coefficients deals with how they are calculated. Given that we use estimates calculated by the World Bank using the same methods for each country, and that our purpose here is looking at trends across countries, the calculation controversy is not as relevant as in other settings; Facundo Alvaredo, "A Note on the Relationship Between Top Income Shares and the Gini Coefficient," *Economics Letters* 110, no. 3 (2011): 274–277.

19. Philip L. Martin. "Competing for Global Talent: The US Experience" in *Competing for Global Talent*, ed. Christiane Kuptsch and Eng Fong Pang (Geneva: ILO International Institute for Labour Studies, 2005), 87–106; Ayelet Shachar, "Race for Talent: Highly Skilled Migrants and Competitive Immigration Regimes," *New York University Law Review* 81 (2006): 148–206.

CHAPTER 3

1. Jonathan A. Plucker, Jacob Hardesty, and Nathan Burroughs, *Talent on the Sidelines: Excellence Gaps and America's Persistent Talent Underclass* (Storrs, CT: Center for Education Policy Analysis, University of Connecticut, 2013), 12–14; David Rutkowski, Leslie Rutkowski, and Jonathan A. Plucker, "Trends in Education Excellence Gaps: A 12-year International Perspective Via the Multilevel Model for Change," *High Ability Studies* 23, no. 2 (2012): 143–166; Jonathan A. Plucker, Nathan Burroughs, and Ruiting Song, *Mind the (Other) Gap!: The Growing Excellence Gap in K–12 Education* (Bloomington, IN: Center for Evaluation and Education Policy Analysis, 2010); Chester E. Finn and Brandon L. Wright, *Failing Our Brightest Kids: The Global Challenge of Educating High-Ability Students*, (Cambridge, MA: Harvard Education Press, 2015).

2. Tina Beveridge, "No Child Left Behind and Fine Arts Classes," Arts Education Policy Review 111, no. 1 (2009): 4–7; Paul G. Fitchett and Tina L. Heafner, "A National Perspective on the Effects of High-Stakes Testing and Standardization on Elementary Social Studies Marginalization," Theory & Research in Social Education 38, no. 1 (2010): 114–130.

3. Rutkowski, Rutkowski, and Plucker, "Trends in Education Excellence Gaps."

4. Finn and Wright, *Failing Our Brightest Kids*, 69–216.

5. Plucker, Hardesty, and Burroughs, *Talent on the Sidelines*

6. Common Core of Data (CCD), "State Nonfiscal Survey of Public Elementary and Secondary Education," 1995–96 through 2012–13 (Washington, DC: US Department of Education, National Center for Education Statistics, n.d.); and National Elementary and Secondary Enrollment Projection Model, 1972 through 2024 (table prepared March 2015), https://nces.ed.gov/programs/digest/d14/tables/dt14_203.50.asp?current=yes.

7. US Department of Education, National Center for Education Statistics, *Annual Report of the Commissioner of Education*, 1870 to 1910; *Biennial Survey of Education in the United States*, 1919-20 through 1949-50; *Statistics of Public Elementary and Secondary School Systems*, 1959 through 1980; Common Core of Data (CCD), "State Nonfiscal Survey of Public Elementary and Secondary Education," 1981–82 through 2010-11; Parent and Family Involvement in Education Survey of the National Household Education Surveys Program (PFI-NHES:2007); Private School Universe Survey (PSS), 1989–90 through 2009–10; *Projections of Education Statistics to 2021*; Opening (Fall) Enrollment in Higher Education, 1959; Higher Education General Information Survey (HEGIS), "Fall Enrollment in Institutions of Higher Education" surveys, 1969 through 1985; Integrated Postsecondary Education Data System.

8. Laura G. Knapp, Janice E. Kelly-Reid, and Scott A. Ginder, "Enrollment in Postsecondary Institutions, Fall 2010; Financial Statistics, Fiscal Year 2010; and Graduation Rates, Selected Cohorts, 2002-07 (NCES 2012-280) (Washington, DC: National Center for Education Statistics, 2012), http://nces.ed.gov/pubs2012/2012280.pdf.

CHAPTER 4

1. National Association for Gifted Children, *State of the States of Gifted Education: 2014–2015* (Washington, DC: National Association for Gifted Children, 2015); Carolyn M. Callahan, Tonya R. Moon, and Sarah Oh, *Status of Elementary Gifted Programs 2013* (Charlottesville, VA: National Research Center on the Gifted and Talented University of Virginia, 2013), http://www.nagc.org/sites/default/files/key%20reports/ELEM%20school%20GT%20Survey%20Report.pdf.

2. Matthew T. McBee, Scott J. Peters, and Craig Waterman, "Combining Scores in Multiple-Criteria Assessment Systems: The Impact of Combination Rules," Gifted Child Quarterly 58, no. 1 (2014): 68–89.

3. *Percentage Distribution of Students Enrolled in Public Elementary and Secondary Schools, by Race/Ethnicity: Fall 2002, Fall 2012, and Fall 2024* (Washington, DC: National Center for Educational Statistics, n.d.), http://nces.ed.gov/programs/coe/indicator_cge.asp.

4. *Total Number of Public School Teachers and Percentage Distribution of School Teachers, by Race/Ethnicity and State: 2011–12* (Washington, DC: National Center for Educational Statistics, n.d.) https://nces.ed.gov/surveys/sass/tables/sass1112_2013314_tls_001.asp.

5. Jean S. Peterson, "Gifted—Through Whose Cultural Lens? An Application of the Postpositivistic Mode of Inquiry," *Journal for the Education of the Gifted* 22, no. 4 (1999): 354–383.

6. Jason A. Grisson and Christopher Redding, "Discretion and Disproportionality: Explaining the Underrepresentation of High-Achieving Students of Color in Gifted Programs," *AERA Open* 2, no. 1 (2016): 1–25.

7. Matthew T. McBee, "A Descriptive Analysis of Referral Sources for Gifted Education

Screening by Race and Socioeconomic Status," *Journal of Secondary Gifted Education*, 17, no. 2 (2006): 103–111.

8. David Card and Laura Giuliano, "Can Universal Screening Increase the Representation of Low Income and Minority Students in Gifted Education?" (Working Paper 21519, National Bureau of Economic Research, September 2015), http://www.nber.org/papers/w21519.

9. Information on test scores from Scott J. Peters and Kenneth G. Engerrand, "Equity and Excellence: Proactive Efforts in the Identification of Underrepresented Students for Gifted and Talented Students," *Gifted Child Quarterly* (in press).

10. Frank C. Worrell, "Ethnically Diverse Students," in *Critical Issues and Practices I Gifted Education: What the Research Says*, 2nd ed., ed. Jonathan A. Plucker and Carolyn M. Callahan (Waco, TX: Prufrock Press, 2014), 237–254.

11. Alena Friedrich, Barbara Flunger, Benjamin Nagengast, Kathrin Jonkmann, and Ulrich Trautwein, "Pygmalion Effects in the Classroom: Teacher Expectancy Effects on Students' Math Achievement," Contemporary Educational Psychology 41, (2015), 1–12.

12. Julie Fox and Terry A. Stinnett, "The Effects of Labeling Bias on Prognostic Outlook for Children as a Function of Diagnostic," *Psychology in the Schools* 33, no. 2 (1996): 143–153.

13. R. Allan Allday, Gary J. Duhon, Sarah Blackburn-Ellis, and Jamie L. Van Dycke, "The Biasing Effect of Labels on Direct Observation by Preservice Teachers," *Teacher Education and Special Education* 34, no. 1 (2011): 52–58.

14. Jillian Gates, "Children with Gifts and Talents: Looking Beyond Traditional Labels," *Roeper Review* 32 (2010): 200–206.

15. Kate E. Snyder, Michael N. Barger, Stephanie V. Wormington, Rochelle Schwartz-Bloom, and Lisa Linnebrink-Garcia, "Identification as Gifted and Implicit Beliefs About Intelligence: An Examination of Potential Moderators, *Journal of Advanced Academics* 24, no. 4 (2013): 242–258.

16. John F. Feldhusen and David Y. Dai, "Gifted Students' Attitudes and Perceptions of the Gifted Label, Special Program, and Peer Relations," *Journal of Secondary Gifted Education* 9, no 1 (1997): 15–20.

17. John P. Papay, Richard J. Murnane, and John B. Willett, "The Impact of Test-Score Labels on Human-Capital Investment," *Journal of Human Resources* (in press).

18. D. Betsy McCoach and Del Siegle, "What Predicts Teachers' Attitudes Towards the Gifted?" *Gifted Child Quarterly* 51, no. 3 (2007): 246–254; Dewey Cornell, "Gifted Children: The Impact of Positive Labeling on the Family System," *American Journal Orthopsychiatry* 53, no. 2 (1983): 322–335; Michael S. Matthews, Jennifer A. Richotte, and Jennifer L. Jolly, "What's Wrong with Giftedness? Parents' Perceptions of the Gifted Label," *International Studies in Sociology of Education* 24, no. 4 (2014): 372–393.

CHAPTER 5

1. David Dai and Fei Chen, "Three Paradigms of Gifted Education: In Search of Conceptual Clarity in Research and Practice" *Gifted Child Quarterly* 57, no. 3 (2013): 151–168.

2. So Yoon Yoon and Marcia Gentry, "Racial and Ethnic Representation in Gifted Programs: Current Status of and Implications for Asian American Students," *Gifted Child Quarterly* 53, no. 2 (2009): 121–136.

3. James H. Borland, "Gifted Education without Gifted Children: The Case for No Conception of Giftedness," in *Conceptions of Giftedness*, ed. Robert J. Sternberg and Janet E. Davidson (New York: Cambridge University Press, 2008), 1–19; Rena F. Subotnik, Paula Olszewski-Kubilius, and Frank C. Worrell, "A Proposed Direction Forward for Gifted Education Based on Psychological Science" *Gifted Child Quarterly* 56, no. 4 (2012): 176–188; Scott J. Peters et al., *Beyond Gifted Education: Designing and Implementing Advanced Academic Programs* (Waco, TX: Prufrock Press, 2014), 1–5.

4. Jonathan A. Plucker, Jacob Hardesty, and Nathan Burroughs, *Talent on the Sidelines: Excellence Gaps and America's Persistent Talent Underclass* (Storrs, CT: Center for Education Policy Analysis, University of Connecticut, 2013).

5. Ibid.

6. Jill L. Adelson, D. Betsy McCoach, and M. Katherine Gavin, "Examining the Effects of Gifted Programming in Mathematics and Reading using EXLS-K," *Gifted Child Quarterly* 56, no. 1 (2012): 25–39; Sa A. Bui, Steven G. Craig, and Scott A. Imberman, "Is Gifted Education a Bright Idea?" *American Economic Journal: Economic Policy* 6, no. 3 (2014): 30–62.

7. Joseph S. Renzulli, "What Makes Giftedness? Reexamining a Definition," *Phi Delta Kappan* 60, no. 3 (1978): 180–184, 261.

8. Dai and Chen, "Three Paradigms of Gifted Education."

9. Joseph S. Renzulli and Sally M. Reis, *The Schoolwide Enrichment Model: A How-To Guide for Educational Excellence* (Mansfield Center, CT: Creative Learning Press, 1985).

10. Karen Rolling, Chrystyna V. Mursky, Sneha Shah-Coltrane, and Susan K. Johnsen, "RtI Models for Gifted Children," *Gifted Child Today* 32, no. 3 (2008): 20–30.

11. Peters et al., *Beyond Gifted Education*.

12. National Association for Gifted Children, *State of the States of Gifted Education: 2012–2013* (Washington, DC: National Association for Gifted Children, n.d.).

13. Vicki L. Vaughn, John F. Feldhusen, and J. W. Asher, "Meta-Analyses and Review of Research on Pull-Out Programs in Gifted Education," *Gifted Child Quarterly* 35, no. 2 (1991): 92–98.

14. Adam Booij, Ferry Haan, and Erik Plug, "Enriching Students Pays Off: Evidence from an Individualized Gifted and Talented Program in Secondary Education" (IZA Discussion Paper 9757, 2016).

15. Jill L. Adelson and Brittany D. Carpenter, "Grouping for Achievement Gains: For Whom Does Achievement Grouping Increase Kindergarten Reading Growth?" *Gifted Child Quarterly* 55, no. 4 (2009): 265–278.

16. Takako Nomi, "The Effects of Within-Class Ability Grouping on Academic Achievement in Early Elementary Years," *Journal of Research on Educational Effectiveness* 3, no. 1 (2010): 56–92.

17. Yiping Lou et al., "Within-Class Grouping: A Meta-Analysis," *Review of Educational Research* 66, no. 4, (1996): 423–458.

18. Daniel L. Reese, Laura M. Argys, and Dominic J. Brewer, "Tracking in the United States: Descriptive Statistics from the NELS," *Economics of Education Review* 15, no. 1 (1996): 83–89.

19. Courtney A. Colling and Li Gan, "Does Sorting Students Improve Scores? An Analysis of Class Composition," (Working Paper 18848, National Bureau of Economic Research, 2013).

20. Saiying Steenbergen-Hu and Sidney M. Moon, "The Effects of Acceleration on High-Ability Learners: A Meta-Analysis," *Gifted Child Quarterly* 55, no. 1 (2011): 39–53.

21. Jonathan A. Plucker and Carolyn M. Callahan, "Research on Giftedness and Gifted Education: Status of the Field and Considerations for the Future," *Exceptional Children* 80 (2014): 390–406.

22. Lou et al., "Within-Class Grouping."

23. Katie L. McClarty, "Life in the Fast Land: Effects of Early Grade Acceleration on High School and College Outcomes," *Gifted Child Quarterly* 59, no. 1 (2015): 3–13.

24. Gregory Park, David Lubinski, and Camilla P. Benbow, "When Less Is More: Effects of Grade Skipping on Adult STEM Productivity Among Mathematically Precocious Adolescents," *Journal of Educational Psychology* 105, no. 1 (2013): 176–198.

25. Steenbergen-Hu and Moon, "The Effects of Acceleration on High-Ability Learners."

26. Russell T. Warne et al., "The Impact of Participation in the Advanced Placement Program on Students' College Admissions Test Scores," *Journal of Educational Research* 108, no. 5 (2015): 400–416.

27. College Board, *10th Annual AP Report to the Nation*, http://media.collegeboard.com/digitalServices/pdf/ap/rtn/10th-annual/10th-annual-ap-report-to-the-nation-single-page.pdf.

28. Jonathan A. Plucker and Bryn Harris, "Acceleration and Economically Vulnerable Children," in A Nation Empowered: Evidence Trumps the Excuses That Hold Back America's Brightest Students, ed. Susan G. Assouline, Nicholas Colangelo, Joyce VanTassel-Baska, and Ann. E. Lupkowski-Shoplik (Iowa City, IA: The Belin-Blank Center for Gifted and Talented Education, 2015), 181–188.

29. "Jacob K. Javits Gifted and Talented Students Education Program: 2015 Awards," United States Department of Education, http://www2.ed.gov/programs/javits/awards.html.

CHAPTER 6

1. Michael T. Kane, "Explicating Validity," *Assessment in Education: Principles, Policy & Practice* (2015): 1–14.

2. Françoys Gagné, "Academic Talent Development and the Equity Issue in Gifted Education," *Talent Development and Excellence* 3, no. 1 (2011), 3–22.

3. College Board, *10th Annual AP Report to the Nation*, http://media.collegeboard.com/digitalServices/pdf/ap/rtn/10th-annual/10th-annual-ap-report-to-the-nation-single-page.pdf.

4. Jay Matthews, "Why Gifted Education Doesn't Make Sense," *Washington Post*, October 8, 2014, https://www.washingtonpost.com/lifestyle/on-parenting/why-gifted-education-doesnt-make-sense/2014/10/07/b2bc0b8a-4930-11e4-b72e-d60a9229cc10_story.html.

5. So Yoon Yoon and Marcia Gentry, "Racial and Ethnic Representation in Gifted Programs: Current Status of and Implications for Asian American Students," *Gifted Child Quarterly* 53, no. 2 (2009): 121–136.

6. Michael S. Matthews and Scott J. Peters, "Methods to Increase the Identification Rate of Students from Traditionally Underrepresented Populations for Gifted Services," in American Psychological Association Handbook on Gifted Education, ed. S. Pfeiffer, E. Shaunessy-Dedrick, and M. Nicpon (Washington, DC: American Psychological Association, in press).

7. Carolyn M. Callahan, Tonya R. Moon, and Sarah Oh, *Status of Elementary Gifted Programs 2013*, http://www.nagc.org/sites/default/files/key%20reports/ELEM%20school%20GT%20Survey%20Report.pdf,

8. *State of the States of Gifted Education: 2014–2015* (Washington, DC: National Association for Gifted Children, 2015).

9. David F. Lohman, "The Role of Nonverbal Ability Tests in Identifying Academically Gifted Students: An Aptitude Perspective," *Gifted Child Quarterly* 49, no. 2 (2005): 111–138.

10. Carol A. Carman and Debra K. Taylor, "Socioeconomic Status Effects on Using the Naglieri Nonverbal Ability Test (NNAT) to Identify Gifted/Talents," *Gifted Child Quarterly* 52, no. 2 (2010): 75–84; Jacob A. Giessman, James L. Gambrell, and Molly S. Stebbins, "Minority Performance on the Naglieri Nonverbal Ability Test, Second Edition, Versus the Cognitive Abilities Test, Form 6: One Gifted Program's Experience," *Gifted Child Quarterly* 57, no. 2 (2013): 101–109.

11. Jack A. Naglieri and Donna Y. Ford, "Addressing Underrepresentation of Gifted Minority Children Using the Naglieri Nonverbal Ability Test (NNAT)," *Gifted Child Quarterly* 47, no. 2 (2003): 155–160; Jack A. Naglieri and Donna Y. Ford, "Increasing Minority Children's Participation in Gifted Classes Using the NNAT: A Response to Lohman," *Gifted Child Quarterly* 49, (no. 1): 29–36.

12. David F. Lohman, "Identifying Academically Talented Students: Some General Principals, Two Specific Procedures," in *International Handbook on Giftedness*, ed. Larisa V. Shavinina (Berlin: Springer Science + Business Media, 2009), 971–997; Matthew T. McBee, Scott J. Peters, and Craig Waterman, "Combining Scores in Multiple-Criteria Assessment Systems: The Impact of Combination Rules," *Gifted Child Quarterly* 58, no. 1 (2014): 69–89.

13. Scott J. Peters et al., *Beyond Gifted Education: Designing and Implementing Advanced Academic Programs* (Waco, TX: Prufrock Press, 2014), 35–36.

14. Carol V. Horn, "Young Scholars: A Talent Development Model for Finding and Nurturing Potential in Underserved Populations," *Gifted Child Today* 38, no. 1 (2015): 19–31; Christine C. Harradine, Mary Ruth B. Coleman, and Donna-Marie

C. Winn, "Recognizing Academic Potential in Students of Color: Findings of U-START~PLUS," *Gifted Child Quarterly* 58, no. 1 (2014): 24–34.

15. Horn, "Young Scholars."

16. "Young Scholar Handbook," Advanced Academic Program Office, Instructional Services Department, Fairfax County Public Schools (n.d.), accessed February 10, 2016, http://www.fcps.edu/is/aap/pdfs/ys/youngscholarhandbookweb1.pdf.

17. Matthew T. McBee, "A Descriptive Analysis of Referral Sources for Gifted Identification Screening by Race and Socioeconomic Status," *Journal of Secondary Gifted Education* 17, no. 2 (2006): 103–111; Jason A. Grissom and Christopher Redding, "Discretion and Disproportionality: Explaining the Underrepresentation of High-Achieving Students of Color in Gifted Programs," *AERA Open* 2, no. 1 (2016): 1–25.

18. Matthew T. McBee, Scott J. Peters, and Erin M. Miller, "The Impact of the Nomination State on Gifted Program Identification: A Comprehensive Psychometric Analysis," *Gifted Child Quarterly* (in press).

19. Ibid.

20. Lohman, "Identifying Academically Talented Students"; Scott J. Peters and Marcia Gentry, "Group-Specific Norms and Teacher Rating Scales: Implications for Underrepresentation," *Journal of Advanced Academics* 23, no. 2 (2012): 125–144.

21. Nicholas Jacobs, "Understanding School Choice Location as a Determinant of Charter School Racial, Economic, and Linguistic Segregation," *Education and Urban Society* 45, no. 4 (2013): 459–482; Rachel R. Ostrander, "School Funding: Inequality in District Funding and the Disparate Impact on Urban and Migrant School Children," *Brigham Young University Education and Law Journal* (2015): 271–295.

22. We acknowledge that some of our colleagues dislike including athletics or extracurricular examples when discussing advanced academics, primarily because those activities are usually voluntary. But in this context, that makes the logic stronger: If we want to promote excellence and our voluntary activities clearly embrace local norms without disastrous consequences for those fields, then why not use such local norms for K–12 academics?

23. Stephanie A. Weisman and Denise C. Gottfredson, "Attrition from After School Programs: Characteristics of Students Who Drop Out," *Prevention Science* 2, no. 3 (2001): 201–205; Jonathan A. Plucker, "The Effect of Relocation on Gifted Students," *Gifted Child Quarterly* 43, no. 2 (1999): 95–106.

24. National Research Council and Institute of Medicine, *Student Mobility: Exploring the Impact of Frequent Moves on Achievement: Summary of a Workshop* (Washington, DC: National Academies Press, 2010).

25. Lohman, "Identifying Academically Talented Students," 975.

26. Peters and Gentry, "Group-Specific Norms and Teacher Rating Scales."

27. David Card and Laura Giuliano, "Can Universal Screening Increase the Representation of Low Income and Minority Students in Gifted Education?" (Working Paper 21519, National Bureau of Economic Research, September 2015), http://www.nber.org/papers/w21519.

CHAPTER 7

1. Jonathan A. Plucker, "The Angry Moderate Reformer, Part IV: Poverty Reduction as Education Reform," *Education Week*, August 15, 2013, http://tinyurl.com/lm65kjb; Jonathan A. Plucker, "Poverty, Ed Reform, and the Most Important Foundation You've Probably Never Heard Of," *Education Week*, December 5, 2014, http://blogs.edweek.org/edweek/rick_hess_straight_up/2014/12/poverty_ed_reform_and_foundation_youve_never_heard_of.html.

2. Michael A. Rebell and Jessica R. Wolff, "Educational Opportunity Is Achievable and Affordable," *Phi Delta Kappan* 93, no. 6 (2012): 62–65.

3. All data, unless otherwise noted, are drawn from databases representing 2013 data.

4. Carmen DeNavas-Walt and Bernadette D. Proctor, *Income and Poverty in the United States: 2013, Current Population Reports*," US Census Bureau, 2014.

5. Carmen DeNavas-Walt and Bernadette D. Proctor, *Income and Poverty in the United States: 2014*. US Census Bureau, 2015.

6. UNICEF Innocenti Research Centre, *Measuring Child Poverty: New League Tables of Child Poverty in the World's Rich Countries* (Innocenti Report Card 10) (Florence: UNICEF Innocenti Research Centre, 2012).

7. Alisha Coleman-Jensen, Christian Gregory, and Anita Singh, *Household Food Security in the United States in 2013*," USDA-ERS Economic Research Report 173 (2014).

8. See https://nces.ed.gov/programs/digest/d14/tables/dt14_204.10.asp?current=yes.

9. See an excellent discussion of these issues in *Measuring Child Poverty*.

10. Michael Harwell and Brandon LeBeau, "Student Eligibility for a Free Lunch as an SES Measure in Education Research," *Educational Researcher* 39, no. 2 (2010): 120–131; Tom Snyder and Lauren Musu-Gillette, "Free or Reduced Price Lunch: A Proxy for Poverty?" April 16, 2015, http://nces.ed.gov/blogs/nces/post/free-or-reduced-price-lunch-a-proxy-for-poverty.

11. To complicate matters further, the family income gap may be a fraction as large as the family wealth gap. See William Darity Jr. and Melba J. Nicholson, "Racial Wealth Inequality and the Black Family," in *African American Family Life: Ecological and Cultural Diversity*, ed. V.C. Mcloyd, N.E. Hill, and K.A. Dodge (New York: Guilford, 2005), 78–85.

12. Coleman-Jensen, Gregory, and Singh, *Household Food Security*.

13. During work on related projects, our colleague James Moore suggested the use of this term, and we use it throughout this chapter. However, for stylistic reasons, we do occasionally use *poverty* and *economic vulnerability* interchangeably to avoid repetition of the longer term.

14. Elizabeth Kneebone, *The Growth and Spread of Concentrated Poverty, 2000 to 2008–2012* (Washington, DC: The Brookings Institution, 2014), http://www.brookings.edu/research/interactives/2014/concentrated-poverty#/M10420.

15. Michael J. Petrilli and Brandon L. Wright, "America's Mediocre Test Scores," *Education Next* 16, no. 1 (2016); Michael J. Petrilli and Brandon L. Wright, "America's Unexceptional Poverty Rate," *National Review Online*, November 3,

2015, http://www.nationalreview.com/article/426478/americas-unexceptional-poverty-rate-michael-j-petrilli-brandon-l-wright.

16. Matt Bruening, "America's Exceptional Child Poverty," *Demos.org*, November 5, 2015, http://www.demos.org/blog/11/5/15/americas-exceptional-child-poverty.

17. Jonathan A. Plucker, Jacob Hardesty, and Nathan Burroughs, *Talent on the Sidelines: Excellence Gaps and America's Persistent Talent Underclass* (Storrs, CT: Center for Education Policy Analysis, University of Connecticut, 2013), 20.

18. Although we restrict our examples to the Grade 4 Mathematics test in this chapter, data trends on other content area tests are similar.

19. Martha S. Hill and Jodi R. Sandfort, "Effects of Childhood Poverty on Productivity Later in Life: Implications for Public Policy," *Children and Youth Services Review* 17, no. 1 (1995): 91–126.

20. Stephen E. Gilman, Ichiro Kawachi, Garrett M. Fitzmaurice, and Stephen L. Buka, "Socioeconomic Status in Childhood and the Lifetime Risk of Major Depression," *International Journal of Epidemiology* 31, no. 2 (2002): 359–367; Jungeun Olivia Lee, Karl G. Hill, Lacey A. Hartigan, Joseph M. Boden, Katarina Guttmannova, Rick Kosterman, Jennifer A. Bailey, and Richard F. Catalano, "Unemployment and Substance Use Problems Among Young Adults: Does Childhood Low Socioeconomic Status Exacerbate the Effect?" *Social Science & Medicine* 143 (2015): 36–44; Nick Spencer, Tu Mai Thanh, and Séguin Louise, "Low Income/Socio-Economic Status in Early Childhood and Physical Health in Later Childhood/Adolescence: A Systematic Review," *Maternal and Child Health Journal* 17, no. 3 (2013): 424–431; Roger T. Staff, Alison D. Murray, Trevor S. Ahearn, Nazahan Mustafa, Helen C. Fox, and Lawrence J. Whalley, "Childhood Socioeconomic Status and Adult Brain Size: Childhood Socioeconomic Status Influences Adult Hippocampal Size," *Annals of Neurology* 71, no. 5 (2012): 653–660; Eileen Y. Chou, Bidhan L. Parmar, and Adam D. Galinsky, "Economic Insecurity Increases Physical Pain," *Psychological Science* (2016), 1–12.

21. Sarah E. Hill, Marjorie L. Prokosch, Danielle J. DelPriore, Vladas Griskevicius, and Andrew Kramer, "The Impact of Perceived Disease Threat on Women's Desire for Novel Dating and Sexual Partners: Is Variety the Best Medicine?" *Psychological Science* (2016): 1–11.

22. OECD, *Income Inequality and Growth: The Role of Taxes and Transfers*, OECD Economics Department Policy Notes, no. 9 (January 2012); UNICEF, 2014, https://www.oecd.org/tax/public-finance/49417295.pdf.

23. OECD, *Income Inequality and Growth*, 9.

24. Duncan Lindsey, *Child Poverty and Inequality: Securing a Better Future for America's Children* (New York: Oxford University Press, 2008).

25. DeNavas-Walt and Proctor, *Income and Poverty*, 14.

26. See Lindsey, *Child Poverty and Inequality*, for a cogent and concise analysis of senior versus child welfare policies.

27. Joseph Rowntree Foundation, *Reducing Poverty in the UK: A Collection of Evidence Reviews* (York, UK: Joseph Rowntree Foundation, 2014).

28. Jonathan A. Plucker and Bryn Harris, "Acceleration and Economically Vulnerable Children," in A Nation Empowered: Evidence Trumps the Excuses That Hold Back America's Brightest Students, vol. 2, ed. S. G. Assouline, N. Colangelo, J. VanTassel-Baska, and A. E. Lupkowski-Shoplik (Iowa City, IA: The Belin-Blank Center for Gifted and Talented Education, 2015), 181–188.

29. Thomas P. Hebert, "Educating Gifted Children from Low Socioeconomic Backgrounds: Creating Visions of a Hopeful Future," Exceptionality 10, no. 2 (2002): 127–138.

30. Paula Olszewski-Kubilius and Jane Clarenbach, Unlocking Emergent Talent: Supporting High Achievement of Low-Income, High Ability Students (Washington, DC: National Association for Gifted Children, 2012).

31. Molly Chamberlin and Jonathan A. Plucker, "P–16 Education: Where Are We Going? Where Have We Been?" Phi Delta Kappan 89, no. 7 (2008): 472–479; Julia Link Roberts, "Talent d\Development: A 'Must' for a Promising Future," Phi Delta Kappan 89, no. 7 (2008): 501–506.

32. Fredrik Andersson, John C. Haltiwanger, Mark J. Kutzbach, Henry O. Pollakowski, and Daniel H. Weinberg, Job Displacement and the Duration of Joblessness: The Role of Spatial Mismatch (Report No. w20066, National Bureau of Economic Research, 2014).

33. Kneebone, Concentrated Poverty.

34. Donald J. Leu, Elena Forzani, Chris Rhoads, Cheryl Maykel, Clint Kennedy, and Nicole Timbrell, "The New Literacies of Online Research and Comprehension: Rethinking the Reading Achievement Gap," Reading Research Quarterly 50, no. 1 (2015): 37–59.

35. See, for instance, Edwin Leuven, Mikael Lindahl, Hessel Oosterbeek, and Dinand Webbink, "Expanding Schooling Opportunities for 4-Year-Olds," Economics of Education Review 29, no. 3 (2010): 319–328.

36. Timothy J. Bartik, Brad Hershbein, and Marta Lachowska, "Longer-Term Effects of the Kalamazoo Promise Scholarship on College Enrollment, Persistence, and Completion" (presented at the American Education Finance and Policy Annual Conference, Washington, DC, February 26–28, 2015); Jeffrey N. Jones, Gary Miron, and Allison J. Kelaher-Young, "The Kalamazoo Promise and Perceived Changes in Teacher Beliefs, Expectations, and Behaviors," Journal of Educational Research 105, no. 1 (2012): 36–51.

37. Jennifer Glynn, unpublished internal evaluation reports, 2012–2015 (Lansdowne, VA: Jack Kent Cooke Foundation). The scholars and non-selected applicants are clearly not highly similar groups. Students in both groups excel academically by sixth and seventh grade, but the JKCF staff tell us that the selected students tend to be higher in "have more sparks of leadership, commitment to service, grit and persistence."

38. Lindsey, Child Poverty and Inequality.

39. Michele Raitano and Francesco Vona, "Assessing Students' Equality of Opportunity in OECD Countries: The Role of National- and School-Level Policies" Applied

Economics (2016): 1–16; Jennifer Riedl Cross, "Gifted Education as a Vehicle for Enhancing Social Equality," *Roeper Review* 35, no. 2 (2013): 115–123.

40. Ying Lu and Sharon L. Weinberg, "Public Pre-K and Test Taking for the NYC Gifted-and-Talented Programs: Forging a Path to Equity," *Educational Researcher* 45 (January/February 2016): 36–47, 2016, as doi:10.3102/0013189X16633441.

41. Keith Witham, Lindsey E. Malcom-Piqueux, Alicia C. Dowd, and Estela Mara Bensimon,. America's Unmet Promise: The Imperative for Equity in Higher Education (Association of American Colleges and Universities, 2015).

42. Esra Altintas and Sükrü Ilgün, "The Perception of Gifted Students' Parents About the Term of Giftedness," *Educational Research and Reviews* 10, no. 5 (2015): 654–659; Kathleen Moritz Rudasill, Jill L. Adelson, Carolyn M. Callahan, Deanna Vogt Houlihan, and Benjamin M. Keizer, "Gifted Students' Perceptions of Parenting Styles: Associations with Cognitive Ability, Sex, Race, and Age," *Gifted Child Quarterly* (2012): 15–24.

43. Thomas W. Sanchez, "Poverty, Policy, and Public Transportation." *Transportation Research Part A: Policy and Practice* 42, no. 5 (2008): 833–841.

CHAPTER 8

1. James A. Kulik and Chen-Lin C. Kulik, "Meta-Analytic Findings on Grouping Programs," *Gifted Child Quarterly* 36, no. 2 (1992): 73–77.

2. James R. Delisle, "Differentiation Doesn't Work." *Education Week*, January 6, 2015. http://www.edweek.org/ew/articles/2015/01/07/differentiation-doesnt-work. html; Carol Ann Tomlinson, "Differentiation Does, in Fact, Work." *Education Week* January 27, 2015, http://www.edweek.org/ew/articles/2015/01/28/differentiation-does-in-fact-work.html.

3. James E. Rosenbaum, "Making Inequality; the Hidden Curriculum of High School Tracking." (New York: John Wiley & Sons, 1976); James E. Rosenbaum, "The Structure of Opportunity in School," *Social Forces* 57, no. 1 (1978): 236–256.

4. Jeannie Oakes, *Keeping Track: How Schools Structure Inequality* (New Haven, CT: Yale University Press, 1985).

5. Tom Loveless, *The Resurgence of Ability Grouping and Persistence of Tracking* (Washington, DC: The Brookings Institution, 2013), 12–21.

6. NEA Resolutions B-16, 1998, 2005, http://www.nea.org/tools/16899.htm.

7. Tom Loveless, *The Tracking Wars: State Reform Meets School Policy* (Washington, DC: Brookings Institution, 1999); Tom Loveless, *How Well are American Students Learning?* (Washington, DC: The Brookings Institution, 2013), 13–20.

8. Adam Gamoran, "Instructional and Institutional Effects of Ability Grouping." *Sociology of Education* (1986): 185–198; Maureen T. Hallinan, "Ability Grouping and Student Learning," in *The Social Organization of Schools* ed. Maureen T. Hallinan (New York: Springer US, 1987), 41–69.

9. Anne Wheelock, *Crossing the Tracks: How "Untracking" Can Save America's Schools* (New York: New Press, 1992), http://teacher.scholastic.com/professional/classmgmt/ abilitygroup.htm

10. We acknowledge that many people we respect use *tracking* to represent ability grouping and *ability grouping* to represent within-class grouping by ability. This usage feels anachronistic to us and perhaps unintentionally insensitive to historical concerns about tracking, and we are sticking to *ability grouping* as used in chapter 5 (including *between-class grouping* and *within-class grouping*).

11. Charles W. Cheng, Emily Brizendine, and Jeannie Oakes, "What Is 'An Equal Chance' for Minority Children?" *Journal of Negro Education* 48, no. 3 (1979): 267–287; John I. Goodlad and Jeannie Oakes, "We Must Offer Equal Access to Knowledge," *Educational Leadership* 45 no. 5 (1988): 16–22.

12. Years ago, one of us called Monticello to get a citation for this famous quote, and they laughed out loud when they heard it. They immediately questioned the attribution, given that, to quote the researcher, "He owned slaves. Lots of them." To the staff's credit, they did search their archives and could not find this quote anywhere in Jefferson's work. Still, it's a good quote. See also https://www.monticello.org/site/research-and-collections/nothing-more-unequalquotation.

13. Holly Hertberg-Davis, "Myth 7: Differentiation in the Regular Classroom Is Equivalent to Gifted Programs and Is Sufficient: Classroom Teachers Have the Time, the Skill, and the Will to Differentiate Adequately," *Gifted Child Quarterly* 53, no. 4 (2009): 251–253; Holly L. Hertberg-Davis and Catherine M. Brighton, "Support and Sabotage: Principals' Influence on Middle School Teachers' Responses to Differentiation," *Prufrock Journal* 17, no. 2 (2006): 90–102; Michael Petrilli, "All Together Now?" *Education Next* 11, no. 1 (2011), http://educationnext.org/all-together-now/.

14. Tom Loveless, *The Resurgence of Ability Grouping and Persistence of Tracking* (Washington, DC: Brown Center on Educational Policy, The Brookings Institution, 2013), 12–21.

15. Yiping Lou et al., "Within-Class Grouping: A Meta-Analysis," *Review of Educational Research* 66, no. 4, (1996): 423–458; Saiying Steenbergen-Hu, Matthew C. Makel, and Paula Olszewski-Kubilius, "What One Hundred Years of Research Says About the Effects of Ability Grouping and Acceleration on Students' Academic Achievement" (paper presented at the annual meeting of the National Association for Gifted Children, Phoenix, AZ, November 13, 2015).

16. Jonathan A. Plucker, Jacob Hardesty, and Nathan Burroughs, *Talent on the Sidelines: Excellence Gaps and America's Persistent Talent Underclass* (Storrs, CT: Center for Education Policy Analysis, The University of Connecticut, 2012), 9–11; Loveless, *The Resurgence of Ability Grouping and Persistence of Tracking*.

17. Jamet W. Schofield, "Grouping with Curriculum Differentiation and the Achievement Gap in Secondary Schools," *Teachers College Record* 112, no. 5 (2010): 1492–1528.

18. Steenbergen-Hu, Makel, and Olszewski-Kubilius, "What One Hundred Years of Research Says About the Effects of Ability Grouping."

19. Joseph P. Robinson, "Evidence of a Differential Effect of Ability Grouping on the Reading Achievement Growth of Language-Minority Hispanics," *Educational Evaluation and Policy Analysis* 30, no. 2 (2008): 141–180.

20. David Card and Laura Giuliano, "Does Gifted Education Work? For Which Students?" (Working Paper 20453, National Bureau of Economic Research, 2014).

CHAPTER 9

1. Jonathan A. Plucker, Jacob Hardesty, and Nathan Burroughs, *Talent on the Sidelines: Excellence Gap and America's Persistent Talent Underclass* (Storrs, CT: Center for Education and Policy Analysis, University of Connecticut, 2012), http://webdev.education.uconn.edu/static/sites/cepa/AG/excellence2013/Excellence-Gap-10-18-13_JP_LK.pdf.

2. Christine J. Briggs, Sally M. Reis, and Erin E. Sullivan, "A National View of Promising Programs and Practices for Culturally, Linguistically, and Ethnically Diverse Gifted and Talented Students," *Gifted Child Quarterly* 52, no. 2 (2008): 131–145.

3. The College Board, *10th Annual Report to the Nation* (New York: The College Board, 2014), http://media.collegeboard.com/digitalServices/pdf/ap/rtn/10th-annual/10th-annual-ap-report-to-the-nation-single-page.pdf.

4. The College Board, *SpringBoard: Compendium of Research*, (New York: The College Board, 2011, https://secure-media.collegeboard.org/digitalServices/pdf/springboard/springboard-research-compendium.pdf.

5. Ibid.

6. Paula Olszewski-Kubilius, Seon-Young Lee, Mephie Ngoi, and Daphne Ngoi, "Addressing the Achievement Gap Between Minority and Nonminority Children by Increasing Access to Gifted Programs," *Journal for the Education of the Gifted* 28, no. 2 (2004): 127–158; Paula Olszewski-Kubilius, "Addressing the Achievement Gap Between Minority and Nonminority Children: Increasing Access and Achievement Through Project EXCITE," *Gifted Child Today* 29, no. 2 (2006): 28–37.

7. M. Katherine Gavin et al., "Mentoring Mathematical Minds—A Research-Based Curriculum for Talented Elementary Students," *Journal of Advanced Academics* 18, no. 4 (2007): 566–585.

8. Seokhee Cho, Jenny Yang, and Marcella Mandracchia, "Effects of M3 Curriculum on Mathematics and English Proficiency Achievement of Mathematically Promising English Language Learners," *Journal of Advanced Academics* 26, no. 2 (2015): 112–142.

9. Ibid.

10. And the fact that, well, it was a math intervention.

11. Paradise Valley Unified School District records.

12. *Guidance on the Voluntary Use of Race to Achieve Diversity and Avoid Racial Isolation in Elementary and Secondary Schools*, US Department of Justice and United States Department of Education, 2011, http://www2.ed.gov/about/offices/list/ocr/docs/guidance-ese-201111.pdf.

13. Briggs, Reis, and Sullivan, "A National View of Promising Programs and Practices."

14. David Card and Laura Giuliano, "Can Universal Screening Increase the Representation of Low Income and Minority Students in Gifted Education?" (Working

Paper 21519, National Bureau of Economic Research, 2015), http://www.nber.org/papers/w21519.

15. Jennifer Giancola and Richard D. Kahlenberg, *True Merit: Ensuring Our Brightest Students have Access to Our Best Colleges and Universities* (Lansdowne, VA: The Jack Kent Cooke Foundation, January 2016), http://www.jkcf.org/assets/1/7/JKCF_True_Merit_Report.pdf.

16. Eric P. Bettinger et al., "The Role of Application Assistance and Information in College Decisions: Results from the H&R Block FAFSA Experiment," *Quarterly Journal of Economics* 127, no. 3 (2012): 1205–1242.

17. Andrew Garrod and Colleen Larimore, eds., *First Person, First Peoples* (Ithaca, NY: Cornell University Press, 1997), 1–19.

18. "Graduation Rate from First Institution Attended for First-Time, Full-Time Bachelor's Degree-Seeking Students at 4-year Postsecondary Institutions, by Race/Ethnicity, Time to Completion, Sex, Control of Institution, and Acceptance Rate: Selected Cohort Entry Years, 1996 Through 2007" (Washington, DC: National Center for Education Statistics, 2014), http://nces.ed.gov/programs/digest/d14/tables/dt14_326.10.asp

19. "Call me MISTER Is Building the Next Generation of African American Male Teachers," W. K. Kellogg Foundation (n.d.), accessed February 2, 2016, http://www.wkkf.org/what-we-do/featured-work/call-me-mister-is-building-the-next-generation-of-african-american-male-teachers.

20. Scott J. Peters and Kenneth G. Engerrand, "Equity and Excellence: Proactive Efforts in the Identification of Underrepresented Students for Gifted and Talented Services," *Gifted Child Quarterly* (in press).

CHAPTER 10

1. Sasha A. Barab and Jonathan A. Plucker, "Smart People or Smart Contexts? Cognition, Ability, and Talent Development in an Age of Situated Approaches to Knowing and Learning," *Educational Psychologist* 37, no. 3 (2002): 165–182; Jonathan A. Plucker and Sasha A. Barab. "The Importance of Contexts in Theories of Giftedness," *Conceptions of Giftedness* (2005): 201–216.

2. Barab and Plucker, "Smart People or Smart Contexts?"

3. Jenna McWilliams and Jonathan A. Plucker, "Brain Cancer, Meat Glue, and Shifting Models of Outstanding Human Behavior: Smart Contexts for the 21st Century," *Talent Development and Excellence* 6, no. 1 (2014): 47–55.

4. Donald J. Leu, Elena Forzani, Chris Rhoads, Cheryl Maykel, Clint Kennedy, and Nicole Timbrell, "The New Literacies of Online Research and Comprehension: Rethinking the Reading Achievement Gap," *Reading Research Quarterly* 50, no. 1 (2015): 37–59.

5. Jia Li, Catherine Snow, and Claire White, "Urban Adolescent Students and Technology: Access, Use and Interest in Learning Language and Literacy," *Innovation in Language Learning and Teaching* 9, no. 2 (2015): 143–162; Patrick Wachir and Jared

Keengwe. "Technology Integration Barriers: Urban School Mathematics Teachers Perspectives," *Journal of Science Education and Technology* 20, no. 1 (2011): 17–25.

6. June Ahn, June, Lauren K. Bivona, and Jeffrey DiScala, "Social Media Access in K–12 Schools: Intractable Policy Controversies in an Evolving World," *Proceedings of the American Society for Information Science and Technology* 48, no. 1 (2011): 1–10; Barbara Jansen. "Internet Filtering 2.0: Checking Intellectual Freedom and Participative Practices at the Schoolhouse Door," *Knowledge Quest* 39, no. 1 (2010): 46; Orrin T. Murray and Nicole R. Olcese, "Teaching and Learning with iPads, Ready or Not?" *TechTrends* 55, no. 6 (2011): 42–48; Mark Warschauer and Tina Matuchniak, "New Technology and Digital Worlds: Analyzing Evidence of Equity in Access, Use, and Outcomes," *Review of Research in Education* 34, no. 1 (2010): 179–225.

7. Benjamin Riley, "Personalized Learning Is Not the Solution," *EducationNext*, July 3, 2015, http://educationnext.org/personalization-future-learning/.

8. Jacob Hardesty, Jenna McWilliams, and Jonathan A. Plucker, "Excellence Gaps: What They Are, Why They Are Bad, and How Smart Contexts Can Address Them . . . or Make Them Worse," *High Ability Studies* 25, no. 1 (2014): 71–80.

9. Mary Ruth Coleman, "Response to Intervention (RtI) Approaches to Identification Practices Within Gifted Education," *Fundamentals of Gifted Education: Considering Multiple Perspectives* (2013): 152–159; Holly Hertberg-Davis, "Myth 7: Differentiation in the Regular Classroom Is Equivalent to Gifted Programs and Is Sufficient: Classroom Teachers Have the Time, the Skill, and the Will to Differentiate Adequately," *Gifted Child Quarterly* 53 no. 4 (2009): 251–253; Robert G. McKenzie, "The Insufficiency of Response to Intervention in Identifying Gifted Students with Learning Disabilities," *Learning Disabilities Research & Practice* 25, no. 3 (2010): 161–168; Harold Pashler, Mark McDaniel, Doug Rohrer, and Robert Bjork, "Learning Styles Concepts and Evidence," *Psychological Science in the Public Interest* 9, no. 3 (2008): 105–119.

10. Coalition for Psychology in Schools and Education, "Top 20 Principles from Psychology for PreK–12 Teaching and Learning (Washington, DC: American Psychological Association, 2015), http://www.apa.org/ed/schools/cpse/top-twenty-principles.pdf.

11. Claude M. Steele and Joshua Aronson, "Stereotype Threat and the Intellectual Test Performance of African Americans," *Journal of Personality and Social Psychology* 69, no. 5 (1995): 797–811.

12. Jacquelynne S. Eccles, "Gender Roles and Women's Achievement-Related Decisions," *Psychology of Women Quarterly* 11, no. 2 (1987): 135–172; Jane Butler Kahle, Lesley H. Parker, Leonie J. Rennie, and Dana Riley, "Gender Differences in Science Education: Building a Model," *Educational Psychologist* 28, no. 4 (1993): 379–404.

13. Jonathan A. Plucker, "Introducing Female Scientists, Mathematicians, and Engineers into the Curriculum: Location and Evaluation of Resources," *Journal of Women and Minorities in Science and Engineering* 1, no. 3 (1994): 209–220; Toni Schmader, "Gender Identification Moderates Stereotype Threat Effects on

Women's Math Performance," *Journal of Experimental Social Psychology* 38, no. 2 (2002): 194–201; Steven J. Spencer, Claude M. Steele, and Diane M. Quinn, "Stereotype Threat and Women's Math Performance," *Journal of Experimental Social Psychology* 35, no. 1 (1999): 4–28.

14. Pamela R. Clinkenbeard, "Motivation and Gifted Students: Implications of Theory and Research," *Psychology in the Schools* 49, no. 7 (2012): 622–630; Joyce VanTassel-Baska, "The World of Cross-Cultural Research: Insights for Gifted Education," *Journal for the Education of the Gifted* 36 no. 1 (2013): 6–18.

15. Lisa S. Blackwell, Kali H. Trzesniewski, and Carol Sorich Dweck, "Implicit Theories of Intelligence Predict Achievement Across an Adolescent Transition: A Longitudinal Study and an Intervention," *Child Development* 78, no. 1 (2007): 246–263; Angela L. Duckworth, Christopher Peterson, Michael D. Matthews, and Dennis R. Kelly, "Grit: Perseverance and Passion for Long-Term Goals," *Journal of Personality and Social Psychology* 92, no. 6 (2007): 1087–1101; Ying-yi Hong, Chi-yue Chiu, Carol S. Dweck, Derrick M-S. Lin, and Wendy Wan, "Implicit Theories, Attributions, and Coping: A Meaning System Approach," *Journal of Personality and Social Psychology* 77, no. 3 (1999): 588–599.

16. Abedrahman Abuhassàn and Timothy C. Bates, "Grit: Distinguishing Effortful Persistence from Conscientiousness," *Journal of Individual Differences* 36 (2015): 205–214; Kaili Rimfeld, Yulia Kovas, Philip S. Dale, and Robert Plomin, "True Grit and Genetics: Predicting Academic Achievement From Personality," *Journal of Personality and Social Psychology* (2016): 1–10; Angela L. Duckworth, Christopher Peterson, Michael D. Matthews, and Dennis R. Kelly, "Grit: Perseverance and Passion for Long-Term Goals," *Journal of Personality and Social Psychology* 92, no. 6 (2007): 1087–1101.

17. Geoffrey L. Cohen and David K. Sherman, "The Psychology of Change: Self-Affirmation and Social Psychological Intervention," *Annual Review of Psychology* 65 (2014): 333–371; Geoffrey L. Cohen, Joshua Aronson, and Claude M. Steele, "When Beliefs Yield to Evidence: Reducing Biased Evaluation by Affirming the Self," *Personality and Social Psychology Bulletin* 26, no. 9 (2000): 1151–1164.

18. Geoffrey L. Cohen, Julio Garcia, Valerie Purdie-Vaughns, Nancy Apfel, and Patricia Brzustoski, "Recursive Processes in Self-Affirmation: Intervening to Close the Minority Achievement Gap," *Science* 324, no. 5925 (2009): 400–403.

19. Geoffrey L. Cohen, Julio Garcia, Nancy Apfel, and Allison Master, "Reducing The Racial Achievement Gap: A Social-Psychological Intervention," *Science* 313, no. 5791 (2006): 1307–1310; Jonathan E. Cook, Valerie Purdie-Vaughns, Julio Garcia, and Geoffrey L. Cohen, "Chronic Threat and Contingent Belonging: Protective Benefits of Values Affirmation on Identity Development," *Journal of Personality and Social Psychology* 102, no. 3 (2012): 479–496.

20. Joseph T. Powers, Jonathan E. Cook, Valerie Purdie-Vaughns, Julio Garcia, Nancy Apfel, and Geoffrey L. Cohen, "Changing Environments by Changing Individuals: The Emergent Effects of Psychological Intervention," *Psychological Science* 27 no. 2 (2015): 150–160.

21. Hannah-Hanh D. Nguyen and Ann Marie Ryan, "Does Stereotype Threat Affect Test Performance of Minorities and Women? A Meta-Analysis of Experimental Evidence," *Journal of Applied Psychology* 93, no. 6 (2008): 1314–1334; David S. Yeager and Gregory M. Walton, "Social-Psychological Interventions in Education: They're Not Magic," *Review of Educational Research* 81, no. 2 (2011): 267–301.

22. Gregory M. Walton and Geoffrey L. Cohen, "A Brief Social-Belonging Intervention Improves Academic and Health Outcomes of Minority Students," *Science* 331, no. 6023 (2011): 1447–1451.

23. Ibid.

24. Catherine Good, Joshua Aronson, and Jayne Ann Harder, "Problems in the Pipeline: Stereotype Threat and Women's Achievement in High-Level Math Courses," *Journal of Applied Developmental Psychology* 29, no. 1 (2008): 17–28.

25. Anne T. Ottenbreit-Leftwich, Thomas A. Brush, Jesse Strycker, Susie Gronseth, Tiffany Roman, Serdar Abaci, Sungwon Shin, Wylie Easterling, and Jonathan Plucker, "Preparation Versus Practice: How Do Teacher Education Programs and Practicing Teachers Align in Their Use of Technology to Support Teaching and Learning?" *Computers & Education* 59, no. 2 (2012): 399–411.

26. David A. Freedman, "Statistical Models and Shoe Leather," *Sociological Methodology* 21, (1991): 291–313; Matthew T. McBee, Scott J. Peters, and Erin M. Miller, "The Impact of the Nomination Stage on Gifted Identification: A Comprehensive Psychometric Analysis," *Gifted Child Quarterly* (in press).

CHAPTER 11

1. "Percentage of 18- to 24-Year-Olds Enrolled in Degree-Granting Institutions, by Level of Institution and Sex and Race/Ethnicity of Student: 1967 Through 2012," (Washington, DC: National Center for Education Statistics, n.d.), accessed November 15, 2015, http://nces.ed.gov/programs/digest/d13/tables/dt13_302.60.asp.

2. "Tuition and Fees and Room and Board over Time, 1975–76 to 2015–16, Selected Years," (New York: The College Board, n.d.), accessed November 15, 2015, http://trends.collegeboard.org/college-pricing/figures-tables/tuition-and-fees-and-room-and-board-over-time-1975-76-2015-16-selected-years.

3. *Federal Aid per Student by Type Over Time* (New York: The College Board, n.d.), accessed November 19, 2015, http://trends.collegeboard.org/student-aid/figures-tables/federal-aid-student-type-over-time.

4. Steven A. Culpepper and Ernest C. Davenport, "Addressing Differential Prediction of College Grades by Race/Ethnicity with a Multilevel Model," Journal of Educational Measurement 46, no. 2 (2009): 220–242.

5. Jason Fletcher and Marta Tienda, "Race and Ethnic Differenced in College Achievement: Does High School Attended Matter" *Annals of the American Academic of Political and Social Science* 627, no. 1 (2010): 144–166.

6. "College Scorecard," US Department of Education, accessed November 19, 2015, https://collegescorecard.ed.gov/.

7. Terris Ross, Grace Kena, Amy Rathbun, Angelina KewalRamani, Jijun Zhang,

Paul Kristapovich, and Eileen Manning, *Higher Education: Gaps in Access and Persistence Study* (Washington, DC: National Center for Education Statistics, August 2012), http://nces.ed.gov/pubs2012/2012046.pdf.

8. Table 326.10, "Graduation Rate from First Institution Attended for First-Time, Full-Time Bachelor's Degree-Seeking Students at 4-Year Postsecondary Institutions, by Race/Ethnicity, Time to Completion, Sex, Control of Institution, and Acceptance Rate: Selected Cohort Entry Years, 1996 Through 2007" (Washington, DC: National Center for Education Statistics, n.d., https://nces.ed.gov/programs/digest/d14/tables/dt14_326.10.asp, accessed November 15, 2015.

9. Regents of the University of California v. Bakke, 438 U.S. 265 (1978).

10. *Grutter v. Bollinger*, 539 U.S. 306 (2003); *Grutter v. Bollinger*, 539 U.S. 306 (2003).

11. Ibid., opinion of S. O'Connor, pp. 329–330, quoting Bakke, opinion of L. Powell, L., p. 307.

12. Ibid., opinion of S. O'Connor, S., p. 334

13. *Hopwood v. Texas*, 78 F.3d 932 (5th Cir. 1996).

14. Marta Tienda, Sigal Alon, and Sunny X. Niu, "Affirmative Action and the Texas Top 10 Percent Admission Law: Balancing Equity and Access to Higher Education," Societes Contemporaines 79 (2010): 19–39, http://theop.princeton.edu/reports/wp/affirmativeaction_topten.pdf.

15. University of Texas at Austin, The Top 10% Law and its impact on the University of Texas at Austin, 2008, http://www.texastop10.princeton.edu/publicity/general/UT_Report_Top_10_Law.pdf.

16. "Talented Twenty Program," Florida Department of Education, n.d., accessed November 21, 2015, http://www.fldoe.org/schools/family-community/activities-programs/talented-twenty-program.

17. Jeannette Cruz, "Understanding the Relationship Between the Talented Twenty Program and College Aspirations for High Ranking students at a High Priority School" (PhD diss., Florida International University, 2011), 19–22.

18. Patricia Marin and Edgar K. Lee, "Appearance and Reality in the Sunshine State: The Talented 20 Program in Florida" (Cambridge, MA: The Civil Rights Project at Harvard University, 2003), http://civilrightsproject.ucla.edu/research/college-access/admissions/appearance-and-reality-in-the-sunshine-state-the-talented-20-program-in-florida/marine-appearnace-reality-sunshine-2003.pdf.

19. "What IS ELC?," University of California Admissions, n.d., accessed November 21, 2015, http://admission.universityofcalifornia.edu/freshman/california-residents/local-path/index.html.

20. See Proposition 209, 1996.

21. "Accountability Sub Report on Diversity" (revised), University of California, September 2010, http://regents.universityofcalifornia.edu/regmeet/sept10/j1attach.pdf.

22. Manuel Alba et al., "Beyond Percentage Plans: The Challenge of Equal Opportunity in Higher Education," Report, accessed November 21, 2015 (Washington, DC: Commission on Civil Rights, November 2002), http://files.eric.ed.gov/fulltext/ED476896.pdf.

23. *Parents Involved in Community Schools v. Seattle School District* No. 1, 551 U.S. 701 (2007).

24. "Guidance on the Voluntary Use of Race to Achieve Diversity in Postsecondary Education," US Department of Justice and US Department of Education, accessed November 15, 2015, http://www2.ed.gov/about/offices/list/ocr/docs/guidance-pse-201111.pdf; "Guidance on the Voluntary Use of Race to Achieve Diversity and Avoid Racial Isolation in Elementary and Secondary Schools," US Department of Justice and US Department of Education, http://www2.ed.gov/about/offices/list/ocr/docs/guidance-ese-201111.pdf, accessed November 15, 2015.

25. Sheryll Cashin, *Place Not Race: A New Vision of Opportunity in America.* (Boston: Beacon Hill Books, 2014), 82.

CHAPTER 12

1. Frank Newport, "Americans Continue to Say U.S. Wealth Distributions Is Unfair," May 4, 2015, http://www.gallup.com/poll/182987/americans-continue-say-wealth-distribution-unfair.aspx.

2. Jonathan A. Plucker, *Common Core and America's High-Achieving Students,* (Washington, DC: Thomas B. Fordham Institute, 2015), http://edex.s3-us-west-2.amazonaws.com/Common20Core%20and%20America%27s%20High-Achieving%20Students_FINAL.pdf.

3. http://www2.ed.gov/programs/javits/awards.html.

4. National Association for Gifted Children, *State of the States of Gifted Education: 2014–2015.* (Washington, DC: National Association for Gifted Children, 2015).

5. Ann Duffett, Steve Farkas, and Tom Loveless, *High-Achieving Students in the Era of No Child Left Behind* (Washington, DC: Thomas Fordham Foundation, 2008); National Research Council Committee on Highly Successful Schools or Programs for K–12 STEM Education, *Successful K–12 STEM Education: Identifying Effective Approaches in Science, Technology, Engineering, and Mathematics* (Washington, DC: National Academies Press, 2011).

6. Marni Bromberg and Christina Theokas, *Falling Out of the Lead Following High Achievers Through High School and Beyond* (Washington, DC: The Education Trust, 2014), http://edtrust.org/wp-content/uploads/2013/10/FallingOutoftheLead.pdf.

7. Marcia Gentry, *Total School Cluster Grouping and Differentiation: A Comprehensive Research-Based Plan for Raising Student Achievement and Improving Teacher Practices* (Waco, TX: Prufrock Press, 2014), 5.

8. Jonathan A. Plucker, Jennifer Giancola, Grace Healey, Daniel Arndt, and Chen Wang, *Equal Talents, Unequal Opportunities: A Report Card on State Support for Academically Talented Low-Income Students* (Lansdowne, VA: Jack Kent Cooke Foundation, 2015), http://www.excellencegap.org/.

9. Higher Education Opportunity Act, PL110-315).

10. NAGC, *State of the States of Gifted Education: 2014–2015*; Plucker et al., *Equal talents, unequal opportunities.*

11. M. Katherine Gavin et al., "Mentoring Mathematical Minds: A Research-Based

Curriculum for Talented Elementary Students," *Journal of Advanced Academics* 18, no. 4 (2007): 566–585; Seokhee Cho, Jenny Yang, and Marcella Mandracchia, "Effects of M3 Curriculum on Mathematics and English Proficiency Achievement of Mathematically Promising English Language Learners," *Journal of Advanced Academics* 26, no. 2 (2015): 112–142.

12. National Academy of Engineering, "*National Academy of Engineering: Grand Challenges for Engineering*," http://www.engineeringchallenges.org/challenges.aspx, accessed February (2016).

13. United Nations, *2030 Agenda for Sustainable Development*, http://www.undp.org/content/undp/en/home/sdgoverview/post-2015-development-agenda/.

ACKNOWLEDGMENTS

THIS BOOK would not have come into existence without the support of many people and groups. Researchers and support staff at the Indiana University Center for Evaluation and Education Policy assisted in the initial, formative work on excellence gaps. Jane Clarenbach at the National Association for Gifted Children and Kim Hynes, formerly of the Council for Exceptional Children, were among the first people to see the power of the excellence gap approach to equity and excellence.

They, in turn, exposed the work to policymakers and leaders in several state associations for gifted education, and over the past six years, the momentum has continued to build. With the assistance of several colleagues, including Nathan Burroughs, Jacob Hardesty, Bryn Harris, Jake McWilliams, David Rutkowski, Leslie Rutkowski, and Ruiting Song, we have now shared this work around the country. Without the help of so many colleagues and educators, this book would not have been possible.

We also appreciate the feedback that several colleagues provided to us on various chapters. They include Carolyn Callahan, Tarek Grantham, Tim Green, Holly Hertberg Davis, Matthew Makel, Michael Matthews, Matthew McBee, Erin Miller, and Anne Rinn-McCann. And, last but not least, Caroline Chauncey at Harvard Education Press helped foster this book from a question—Do we know enough about excellence gaps to guide intervention efforts?—to the book you are currently holding in your hand. Nancy Walser at HEP helped us bring the book to the finish line, for which we are grateful.

ABOUT THE AUTHORS

JONATHAN A. PLUCKER is the Julian C. Stanley Professor of Talent Development at Johns Hopkins University, with a joint appointment at the Center for Talented Youth and School of Education. He is one of the original developers of the concept of excellence gaps and first wrote about them in the report *Mind the Other Gap* (2010) and then in *Talent on the Sidelines* (2013), in addition to several other studies and papers on the topic. In addition to more than $30 million in externally funded research and over two hundred publications, he has edited or authored the books *Critical Issues and Practices in Gifted Education: What the Research Says* (with Carolyn Callahan), *Essentials of Creativity Assessment* (with James Kaufman and John Baer), *Intelligence 101* (with Amber Esping), *Doing Good Social Science: Trust, Accuracy, Transparency* (with Matthew Makel), and *Creativity and Innovation: Theory, Research, and Practice*. He is a recipient of the National Association for Gifted Children's Distinguished Scholar Award and American Psychological Association's Rudolf Arnheim Award for Outstanding Achievement in Creativity Research and an elected Fellow of the APA and the American Association for the Advancement of Science. He received his PhD from the University of Virginia and has previously taught at the University of Maine, Indiana University, and the University of Connecticut. Professor Plucker currently serves on the NAGC board of directors.

SCOTT J. PETERS is an associate professor of Educational Foundations at the University of Wisconsin–Whitewater. He received his PhD from Purdue University, specializing in gifted and talented education and applied research methodology. His research focuses on educational assessment, identification of student exceptionalities (particularly those from low-income or underrepresented groups) and gifted and talented programming outcomes. He has published in *Teaching for High Potential*, *Gifted Child Quarterly*, *Journal of Advanced Academics*, *Gifted and Talented International*, *Gifted Children*, *Journal of Career and Technical Education Research*, *Educational Leadership*, *Education Week*, and *Pedagogies*. He is the recipient of the Feldhusen Doctoral Fellowship in Gifted Education, the NAGC Research an Evaluation Network Dissertation Award, the NAGC Doctoral Student of the Year Award, the NAGC Early Scholar Award, the Michael Pyryt Collaboration Award, and the University of Wisconsin–Whitewater Innovation and Outstanding Research Awards. He has served as the program chair of the AERA Research on Giftedness, Creativity, and Talent SIG; on the board of the Wisconsin Association for Talented and Gifted; and as the National Association for Gifted Children Research and Evaluation Network Secretary. He is the lead author of *Beyond Gifted Education: Designing and Implementing Advanced Academic Programs* (with Michael Matthews, Matthew McBee, and D. Betsy McCoach) (Prufrock Press).

INDEX

ability grouping
    anti-grouping policies concerns, 127–128
    arguments against, 123
    benefits for ELL students, 125–126, 135
    benefits for high achievers, 124, 125, 128
    challenges in heterogeneously grouped classes, 127
    differences in attitudes toward, 120
    educators' denial of using, 119–120
    extent of the use of, 123–124, 126–127
    impact on excellence gaps, 124–126
    promise of, 126, 128, 183–184
    questioning of, 121–122
    talent development and, 77–78
    tracking versus, 121, 122
acceleration, 78–79
accountability systems, 176–177, 184–185
achievement gaps. *See also* excellence gaps
    correlation between educational achievement and family income, 6
    ESEA's goal of closing, 10
    factor of parental resources in, 15
    illustration of the factors in student success, 3–5
    impact of exposure to high-quality early education programs, 6
    low-income students' NAEP scores, 43–44
    minimum proficiency goal, 14
    NCLB and, 11–13
    nominal effect of raising academic standards, 14–15

non-low-income students' NAEP scores, 44–45
    origin of the idea of, 7–8
adaptive tests, 177–179
advanced placement (AP)
    front-loading program, 131–132
    percent of blacks taking an exam, 85
    talent development and, 80–81
affirmative action policies
    court ruling on a diversity-based points system, 164
    court ruling on a subjective admissions policy, 161–164
    implementation of, 157
    lawsuit against a quota system, 160–161
    percentage plans, 164–167, 168–169
    restrictions on closing excellence gaps in enrollments, 164
alternative identification
    arbitrary classifications and, 99–100
    basis for judging a system, 88–89
    disparities in areas of high achievement, 85
    ethnic representation rates in gifted and talented programs, 86
    group-specific comparisons, 96–99
    local norms comparisons, 93–96
    nonverbal ability testing, 87–90
    presumptions underlying methods for, 92
    rationale for, 87
    role of identification policies in excellence gaps, 86